SOCIAL WELFARE IN BRITAIN 1885–1985

SOCIAL WELFARE IN BRITAIN
1885–1985

Edited by
REX POPE, ALAN PRATT AND BERNARD HOYLE

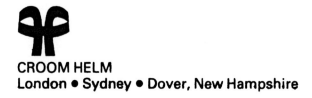

CROOM HELM
London • Sydney • Dover, New Hampshire

Selection and editorial matter © 1986 Rex Pope, Alan Pratt and Bernard Hoyle
Croom Helm Ltd, Provident House, Burrell Row,
Beckenham, Kent BR3 1AT

Croom Helm Australia Pty Ltd, Suite 4, 6th Floor, 64–76 Kippax Street, Surry Hills,
NSW 2010, Australia

British Library Cataloguing in Publication Data

Social welfare in Britain 1885–1985
  1. Great Britain —— Social Policy
  I. Pope, Rex   II. Pratta, Alan   III. Hoyle, Bernard
  361.6'1'0941   HN390

  ISBN 0–7099–4001–7
  ISBN 0–7099–4035–1 Pbk

Croom Helm Ltd, 51 Washington Street,
Dover, New Hampshire, 03820 USA

Library of Congress Cataloging in Publication Data

Main entry under title:
Social welfare in Britain, 1885–1985.

  Bibliography: p.
  Includes index.
  1. Social service —— Great Britain —— History —— 19th century. 2. Social
service —— Great Britain —— History —— 20th century. 3. Great Britain ——
Social policy. 4. Great Britain —— Economic conditions —— 19th century. 5.
Great Britain —— Economic conditions —— 20th century. I. Pope, Rex. II. Pratt,
Alan. III. Hoyle, Bernard. HN385.S66 1986   361'.941   85–28046
ISBN 0–7099–4001–7
ISBN 0–7099–4035–1 (pbk.)

Phototypeset by Sunrise Setting, Torquay, Devon

CONTENTS

Preface

Acknowledgements

Section A: 1885–1940

Section C: Statistics

PREFACE

The increased use of primary source materials is a marked characteristic of recent trends in the study of subjects such as History, Politics or Social Policy and Administration. This book is intended to add significantly to the stock of readily-available material of this type. It is unique in its timespan, not only covering the conventional era of developments in welfare thinking and provision from the late-nineteenth to the mid-twentieth century, but also including the recent past with its quest for redefinitions or a new approach.

The primary sources have been presented in two sections, covering the periods 1885–c.1940 and c.1940 to 1985. During the former, ideas on, and the scope of, welfare provision broadened greatly. There was a sense of progress. Developments, though, were piecemeal; there was no concept of a 'Welfare State'. The second period begins with he changes of the 1940s and the widespread assumption that Britain was establishing a 'Welfare State'. Subsequently, however, there has been mounting speculation as to whether such organisation of society is necessary or desirable and it has been apparent that the hopes of the 1940s have not been fulfilled.

In both these sections, extracts have been grouped under headings. This grouping seemed preferable to a simple chronological organisation. The emphasis throughout is on issues, influences and ideas. This is presented as an alternative or complement to the service-orientated approach of some other documentary collections. Section C aims at providing useful background information in graph or chart form.

The target group for the volume in primarily students on A-level, first degree and professional training courses. This consideration has influenced the price and hence the size of the book. This, in turn, has meant the omission of much that is both interesting and important. What is *most* interesting and *most* important does, we hope, remain.

Rex Pope
Alan Pratt
Bernard Hoyle

ACKNOWLEDGEMENTS

The editors are extremely grateful to the copyright-holders who have kindly allowed their material to be reproduced in this book. In particular, acknowledgement is due in the cases listed below. If the editors have inadvertently included copyright material without making due acknowledgement, they offer their sincere apologies.

George Allen and Unwin Publishers Ltd (B21, B24); Basil Blackwell Publishers Ltd (B29); Bell and Hyman Ltd (B25); Chapman and Hall Ltd (A1); The Conservative and Unionist Central Office (B12); The Conservative Political Centre (B13, B16, B17, B30); The Estate of C.A.R. Crosland (B20); The Fabian Society (A24, B36); Gower Publishing Company Ltd (B23, B26); Victor Gollancz Ltd (B6); The Controller of Her Majesty's Stationery Office (A4, A6, A7, A8, A9, A10, A11, A12, A14, A15, A16, A18, A19, A20, A21, A22, A23, A27, A31, B2, B3, B4, B5, B7, B8, B9, B10, B11, B28, B37); The Institute of Economic Affairs, London (B22); The Labour Party (A26, A34, A35, B14, B15); Lawrence and Wishart Ltd (B34); Longman Group Ltd (A25, A32, A33); Macmillan Publishers Ltd (A3, B31); Methuen and Company Ltd (A2); John Murray Publishers Ltd (B32); The National Council for Voluntary Organisations (A5, A17); Penguin Books Ltd (B27); The Political Quarterly (B18, B19); Pluto Press Ltd (B35); Routledge and Kegan Paul PLC (B1); The Joseph Rowntree Charitable Trust (A29, A30); Salvationist Publishing and Supplies Ltd (A28); The Social Affairs Unit (B33); University of California Press (B27).

SOCIAL WELFARE IN BRITAIN 1885–1985

SECTION A: 1885–1940

Introduction

In the 1880s, social policy was still largely restricted to the deterrent Poor Law. The twin ideologies of self-help and *laissez-faire* dominated welfare thinking. Outside the Poor Law, only in relation to schools and factories had there been effective legislation. Even in these areas, coverage was restricted: to women and children in the factories and to elementary education for the working classes in the case of schooling. At the other extreme was housing where the ideology of the market economy, coupled with belief in the rights of property holders, was to delay any real advance until after the First World War.

Nevertheless, the pressures for action were mounting. Moral and physical degeneracy were seen as linked consequences of the deprivation of the urban poor. Statistical evidence of poverty and analyses of its causes indicated that the 'personal failing' explanation of poverty was insufficient, as was charity as a remedy. Increasing longevity threatened to destroy the financial stability of the friendly societies and to overwhelm the Boards of Guardians. Unemployment and under-employment were found to be problems as much of the labour market as of individuals. Concern for public order motivated the state's early initiatives towards alleviating the conditions of the unemployed. A quest for economic efficiency motivated those who sought to attack the problem at its root — to prevent unemployment.

The administrative and military needs of empire combined with a growing awareness of economic competition as further stimulants to action. So, too, did the example set by Germany, ostensibly Britain's major rival. The need to combat the appeal of labourism or socialism (and, in the case of the Liberals, to fight tariff reform) were further influences.

As a result, the early twentieth century saw increased state intervention in social welfare. Local authorities were permitted to use the rates to support secondary education (1902), to adopt measures such as labour exchanges, farm colonies or emigration to relieve unemployment (1905) and to provide free or subsidised school meals (1906). Compulsion was used with regard to the establishment of Distress Committees (1905), the introduction of school medical inspection (1907) and membership of the Health and Unemployment Insurance schemes (1911). The commitment to income maintenance outside the Poor Law, represented in the 1911 Acts, could also be seen in the provision of Old Age Pensions (1908). The quest for labour market efficiency was a factor in the unemployment insurance section of the 1911 scheme and in the establishment, from 1910, of a national system of labour exchanges. Additional measures, catering for particular groups, included the greater provision of free places in secondary education (1907), together with the protection of children (1908) and of the low paid (1909).

It would be wrong, however, to suggest any radical change either in the scope of provision or in the principles and attitudes governing action. The use of rate income was strictly limited and, in the cases of secondary education, the 1905 unemployment relief measures and the provision of free school meals, local authority action was designed simply to supplement that of voluntary bodies. Nor, in 1905, were rate monies to be used to provide work. The gap-filling nature of state action was seen, too, in the means-testing of applicants for old age pensions. The pensions scheme also included attempts to distinguish the deserving from the undeserving as, in spite of Churchill's opposition, did that for unemployment insurance. The belief that individuals should provide for themselves and their dependants pervaded not only the debates on pensions but also those on school meals.

Large areas of welfare and sections of the population were neglected. School medical *treatment* was not introduced until 1912. Hospital and specialist care was not part of the statutory provision under the 1911 Health Insurance scheme. Housing legislation remained ineffective. Most adult men were still untouched by protective legislation. Only seven trades were included in the original Unemployment Insurance scheme (1911) and, before 1914, only a handful of trades gained protection under the Trade Boards Act. Dependants were excluded from health insurance. Benefits were universally low, a supplement to savings rather than a means of subsistence. Provision, where it existed, was class-based, giving a minimum to the needy. Support for the Poor Law and for the principles of 1834 lived on.

War, during the twentieth century, has served to promote social welfare. The needs of the state have focused attention on the size, physical well-being and mental capabilities of the population. The destruction or disruption of facilities and services has meant a post-war commitment to remedying deficiencies. Deaths and maiming have forced extensions in pension arrangements. A need to maintain morale, coupled with a usually temporary emotional commitment to reducing social divisions and 'improving' society, has brought promises of a better future. War, too, has created an environment where economic issues no longer have priority. Radical reform has become a possibility — what the country needs rather than what it can afford.

The years 1918–19 brought an intention to extend educational facilities, in particular for adolescents through continuation schools. They saw, too, the provision of a relatively generous 'donation' to keep servicemen and redundant civilian war workers from the Poor Law. They saw the raising of pensions to counter inflation, the creation of a Ministry of Health and the establishment of the important principle of state-subsidised, working-class housing to deal with a shortage greatly exacerbated by the virtual cessation of house-building that war had brought about.

From 1920, however, economic difficulties and unemployment dominated social policy. Economies not only thwarted attempts to raise the school leaving age or to establish 'secondary education for all' but also destroyed the continuation schools and, in 1931, forced changes in the free place arrangements for secondary education. An anti-waste campaign saw the abandonment of Addison's 1919 housing scheme, while the political strength of the Approved Societies frustrated attempts to extend and reform provision for health insurance. Against this, the principle of subsidised housing was adopted in subsequent attempts to boost the overall housing stock (1923, 1924) and, in the 1930s, to curb slums and overcrowding.

There were substantial extensions to schemes of benefit and allowances for the unemployed. The concessions of 1918, once given, proved difficult to withdraw. Thus unemployment insurance, as it evolved in the 1920s, incorporated the bulk of the manual working class, and the characteristics of the 1918 donation — relatively generous levels of benefit, dependants' allowances and benefit without contribution — were built into the scheme. In spite of the introduction of the household means test (1931) and the unintentional cuts associated with the introduction of unemployment assistance (1935), the inter-war years saw the unemployed treated separately from, and better than, other groups of the needy.

Between 1918 and 1940, then, there had been an expansion of social welfare provision but it had been ill-co-ordinated and many of the earlier deficiencies remained. Attempts to relieve the unemployed were not matched by any real effort to prevent unemployment. There were major gaps (e.g. in health care for non-earners, in hospital care, in family allowances) and inadequacies (e.g. in the level of pensions, the extent of slum clearance). Old values were still in evidence, including the assumption that people had to be persuaded to take work rather than maintenance. The administration of welfare was divided between a number of bodies (Approved Societies, Public Assistance Committees, Employment Exchanges, Unemployment Assistance Offices) and the Poor Law still survived, albeit broken up to a substantial extent by the Local Government Act of 1929.

Extracts in Section A are grouped under six headings. The first of these, 'Political Economy and Social Policy', might, of course, have subsumed virtually all the passages in the section. Instead, just three are included where the emphasis is clearly on general principles rather than particular aspects of policy. *A1* (*The Radical Programme*, 1885) suggests that political expediency demands an extension of state welfare. *A2* (Chiozza Money, 1912) welcomes compulsion in insurance as a rejection of *laissez-faire*. In *A3* (*The Middle Way*, 1939), Macmillan calls for a new approach to social reform; one based on economic reconstruction.

'Public Economy and Social Welfare' incorporates examples of welfare being subordinated to economic policy and of the responses to this. *A4* ('The Geddes "Axe"', 1921') comprises a savage assault on the education service. *A5* (*Social Service Review*, 1922) accepts the cuts but warns against false economies while urging that individuals have a role to play in the 'crisis'. *A6* (The May Committee Report, 1931) also incorporates an attack on social services, concentrating in this extract on ways to cut the cost of unemployment benefit. *A7* (Sir Ben Turner, 1931) opposes the cuts and the manner of their implementation.

'The Administration of Welfare' gave rise to a number of important issues. *A8* (Old Age Pensions, 1908) deals with the question of contributory or non-contributory benefits. *A9* (Minority Report on the Poor Law, 1909) and *A10* (Majority Report) are for and against the break-up of the Poor Law. *A11* (Majority Report) makes recommendations on the giving of out-relief and on the relationship between the Poor Law and the voluntary agencies, whilst *A12* (Sidney Buxton, 1911) states the case for a compulsory scheme of unemployment insurance. *A13* (Eleanor Rathbone, 1924) outlines the pros and cons of the 'pool' and 'state' systems of providing family allowances. *A14* (*Majority Report on Health Insurance*, 1926) and *A15* (Minority Report) state the case for and against Approved Societies, while both *A16* (*Annual Report of the UAB*, 1935) and *A17* (Ronald Davison, 1935) deal with problems relating to the administration of transitional payments and unemployment assistance.

'Tests of Need or Desert' include the issue of selectivity or universality in welfare services. *A18* (*Report of the Commission on the Aged Poor*, 1895) argues for selectivity and for tests of industry or independence in the granting of old age pensions whereas *A19* (Charles Booth, 1895) supports universal provision. *A20* (Old Age Pensions, 1908) explains the exclusions from the original pensions scheme. *A21* (Keir Hardie, Lloyd George and Austen Chamberlain, 1911) deals with the exclusion of wives of the employed from National Health Insurance. *A22* (Morris Report, 1929) condemns the operation of the 'Genuinely Seeking Work' clause in unemployment insurance.

'The Role of Charity and Voluntary Effort' was considerable throughout this period. *A23* (Octavia Hill, 1888) indicates possible ill-effects of charity, while *A24* (Mrs Townsend, 1911) condemns the principles and policies of the Charity Organisation Society. In *A25* ('Charity Up-to-date', 1912), Samuel Barnett calls for a more thoughtful charity. *A26* (Labour Party, 1922) deals with the failings of the voluntary hospitals.

The final group of extracts is on 'The Identification of Problems'. *A27* (Chamberlain Circular, 1886) urges work schemes to keep the unemployed from pauperism. In *A28* ('Cab-Horse Charter', 1890), William Booth suggests a minimum objective for social welfare. Rowntree in *A29* (*Poverty*, 1901) and *A30* (*Poverty and Progress*, 1941) explains the nature, incidence and causes of poverty at the end of the nineteenth century and in 1936. *A31* (*Physical Deterioration Report*, 1904) demonstrates the need for school meals but, at the same time, a concern that parental responsibility should not be undermined. In *A32* (*Unemployment*, 1909) and *A33* (*Unemployment*, 1930), Beveridge calls for an assault on unemployment. *A34* (Labour Party, 1917) assesses the scale of the housing shortage and calls for state action to cure it. *A35* (Tawney, 1922) attacks the elementary/secondary divide in education and the injustices and inefficiencies that result.

POLITICAL ECONOMY AND SOCIAL POLICY

A1 The Radical Programme, 1885

The evil effects of overcrowding upon the poorer classes of our large towns is now generally recognised, but it is not so widely understood that it is to the interest of all in the community to do away with these evils. Self-interest enforces the dictates of humanity. For under such conditions of life the workman, even if looked upon merely as an instrument to produce wealth, is not nearly so valuable to the community as he might be. As Mr Sidgwick puts it, 'Competition does not tend to give the labourer the real wages required to make his labour most efficient.' The vital statistics alone would prove this. The result of the improvements undertaken in Paris under Napoleon has been to reduce the mortality by one-half. But medical statistics show that for every person who dies in this way, six persons are ill, and the consequent loss to the community of wealth-producing power is enormous. The interests of one class cannot be separated from those of another. 'The advance of pathological knowledge', writes Dr Bristowe, 'proves that most, if not all, epidemic disorders spread by contagion.' According to the same authority the contagion of some disorders, influenza, for instance, is remarkable for its 'amazing diffusibility', while that of others, such as scarlet fever, 'remain dormant for months in articles of clothing'. Now it must be borne in mind that the milk, the food, the linen used in the better classes pass through the hands of those who live in courts and alleys, and whose conditions of lives, although concealed, have the most serious influence upon the lives and health of those whose circumstances appear to place them above all danger, and who may live at a great distance from the source of contagion. Dr Aubrey Husband, in his book upon *Forensic Medicine*, after showing that the poison of typhoid fever may be carried by water and by food, instances the recent outbreaks in the West-end of London, where the carriage of the poison was traced to the milk used by those attacked.

While re-housing may be looked upon as an insurance paid by the better class against disease, it may also be regarded as an insurance paid by the rich against revolution. The Peabody Dwellings show that it is possible to house the poor properly, and to make the improvement, in a pecuniary sense, a fairly profitable investment. Two rooms in these dwellings are let at from 3s. to 4s. 6d. per week, three rooms cost from 4s. 6d. to 7s., but it must not be forgotten that the Peabody trustees require a larger return from their investment than would the municipality. It is useless to increase wages and to lessen the hours of toil so long as the workman is compelled to live in . . . pest-houses . . .; nay, it is almost worse than useless, inasmuch as the extra wage and increased leisure operate as incentives to drunkenness and vice. The surplus wages would be used (this can be seen in the Peabody and Ashley Dwellings) to make two or three rooms comfortable; it is absurd to hope that they will be expended in a vain attempt to make one room habitable. It is to the interest of all in the community that the workman should become a better instrument of production, that his dwelling should not be a hotbed of disease, that his degradation and misery should not be a constant source of danger to the State. The warning of Danton must be heeded, 'If you suffer the poor to grow up as animals they may chance to become wild beasts and rend you.'

The question of cost is the all-important one. All experience demonstrates that it is impossible under our present statutory powers to acquire urban property, compulsorily, for public purposes, at prices which do not inflict a heavy fine on the community . . . How are unsanitary areas to be acquired without paying exorbitant prices for them? Mr Chamberlain's answer is contained in a series of propositions, the chief of which we proceed to enumerate.

The cost of a scheme for the reconstruction of an unhealthy area should be levied on all owners of property within a certain district wherein the improvement is to be made, in proportion to the value of their holdings. A contributory district should be defined, which might be the whole of the metropolis or the whole of a borough; but if the improvement were essentially local, and for the advantage of an immediate district, the cost might be thrown on the owners within that district. The Artisans' Dwellings Act, 1882, already provides that where the demolition of property dealt with adds to the value of other property belonging to the same owner, an improvement rate may be levied on the increased value.

The local authority should be empowered to acquire lands or buildings compulsorily, at a price to be settled by an arbitrator, who shall be instructed to give in all cases *the value which a willing seller would obtain in the open market from a private purchaser, with no*

allowance for prospective value or compulsory sale'.
The arbitrator should have power to deduct from the ascertained value a sum in the shape of a fine for the misuse of property, or for allowing it to become a cause of disease and crime. Other essentials are that it should be made an offence, punishable by heavy penalties, to hold property unfit for human habitation; that greater independence and power should be given to sanitary and medical officers, and that their responsibility should be enlarged; that powers to destroy unhealthy buildings without compensation should be vested in local authorities, and that they should have more stringent and summary provisions for abating nuisances at the cost of proprietors.

It is between these pointed, definite, and it may be admitted, drastic proposals, based on just principles, and conceived in a generous spirit for the advantage of the community, and the weak, short-sighted, half-hearted and selfish conceptions of the Tory Prime Minister that the new democracy will have to choose.

The proprietors of the pest-houses will, of course, exclaim loudly against these proposals; but their remonstrances may be answered with, 'Salus populi suprema lex.' Not only does this measure formulated as above make for the welfare of the community by improving the public health and by increasing the productivity of labour, it also aims at a more equitable distribution of wealth; it makes for Justice. One would wish that it were superfluous to bring forward these obvious considerations, that it were sufficient to appeal to humanity alone! The Peabody and Ashley Dwellings show what may be done towards the humanisation of the poorer classes while increasing their independence of character.

The State has too long made itself the champion of the rights of the individual; it must now assert the rights of the many — of all. It is apparent that in open competition the fittest obtain more than they deserve, and the less fit come too near perishing. If co-operation is not to supersede competition, the worst effects of this struggle for existence must be at once mitigated. The generation of workmen now coming to manhood will at least be able to read; no doubt they will quickly learn that their claims were long ago admitted to be right and equitable. For the privileged classes long to refuse payment of these claims is impossible; to refuse to pay by instalments is equally impolitic and unjust.

From *The Radical Programme* (Chapman & Hall, 1885)

A2   The Case for Compulsion, 1912

When on the 4th of May, 1911, a British Chancellor of the Exchequer rose in the Mother of Parliaments to move for leave to introduce a Bill 'To provide for insurance against loss of health, and for the prevention and cure of sickness, and for insurance against unemployment, and for purposes incidental thereto', a new landmark was set up in the field of British legislation.

For the Bill so introduced by Mr Lloyd George, which became the National Insurance Act of 1911, is a measure of compulsion, out of the pages of which hundreds of 'shalls' and 'shall nots' leap to the eye. Of these the 'shalls' are the things remarkable and significant. The imaginative mind may hear the Act intoning 'Shall', 'Shall', 'Shall', to toll the knell of *laissez faire*. We have won out of the dark days of 'let be', through an intermediate stage of 'shall not', to the beginning of 'shall'. There are to be positive laws as well as laws of negation. There are to be duties as well as restraints. It was good for freedom when we began to deny the right of a man to do what he liked with his own, and to learn that liberty comes through law. We shall gain a larger freedom by each common rule of positive action that we apply to our society, and to the industry which is the basis of our society. We shall never gain the maximum of freedom until, being sufficiently civilised to agree upon, and to perform, and to share, a minimum of necessary working functions, we give leisure as well as labour to every man through organised work.

There has been for long a conviction in the minds of British politicians and British publicists, born of I know not what evidence or observation, that the British working man would never submit to compulsion. Britons never, never would be slaves. Laws enacting compulsory contributions were all very well for Germans, but British workmen would never submit to such an infringement of the inherent rights of liberty-loving Islanders. We have now put the enactment of the compulsory principle to proof, and what has become of the long-cherished and often expressed opinion as to the views of British workmen on compulsion? We have found that the principle is accepted by all but an insignificant minority without murmur, and that where the Act is disliked it is not because of the application of the principle of compulsory insurance, but because of false representations, which go the length of alleging that the Act cheats the workman by taking part of his wages and giving him little or nothing in return.

From Chiozza Money, *Insurance Versus Poverty* (Methuen, 1912)

A3 Macmillan: The End of Radical Reformism, 1939

At first glance it might appear that the obligations of society to its citizens . . . are already being fulfilled. But the picture is not so rosy when we look at it more closely. Admirable as it is, our system of public health, environmental and social services, falls very far short of providing an adequate basis of physical well-being and security. We shall be left with no doubt on that point when we begin to examine the statistics of poverty and the existing standards of nutrition and physical efficiency. I do not intend to go into the question of the anomalies and inadequacies of the existing social services . . . The larger purpose I have in mind cannot be achieved by the methods on which the social services rely, and it is to these methods I want here to draw attention.

Our expenditure on the social services is maintained out of different forms of taxation or levy. The expenditure represents a transference of wealth from the more fortunate members of society to the less fortunate. Out of the £504 million spent on the social services in 1935, over £234 million was provided by Parliamentary votes from the National Exchequer, over £119 million by local rates or from block grants,[1] and over £147 million out of contributions paid by employers and workers to the Insurance Funds, plus some smaller amounts from fees, interest, rents, etc., accruing under the Education, Housing, and other Acts.

The extent to which a system of social services financed in this way can be extended and improved, is governed by two main factors: first, the weight of the burden thrown upon them by faulty functioning in the economic system, and second, the limits of taxable capacity — whether in the form of income tax or wage-levies upon both employers and workers. If unemployment is acute and/or wages and other incomes are low, the burden on the social services increases. If these conditions of economic depression exist, the taxable capacity of the more fortunate members of society is correspondingly reduced.

But, even apart from any reduction of the incomes of the more fortunate due to trade depression, there is at all times a limit to the taxation that can be levied without discouraging enterprise. What is the limit of taxable capacity is, of course, a highly controversial question. It cannot, however, be disassociated from that of the level of general economic prosperity. The limit fluctuates with depression and boom and, to say the least of it, makes the income foundation for any further extensions of the system unstable and insecure. While I think that, given the other circumstances by which confidence of enterprise is maintained, there is room for *some* improvement in the social services financed by these means, I feel that it has become quite clear that, in any circumstances which are conceivable under the existing conditions of economic life, *the limit of taxable capacity would be reached long before a satisfactory minimum standard of comfort and security could be guaranteed by this method alone.*

Our present system of social services is, in fact, a product of the rapid and more or less automatically expanding phase of a capitalist economy. In the earlier period individual and small group methods of production had produced a lower output, but there was a greater stability and security of employment by which the individual could maintain himself by his own efforts. With the growth of industrialism, the individual producers were drawn into the factories and works which were employing the more efficient methods of co-operation and specialisation necessary to machine production. They became, therefore, more dependent upon the social organisation. They constituted a large and growing mass of the population with no independent resources of production to fall back upon. They were not only poor but had been rendered helpless by their divorce from the circumstances in which self-reliance was possible.

In the ruthless thrust forward to exploit the new methods of the machine age, this social problem became more acute. The more intricate and highly developed the industrial system became, and the further the worker was removed from access to natural resources, the greater became the need for social provision against the risks of his employment. At the same time the more highly skilled industrial operations required better-educated labour, and the great growth of towns and cities made the provision of public health services of some kind absolutely essential.

While these new problems were growing and the social will to deal with them was gradually being expressed in a policy of social provision, the profitability of enterprise was also increasing. It was not merely that profits were high, but the opportunities for remunerative investment appeared to be limitless. The resources of the rich on the one hand, and the needs of the poor on the other, led inevitably to the demand that wealth should be transferred from the rich through the agency of taxation and used to finance the elementary obligations which society had to undertake towards the 'poor and the unfortunate'. The social services were definitely eleemosynary in character and have remained so even while the basis has been broadened.

For a long time it was possible to develop the health insurance and other social provisions against poverty in this way. They grew slowly, lagging behind the growing needs. But the resources of the rich were there to finance improvement on an increasing scale; and it was through this combination of circumstances that opportunity was given to that powerful political movement of reformist radicalism which lasted up to the war.

Despite the interruptions of economic expansion which inevitably occurred, and the political resistance of certain sections of the community, the system of social services was able to grow and the expenditure to increase throughout the whole of the post-war period. By that time the sense of society's duty to its citizens had grown to great strength, and the idea of maintaining the social services at as high a standard as possible was part of the accepted policy of all political parties. So firmly has this policy been accepted, that, in spite of the change in the economic circumstances, involving both the reduction in the profitable opportunities of enterprise and the enormously increased social burdens of the post-war years, the system of social services which had been built up has not only never been in jeopardy, but has been tremendously improved in that period. We have added enormously to our expenditure on social care and protection and sought new methods of financing it, both out of increased taxation and by the adoption of the contributory system.

And yet these services are inadequate. Judged from the standpoint of the benefits to its citizens which a well-organised society, with its enormous resources of production, ought to be able to deliver, our social services are only touching the fringe of social needs. The needs have grown as rapidly as the services. The burdens have increased as quickly as our political willingness to bear them. Our expenditure is diffused over a wider area. Nevertheless we are approaching nearer and nearer to the limits of what can be accomplished by the negative procedure of transferring wealth through taxation or levy.

We have lived through half a century in which the dominant political issues were in essence humanitarian. The social policies that were the subject of controversy could all be paid for out of the expanding revenues of profitable enterprise, or by the newer procedure of contributory schemes which widen the area of taxation. On the basis of the political thinking of the Victorian reformers and their immediate successors we have travelled a long way. But we have now almost exhausted the possibilities of progress on the lines that were suitable to their time. We have reached the end of an era of radical reformism. It has become essential that we should do some fresh thinking for ourselves and try to discover the route of progress in the new circumstances of our time. A new age of radicalism would not be able to rely upon the negative method of meeting social obligations out of the transference of wealth. It must take a firmer hold upon the economic system than that. It must improve economic and social organisation so that the weight of the social burdens will be reduced. And it must achieve an increased production of wealth out of which to support the satisfactory minimum standards that so obviously are essential. Economic reconstruction has today become the only possible or sound basis for social reform.

From Harold Macmillan, *The Middle Way* (Macmillan, 1939)

Notes

1. The block grants are provided out of the National Exchequer, but there is no separation of the amounts spent out of the block grants and out of local rates.

PUBLIC ECONOMY AND SOCIAL WELFARE

A4 The Geddes 'Axe', 1921

As a result of our consideration, we are of the opinion:—

(1) That of recent years the national expenditure on Education has far exceeded what the country can at present afford. The cost of Elementary and Secondary Education *per pupil* has increased unreasonably. The incidence of cost has been transferred increasingly from the local Ratepayer to the Taxpayer, and this has had the serious effect of decreasing the financial responsibility of those who actually spend the money. The Board of Education Vote has since 1918/19 grown from £19 millions to £50 millions.

(2) That children should not be taken into State-aided Schools until they have reached the age of 6.

(3) That the cost of teaching must be brought down by the Local Authorities, and that the only way to effect this is to tell each Local Authority how much money it can have, and leave it to the Local Authority to reap thereafter the full benefit of any economies it may make, and we have suggested ways in which we think that such economies can be made. We are impressed by the position of impotence of the Board of Education in either controlling expenditure or effecting economies, once the policy has been determined. There is no doubt, on the other hand, that Local Authorities have been urged into expenditure upon a scale which they would not have contemplated if left free.

(4) That the grants for Secondary Education are providing State-aided or free education to a class which can afford to pay an increased proportion or even the full cost of education, and that children whose mental capabilities do not justify this higher and much more costly education are receiving it. We wish to make it clear that we do not recommend any serious reduction in free Secondary Education, but suggest that it should be confined to children whose mental calibre justifies it and whose parents cannot afford to pay for it.

(5) That as regards Higher Education generally and Scholarships, the expenditure is in excess of the nation's ability to pay, and must be reduced.

(6) That the Estimates for the Board of Education for the year 1922/

23 should be reduced from £50,600,000 to £34,500,000 (which is approaching twice the 1918/19 provision), a reduction of £16,100,000, which, with the automatic reductions in Scotland, will yield £18,000,000, and we recommend that whatever proportion of the reduced sum is to be paid to Local Authorities should be so allotted by the Board of Education that the vicious results of the percentage grant system shall be terminated forthwith.

(7) That the question of Superannuation of Teachers should be examined, and we suggest that this should be put upon a contributory basis. We view with alarm the liability under this head which is accruing, and which, we are told, may well amount ultimately to £12 millions per annum.

We have suggested that a 5 per cent. contribution on salaries should be made by teachers, which would have an immediate effect upon the Exchequer, but the whole question should be gone into forthwith before the growth of vested interests makes it incapable of modification.

From the *First Interim Report of the Committee on National Expenditure*, Cmd 1581 (1921)

A5 Public Economy and Personal Responsibility: A Response to Geddes, 1922

1. The need for 'economy' at the present time is paramount. We, who are actively concerned in voluntary social service, offer our whole-hearted support to any and every measure which will secure *the best possible use of national resources*. If heavy cuts in expenditure on public social services are inevitable we trust that the Government will try to make the cuts where they will be least harmful, but we desire earnestly to draw public attention to certain considerations.

2. It has been stated in the Press that a saving on public services amounting to £130,000,000 is to be effected during the next financial year. We do not yet know where the cuts are to be made, but the following are some of the services which are already affected:—

Provision for maternity and for infant and child welfare.

School medical services.

The care of the mentally defective.

Provision for the welfare of the blind.

Provision for those suffering from tuberculosis.

The treatment of venereal diseases.

Provision for educational developments and for the normal expansion of educational services.

3. Knowing the waste of human life which is never revealed in balance sheets, we would state publicly three convictions, while the 'big axe' is still uplifted.

(i) Merely to urge 'saving' is to state the needs of the present time in negative form; the positive need is wise spending — 'the best possible use of national resources.'

It is wise to spend on productive investment, foolish to pay a 'fancy' price even for things useful in themselves, and worse than foolish to waste money on unproductive luxuries. **Those of the public services which bring in an annual return of social well-being cannot in themselves be regarded as extravagances.** The cost of their administration must be reduced to the lowest point consistent with efficiency, but if that efficiency is impaired the community will in the end pay more — for police and prisons, workhouses, hospitals, asylums, etc. — while the indirect loss will be incalculable.

(ii) One of the chief glories of this country is the spirit of voluntary service. While that spirit lives, there is an immense reserve of power on which to draw. We must make the best possible use of this reserve, for it is perhaps the greatest of all the nation's resources. **Voluntary service must be mobilised now as it was during the war, for with its aid many services, instead of being curtailed, might be extended.**

(iii) The individual citizen has a heavy responsibility at the present time. He must support the wise control of expenditure on public services, but he can only do so if he is prepared at the same time to exercise a similarly wise control of his own expenditure. **The first and clearest duty of every citizen is to make the best possible use of his individual resources, both personal and financial.**

4. It is hardly possible to exaggerate the importance of the part played by the individual citizen at this time of crisis. His personal responsibility cannot be over-emphasised.

As an illustration, we point to the immediate problem of unemployment, which at the moment overshadows all others. The steps that have been taken to meet this problem are all based upon an expansion of credit. Credit for international trade, loans for works by local authorities, loans to the Unemployed Insurance Fund, or loans raised by Boards of Guardians to meet abnormal relief payments, are all forms of inflation. Taken by themselves they must tend to delay the recovery of trade; but if these loans are accompanied by a corresponding measure of abstinence and real saving by the individual they will not add to the inflation. In fact the individual who spends his money by investing in Treasury Bonds, Local Stock or Savings Certificates, is providing work far more surely than if he uses it to buy things which give only temporary satisfaction.

The moral issue is clear. We appeal with confidence to the individual conscience.

ULLSWATER, *President.*
W.G.S. ADAMS, *Chairman.*
PERCY ALDEN, *Vice-Chairman.*
F.G. D'AETH, *Vice-Chairman.*
R. HENRY REW, *Vice-Chairman.*
CHARLES STEWART. *Hon. Treasurer.*
S. P. GRUNDY *Hon. Secretary.*
LIONEL F. ELLIS. *Secretary.*
National Council of Social Service

Reproduced, with permission, from the *Social Service Review,* January 1922, published by the National Council of Social Service (now the National Council for Voluntary Organisations)

A6   The May Committee: Cuts in Social Services and the Means Test, 1931

[A] general review of the increase of Government expenditure since 1924 shows that of the total increases on various heads likely to reach about £130,000,000 this year, about £80,000,000 could be ascribed to developments of social services, including both those administered by the Government and those under the direct control of local authorities. As regards the latter class, the State contribution represents only a part of the cost and for a complete picture it would be necessary to look also at the accounts of local authorities. Indeed, as regards some social services a large part is played also by private effort.

Between 1911 and 1929 the total cost of these services grew to more than five times its former figure, the charge on rates was trebled, and the charge on the Exchequer was multiplied four and a half times. It is, however, satisfactory to note how very great has been the extension in this period of the policy of requiring contributions towards the cost of social services from those who benefit from them, directly or indirectly.

Since 1929 there has been a further increase of roughly £70,000,000 in the gross cost of unemployment insurance and a steady growth of most . . . other items . . ., and it is roughly correct to say that the above services in the current year are costing the country in one form or another about seven times what they cost in 1911. An increase of this charge on the country's productive capacity would have been a serious matter, notwithstanding the change in the value of money, had our trade continued to develop as in the years immediately prior to the war. Under the difficult conditions of the post war period, the increase of burden has been a grave handicap, and we cannot shut our eyes to the fact that the enormous increase in the Exchequer charge for these services has been the prime cause of the present crisis in the national finances.

Had it been possible to make sufficient reductions in other fields of expenditure we would gladly have been content with comparatively minor adjustments in this field. No such alternative is open and we cannot escape the conclusion that, under existing conditions and bearing in mind the rapid downward tendency in the price level with its inevitable reactions on the cost of living and wages, the rapid growth of this expenditure should be stopped and a large reduction made in the existing charge on the Exchequer.

Transitional Benefit Scheme

The Royal Commission[1] submit interim recommendations in regard to this scheme which have the effect of bringing the cost (which would be increased from £35,000,000 to £44,100,000 by the operation of the 26 weeks limit in benefit) down to £34,000,000. **These recommendations include the introduction of a condition as to need in regard to certain special categories. We are, however, of the opinion that this condition should apply to all applicants for benefit who have exhausted their insurance rights.** Government Departments have not the machinery for inquiring into personal circumstances and to set up special machinery for this national scale. For the time being that principle is in abeyance. Now the Board has to accept local determinations or raise them. Thus, once again, the expenditure of national money according to local standards is the order of the day. But the pendulum swung too far back on 5 February. The wise course now would be to redress the extravagances of the swing, though not to reverse it.

Reproduced, with permission, from R.C. Davison, 'Unemployment Assistance: The Next Move', *Social Service Review* (April 1935), published by the National Council of Social Service (now the National Council for Voluntary Organisations)

Note

1. 'The Turk complex . . . the satisfaction the institution of a dependent family gives to all sorts and conditions of men.'

the case of men) of 11d. each by the State, the employer and the employed person.

From the *Report of the Committee on National Expenditure*, Cmd 3920 (1931)

A7 A Response to the National Economy Bill, 1931

Sir Ben Turner   The burdens of the financial crisis are such, we are told, that we must have some sacrifices from somewhere. The sacrifices always seem to come from those least able to bear them, and they are now coming from them to a very extreme extent indeed. There is something wrong with the method also. An imposition is now being applied. It is not an agreed arrangement between contending or opposite parties, but an imposition on the part of the Government by means of Orders-in-Council and similar things, breaking down the machinery that has been established at great cost and trouble by teachers, trade unionists and professional men in connection with salaries and wages.

The Government have never tried to meet the teachers or any other organisation with the object of making an arrangement in regard to wages or salaries to meet the situation. They have been breaking down one of the best agencies possible for peace in the national sense and peace by negotiation. They are, in this Bill, doing something which is very vile indeed. Many hon. Members will have read more about history than I have, but I have read a great deal about the hungry forties and about the Poor Law of 1830 or thereabouts. We are now re-enacting in the Economy Bill not a reformation of the Poor Law system but a Poor Law inquisition. The Bastille was a great word used in the French Revolution. The Bastille system is to be operated under this inquisition by what is termed the public assistance committee. You may call it the public assistance committee, but it is the Poor Law in the very essence. Our respectable, decent working men and women will have to undergo the inquisition of the former Poor Law system, which is not the right way to deal with this business. Most unemployed people and partly unemployed people are decent, God-fearing men and women. Indeed the whole working-class population of the Kingdom are upright, decent folk. But you are going to penalise them in a cruel and heartless fashion by compelling them to go to the public assistance committee to sign documents and forms under what is termed an Act of necessity. How is the Economy Bill going to work? I am the father of a family, and I have worked out the position in this way. A man, his wife and two children are to get under the Economy Act, 27s. 3d. What does 27s. 3d. mean in brutal, hard facts? It means 10s. for rent and rates. It may be more and it may be less, but that is the average in our provincial industrial towns. There are 84 meals per week for a family of four persons. That only allows for three meals a day, whereas a lad or a lass wants five. Allowing for three meals a day at 2d. a meal per person, the amount comes to 14s. and thus, with the allowance for rent, 24s. has gone out of the 27s. 3d. Then there are coals and gas and all the other accessories of life to be paid for out of the remaining 3s. 3d. It is impossible. It puts them absolutely below the bread line straight away. In the name of national economy, we are going to starve the bairns and break the hearts of the women.

From Hansard, *Parliamentary Debates*, House of Commons, 5th Series, vol. 259, Cols 238–40, September 1931

Note

1. Royal Commission on Unemployment Insurance, *First Report* (1931) Cmd 3872.

THE ADMINISTRATION OF WELFARE

A8   Old Age Pensions Contributory or Non-contributory, 1908

Mr Lloyd-George   The first general criticism is that this is a non-contributory scheme. So long as you have taxes imposed upon commodities which are consumed practically by every family in the country there is no such thing as a non-contributory scheme. A workman who has contributed health and strength, vigour and skill, to the creation of the wealth by which taxation is borne has made his contribution already to the fund which is to give him a pension when he is no longer fit to create that wealth. Therefore, I object altogether to the general division of these schemes into contributory and non-contributory schemes. There is, however, a class of scheme which is known as a contributory one. There is the German scheme, in which the workmen pay into a fund. It is rather a remarkable fact that most social reformers who have taken up this question have at first favoured contributory schemes, but a closer examination has almost invariably led them to abandon them on the ground that they are unequal in their treatment of the working classes, cumbersome, and very expensive, and in a country like ours hopelessly impracticable. Let me give now two or three considerations why, in my judgment, a contributory scheme is impossible in this country. In the first place, it would practically exclude women from its benefits. Out of the millions of members of friendly societies there is but a small proportion, comparatively, of women. Another consideration is that the vast majority are not earning anything and cannot pay their contributions. The second reason is that the majority of working men are unable to deflect from their weekly earnings a sufficient sum of money to make adequate provision for old age in addition to that which they are now making for sickness, infirmity, and unemployment. I do not know what the average weekly wage in this country is; we have not had a wages census since 1886 . . . The average weekly wage in 1886 was 24s. 9d., and 57 per cent. of the working classes in this country were then earning 25s. or less. It is quite clear, therefore, that out of such wages they cannot make provision for sickness, for all the accidents and expenses of life, and also set aside a sufficient sum to provide a competence for old age as well . . .

I find that some of the friendly societies which have superannuation benefits demand that if you fail in your subscriptions you either make it up afterwards, sometimes with interest, or you forfeit your benefit altogether. Now it is obviously impossible that that could be done with the great majority of workmen. The friendly societies of this country have a membership of about 12,000,000. So far from the number being over 12,000,000 it would very likely be under, because a good many members of trade unions are also members of benefit societies. It is very gratifying that such a large number of workmen should have the prudence, foresight, and restraint to enable them to set aside out of earnings money which they might have spent on necessaries or the comforts of the moment. I point that out for this reason, that the House may depend upon it that, if it were within the compass of the means of the working classes to make provision for old age, the fact that they had provided for sickness, that a good many have provided against unemployment and accidents of that kind, would in itself be a proof that they would have provided superannuation for old age if they could have done it. Besides that, I do not think the State has a right to invite the workman earning from 15s. to 20s. or 25s. a week to make the sacrifice which is necessary — the sacrifice, really, of some of the absolute necessaries of life as far as he and his children are concerned, in order to make provision for old age, but that the State itself ought to make it.

Lord R. Cecil   He did not wish to attempt to define socialism and individualism, but there were two very distinct principles on which they might proceed in approaching this question of old-age pensions. There was the principle that primarily it was the duty of everybody to provide for his own old-age, and provide for himself generally. That was the principle that he himself held, and he quite admitted that they were entitled to add to that that where for some reason or another the individual was unable to provide for himself, it was reasonable for the State to come in and give assistance to that individual. That was the principle on which the contributory system rested. The Chancellor of the Exchequer had a very strange view of what was meant by the contributory scheme. He said that all schemes of old-age pensions were contributory because everybody paid taxes. Of course it was quite true that every expenditure was to some extent contributed to by the general body of taxpayers, but nobody knew better than the Chancellor of the Exchequer that that was not what was intended by a contributory scheme at all. The essential theory upon which the contributory scheme was based was that there was to be no out and out gift of money by the State to a class, but that there was to be a subvention to thrift and a gift of money which was to be in return for some contribution made by the recipient. The contrary was that the State was bound to provide for all who required assistance. It might well be said that that was the socialistic theory, that it was the business of the State to step in and take upon itself the duty which ordinarily lay upon the individual. That appeared to him to be the true definition of socialism. When they looked at this measure and asked upon which of those two principles it was based, could anyone doubt that it was based upon the second?

From Hansard, *Parliamentary Debates*, House of Commons, 4th Series, vol. 140, Cols 565–586, June 1908

A9   For Breaking up the Poor Law, 1909

The Scheme We Recommend

We have now to present the scheme of reform to which we ourselves have been driven by the facts of the situation. The dominant exigencies of which we have to take account are:

(i) The overlapping confusion and waste that result from the provision for each separate class being undertaken in one and the same district, by two, three, and sometimes even by four separate Local Authorities, as well as by voluntary agencies.

(ii) The demoralisation of character and the slackening of personal effort that result from the unnecessary spreading of indiscriminate, unconditional and gratuitous provision, through this unco-ordinated rivalry.

(iii) The paramount importance of subordinating mere relief to the specialised treatment of each separate class, with the object of preventing or curing its distress.

(iv) The expediency of intimately associating this specialised treatment of each class with the standing machinery for enforcing, both before and after the period of distress, the fulfilment of personal and family obligations.

We have seen that it is not practicable to oust the various specialised

Local Authorities that have grown up since the Boards of Guardians were established. There remains only the alternative — to which, indeed, the conclusions of each of our chapters seem to us to point — completing the process of breaking up the Poor Law, which has been going on for the last three decades. The scheme of reform that we recommend involves:

(i) The final supersession of the Poor Law Authority by the newer specialised Authorities already at work.

(ii) The appropriate distribution of the remaining functions of the Poor Law among those existing Authorities.

(iii) The establishment of suitable machinery for registering and co-ordinating all the assistance afforded to any given person or family; and

(iv) The more systematic enforcement, by means of this co-ordinating machinery, of the obligation of able-bodied persons to support themselves and their families.

The Supersession of the Destitution Authority

We think that the time has arrived for the abolition of the Boards of Guardians in England, Wales and Ireland; and, so far as any Poor Law duties are concerned, of the Parish Councils in Scotland . . . It has become increasingly plain to us in the course of our inquiry — it is, in fact, recognised by many of the members of these bodies themselves — that the character of the functions entrusted in the Poor Law Authorities is such as to render the task, at best, nugatory and, at most, seriously mischievous. The mere keeping of people from starving — which is essentially what the Poor Law sets out to do — may have been useful as averting social revolution: it cannot, in the twentieth century, be regarded as any adequate fulfilment of social duty. The very conception of relieving destitution starts the whole service on a demoralising tack. An Authority having for its function merely the provision of maintenance for those who are starving is necessarily limited in its dealings to the brief period in each person's life [in] which he is actually destitute; and has, therefore, even if it could go beyond the demoralising dole — too bad for the good, and too good for the bad — no opportunity of influencing that person's life, both before he becomes destitute and after he has ceased to be destitute, in such a way as to stimulate personal effort to strengthen character and capacity, to ward off dangers, and generally to keep the individual on his feet. As regards the effect on individual character and the result in enforcing personal and family responsibilities, of the activities of the Destitution Authority on the one hand, and those of the Local Education Authority and Local Health Authority on the other — even where these latter give food as well as treatment — there is, as all our evidence shows, no possible doubt on which side the advantage lies. Yet if a Poor Law Authority attempts to do more than provide bare subsistence for those who are actually destitute, for the period in which they are destitute; if it sets itself to give the necessary specialised treatment required for birth and infancy; if it provides education for children, medical treatment for the sick, satisfactory provision for the aged, and specialised compulsion for the able-bodied, it ceases to be an 'ad hoc' Authority, with a single tradition and a single purpose, and becomes a 'mixed' Authority, without either the diversified professional staff, the variety of technical experience, or even a sufficiency and continuity of work in any one branch to enable it to cope with its multifarious problems. Moreover, as has been abundantly demonstrated by experience, every increase in the advantage-ousness of the 'relief' afforded by the Destitution Authority, and every enlargement of its powers of compulsory removal and deten-tion, brings it into new rivalry with the other Local Authorities, and drags into the net of pauperism those who might otherwise have been dealt with as self-supporting citizens. If, as it seems to us, it has become imperative to put an end to the present wasteful and demoralising overlapping between Local Authorities, it is plain that it is the Destitution Authority — already denuded of several of its functions — that must give way to its younger rivals.

Besides this paramount consideration, there are two incidental reasons which support our recommendation for the abolition of the Boards of Guardians in England, Wales and Ireland, and, so far at any rate as their Poor Law work is concerned, of the Parish Councils in Scotland. These are:

(a) The grave economic and administrative inconveniences of the existing Poor Law areas; and

(b) The unnecessary multiplication of elected Local Authorities.

In the great majority of cases the population dealt with by the Destitution Authority is too small to permit either of economical administration or of proper provision being made in separate institu-tions for all the various classes of paupers. Out of the 1,879 districts into which the United Kingdom is divided for Poor Law purposes, four-fifths have populations which do not amount to 20,000 families each. Even in England and Wales more than two-thirds of the Unions include fewer than 10,000 families; and 81 of those Unions actually have populations of fewer than 2,000 families each. In Scotland . . . a population smaller than that of London is dealt with by 874 separate Poor Law Authorities, nearly three-eighths of which rule over fewer than 200 families each. Any paper provision of specialised institutions for such small groups of people is absolutely impossible. In short, even apart from any other considerations, there are not more than about 100, out of all the 1,679 Poor Law districts of the United Kingdom, in which it would be possible to make decent provision for the many separate classes which have to be differentially dealt with. We have received a large amount of evidence demonstrating conclusively that, if any new area is adopted for administration and rating it cannot . . . practically be any other than that of the County and County Borough . . .

If the new area adopted be that of the County and County Borough, the Local Authority to be entrusted with the work cannot . . . be any other than the County Council and County Borough Council acting through its several committees. 'You could not have two Authorities in the County area' declared to us a practical County administrator, 'we should always be clashing.' 'It would have to be done by the County Council', Mr Walter Long informed us . . . The same testimony was given by Lord Fitzmaurice, who has so long worked in County government, and who declared himself opposed to any new County Authority for Poor Law purposes only. The setting up in London, or in the County Boroughs, of any separately elected body, for the same area, and levying rates on the same occupiers, appears equally impracticable. We therefore come inevitably to the proposal to transfer the duties of the Boards of Guardians to the Councils of the Counties and County Boroughs.

In favour of this course there are many different arguments. We think that it will be generally recognised that the mere reduction in the number of separate Local Authorities, having separate powers of expenditure of the rates, and making separate demands on the time and service of the citizens willing to stand for election, is an advantage in itself. It unfortunately happens that, at any rate in the County Boroughs of England and Wales which comprise one-third of all the population of that country, the various rivals to the Poor Law — the Local Education Authority, the Local Health Authority, the Local Pension Authority, the Local Unemployment Authority, the Local Police Authority and the Local Authority for the Mentally Defective — have one and all become committees of the Town Council. In the Metropolis and in the Counties, the several committees of the County Council already deal with the same services, though they may share their administration, so far as local duties are concerned, with corresponding committees of minor local authorities. The abolition of the Boards of Guardians, and the adoption of the area of the County and County Borough would, in England and Wales at any rate — with appropriate arrangements to meet the cases of the Metropolitan Boroughs in London and of the non-County Boroughs and Urban and Rural District Councils in the other Counties — enable a very desirable unification of Local Government to be carried out. In this proposal to make the County Borough Councils financially responsible for all the duties at present performed by the Boards of Guardians, we are glad to find ourselves in agreement with a majority of our colleagues. We differ from them in this matter in the extent to which they seek to withdraw the new services from the control of the County or County Borough Council itself, and in the way in which they attempt to determine by what machinery of committees and sub-committees the Councils shall carry out the work entrusted to them. We cannot help thinking that these are matters which, in practice, the Councils will decide for themselves. We doubt, whether any provision of Parliament will prevent a Town or County Council exercising whatever measure of control it chooses over a service entrusted to one of its committees for which it has to find the money. And we cannot help thinking that in adopting as their own the proposal that the unit of area should henceforth be the County and County Borough, and that the supreme authority should be the County Council and County Borough Council, the majority of our colleagues have rendered inevitable the adoption of the principle of distributing the Poor Law services among the committees already concerned in those very services. We cannot imagine, for instance, the Education Committee of the Manchester Town Council handing over to the tender mercies of any new statutory Poor Law Committee, the residential schools for defective children, the Day Industrial Schools, or the provision of dinners for hungry children, in which the Councillors take so much pride; or the Health Committee handing over to the new Poor Law Committee the exact contingent of the patients in its Isolation Hospitals and Isolation Wards who are declared to be destitute. If the responsibility for the administration of the various services of the Poor Law is imposed on the Manchester Town Council at all — if it has to levy the Poor Rate to support the Poor Law Schools at Swinton and the Poor Law Infirmary at New Bridge Street — it may confidently be predicted that it will make its own Education Committee and its Director of Education answerable for the one, and its own Health Committee and Medical Officer of Health answerable for the other.

From the Royal Commission on the Poor Law, *Minority Report*, Cd 4499 (1909)

A10   And Against, 1909

Breaking Up of the Poor Law

There was a scheme brought to our notice known as the 'Breaking up of the Poor Law'. Its ideas appear to be the foundation of the alternative proposals recommended by certain of our colleagues who dissent from our Report. Under the scheme the whole existing machinery of Poor Law administration would disappear with the abolition of the Guardians and the work previously performed by them would be broken up into sections and transferred to existing Committees of County and County Borough Councils.

Though we have had the scheme fully before us, we do not propose to criticise it in detail. It seems clear to us that the idea upon which it is founded is faulty and unworkable. The question at issue is whether the work of maintaining those members of the community who have lost their economic independence can be safely entrusted to authorities whose primary duty is something quite distinct — such as that of Education or Sanitation — or whether it is essential that there should be an authority devoting itself entirely to the work. We consider that the many and subtle problems associated with Public Assistance, especially when it is a family rather than an individual that requires rehabilitation, cannot be solved by the simple process of sending off each unit to a separate authority for maintenance and treatment. What is needed is a disinterested authority, practised in looking at all sides of a question, and able to call in skilled assistance. The specialist is too apt to see only what interests him in the first instance and to disregard wider issues.

Moreover the existing education and sanitary authorities ought not, in our judgement, to be converted into agencies for the distribution of relief; and the less their functions are associated with the idea of relief, the better will they perform the public work for which they were called into existence. To thrust upon these Authorities, while their work is still incomplete, the far more difficult and delicate duties of dealing with families which have already broken down would be to court failure in both directions — that of prevention and that of cure.

There are further difficulties which would inevitably arise from this multiplication of agencies authorised to grant public relief. Whilst a combination of incompatible duties is imposed upon the Education and Health Committees by the scheme, its operation in another direction is to dislocate and separate work which cannot be effectively discharged unless it is combined and under the control of one authority or committee. The functions of granting relief and of the recovery of the cost either from the recipients or those legally liable for them should be in the hands of one body and not divided between two or more organisations with separate staffs and methods of investigation. Such a separation must result in a multiplication of inquiries and visitations, causing annoyance and waste of time and money. The same criticism applies to domiciliary and institutional relief. Being the two recognised methods of Public Assistance they should be utilised together as one system under one supervision. Their disconnection by being placed under two tribunals must lead to administrative inefficiency and confusion. Whilst a multiplication of authorities and organisations for the discharge of local duties is to be deprecated as tending to delay and friction, care must be taken not to run to the other extreme by the abolition of organisations specially qualified for a certain class of work and the transfer of such work to existing bodies who are not specially qualified for its discharge.

From the Royal Commission on the Poor Law, *Majority Report*, Cd 4499 (1909)

A11   Outdoor Relief or Home Assistance, 1909

We have dealt at some length with the history of outdoor relief and the problems which are bound up with it. We have seen that the Royal Commission of 1832 proposed the abolition of outdoor relief in the case of the able bodied and that Parliament accepted that principle. We have described the various orders issued from time to time by the Poor Law Commissioners, the Poor Law Board and the Local Government Board for its prohibition or regulation. We have also traced the fluctuations of public opinion which have greatly influenced its administration in the cases in which it is permitted.

The results of our investigation into its history, of our own observation in visiting Boards of Guardians in different parts of the country, and of the evidence given before us, may be summarised as follows:

We have found a total want of principle and of uniformity in its administration, due, as we think, in part at least, to a lack of sufficient supervision. This want of uniformity does not necessarily arise from a difference in circumstances of unions, but is generally the result of careless administration. We have been impressed by the inadequacy which often characterises it, particularly in the case of widows with families, and by the absence of thorough knowledge of applicants on the part of Boards of Guardians and sometimes even of their officers. We have had to record cases in which it was distributed with a complete disregard of sound policy, and, though rarely, on grounds, so far as we could judge, inconsistent with any high standard of administrative honesty. We have found that in few cases is any care or thought given to the conditions under which those who receive it are living. We do not recommend its abolition, partly because we hope that, if our proposals are adopted, the need for it will gradually disappear and, in any case, its mischiefs will be reduced to a minimum, and partly because we feel that time is needed for the development of a curative system of treatment and that the abolition of out-relief might cause hardship. We also feel that it may be, if used wisely, a means of restoring to independence those to whom it is given and that the strict supervision which we recommend of the housing, surroundings and habits of the recipients may do much to raise the level of a neighbourhood.

We think that the work done by out-relief, so far as it is useful, might be better done by voluntary agencies, and we hope that in the future it will be so and that a clear line will be drawn between the 'necessitous', who are properly relieved by the community, and the 'poor' who are the proper objects of voluntary aid.

Our chief recommendations are:

(1) That Out-relief, or as we shall call it, Home Assistance, should

be given only after thorough inquiry, except in cases of sudden and urgent necessity.

(2) That it should be adequate to meet the needs of those to whom it is given.

(3) That persons so assisted should be subject to supervision.

(4) That, with a view to inquiry and supervision, the case-paper system should be everywhere adopted.

(5) That such supervision should include in its purview the conditions, moral and sanitary, under which the recipient is living.

(6) That voluntary agencies should be utilised as far as possible for the personal care of individual cases.

(7) That there should be one uniform Order governing Outdoor Relief or Home Assistance.

From the Royal Commission on the Poor Law, *Majority Report*, Cd 4499 (1909)

A12 Introducing Unemployment Insurance, 1911

Mr S. Buxton The scheme is automatic. It adapts itself to contingencies. The benefits are strictly limited in duration and to a large extent proportionate to the contributions, and we start with a considerable estimated margin of over £200,000 a year, or 10 per cent. If, therefore, our estimate is not over-sanguine we shall be able to improve the benefits conferred by the scheme if we are allowed to start at once, as I hope we shall be, and we shall, under this Bill, rapidly accumulate a large reserve, which will be of assistance when times of depression come, and if continuous good or medium times come, we shall be able to vary the benefits from time to time either in the amount or in the period. So that we have elasticity in that way, and we can call upon the Treasury in time of prolonged depression to come to the assistance of the Fund and to make advances to be subsequently repaid without burden on the public as better times come along. Finally we are able to vary the contribution within strict limits, because no one desires an unlimited liability contribution should be thrown upon either the employers or the workmen, and we are able within limits to alter and change the contribution . . .

It is [said] that we should not carry out the compulsory part of this scheme, but make a beginning with voluntary insurance alone. That also, I hope, will be strenuously resisted by the House, because without the compulsory part we cannot make a real effort — we cannot carry out a comprehensive system of National Insurance against unemployment. All the experience abroad goes to show that a purely voluntary scheme will not really be of an effective character. It naturally includes bad risks, and almost from the beginning it is bound to be more or less financially unsound.

If the scheme is based upon compulsion it must obviously be based on a trade basis, and I think everyone who has considered the subject recognises that in this matter you must have the foundation of a trade basis. On this part I know there has been a great deal of criticism. This Bill starts on the system of a limited number of employments, and we include in this proposal certain trades, the ship-building trade, engineering, building, the construction of vehicles, and we have for the moment excluded other trades and interests from the purview of the Bill. We have done that on two grounds. In the first place this is an experimental measure, and we want, before extending it further, some greater financial experience to enable us to decide whether and to what extent other trades ought to be brought into the scheme.

Then, assuming that there are selected classes, the House may ask why particular classes are in fact chosen. The trades to which I have referred are the trades in which we found, on the whole, that the fluctuations of employment were the greatest and, on the whole, they were the trades most sensitive to ups and downs of depression and good times. I find that in the trades concerning which we have information in the twenty years on which we have actually based our estimates, taking the trades as a whole, the unemployment percentage varies between 2 per cent and 7.8 per cent, while in regard to these particular trades the figures vary between 2.7 per cent and 18.4 per cent, which shows that in these trades the fluctuations are greater than in the rest of the industrial field. They are trades also in which the difficulty is met rather by discharges than by short time.

From Hansard, *Parliamentary Debates*, House of Commons, 5th Series, vol. 26, Cols 273–9, May 1911

A13   Alternative Means of Providing for Family Allowances, 1924

. . . The reader should now . . . judge for himself as to the relative merits of direct provision for families through occupational pools or through State endowment.

To sum them up briefly: the advantages of the pool system are chiefly psychological, in the sense that they are concerned with the reaction to the scheme of those it affects. Because it can be adopted piecemeal and experimentally, it is more likely to commend itself, at least as a first step, to a conservative-minded, cautious nation. It will be easier to get it going because it is a smaller matter to convince a group of people, experienced in the difficulties of providing for families through the present wage-system and conscious of their own direct responsibility as employers or leaders of working-class opinion, than to convince a Parliament or a Government. The grading of allowances to suit the different standards of life and eugenic needs of different sections of the population, which is essential if the full advantages of direct provision are to be reaped, will come about much more easily and naturally through occupational pools than under a State system, though it is technically quite possible under the latter. For the same reason, the pool scheme is better suited to allay . . . the fear of stimulating population in the wrong places and the fear of diminishing the incentive to industry — since it is plain that if either of these results did happen, those who are responsible for the pool covering the occupations adversely affected could check it by varying the amount and conditions of the allowance.

On the other hand, the State system has many material and a few psychological advantages. It would be a far more complete treatment of the whole difficulty. It could be made to cover, by a single Act of Parliament, all classes and occupations, including some which it will be very difficult, for technical or psychological reasons or both, to bring under occupational schemes. It could be more economically administered, since the State has already nearly all the necessary machinery of administration — the post office, the educational and public health services. It would rectify the very serious anomaly by which the industries employing little adult male labour are enabled to escape their fair share of what should be a national burden by shifting it on to the other trades. This again could technically be done under the occupational system, but it would practically be difficult to enforce it.

On the psychological side, the advantages of a State system are that it implies a more complete act of restitution to the family, by acknowledging that its claim on the nation rests on its own value and not on the occupational services of the father. For the same reason it would do more to raise the status of motherhood. But the opportunist who values a bird in the hand more than two in the bush, might perhaps rather deem these two points a disadvantage, since they are a direct challenge to the hidden Turk.[1]

Lastly — and I leave it to the reader to determine whether the point tells in favour of an occupational scheme or a State system — under the former the question of whether family allowances should constitute an addition to the existing wage bill, or a redistribution, or a mixture of both, would be fought out within the industry and decided according to its circumstances and the bargaining strength of the parties concerned; under a State system, the incidence of the cost on the various classes of the community would depend in the first instance on the Government which happened to be in power when the system was introduced. What its ultimate reaction might be on wages is a question I will not discuss, but will content myself with the surely safe generalisation that, in the long run, the share which each class in the community secures for itself of the nation's wealth will depend, not on whether the share comes to it in the shape of profits only, or wages only, or profits and wages plus family allowances, but first, on the size of the divisible heap; secondly, on the value of the contribution made by the class to the heap; thirdly, on the skill with which it uses its economic and political bargaining power to secure the equivalent of its contribution.

As a security, however, against extravagant demands on the one hand and unfair attacks on wages on the other, the solution proposed by the New South Wales Labour Party might some day provide a satisfactory basis for a compromise between the two sections of opinion. At their Conference in 1921 they proposed

(a) The fixation of a basic wage for a man and wife, based on the stabilized cost of living.
(b) The maintenance of all children of the nation by a direct charge on the whole community by means of a graduated tax on all incomes.

Such a solution would imply a definite abandonment by Labour of the attempt 'to eat their cake and have it' by drawing maintenance for their children from the nation and simultaneously including it in the wage bill. On the other hand it would prevent employers from using family allowances as an excuse for forcing the lower grades of workers below a reasonable standard of life.

From Eleanor Rathbone, *The Disinherited Family* (Allen & Unwin, 1924)

A14   For 'Approved Societies' in National Health Insurance, 1926

We come, therefore, to the question whether the Approved Society system should be continued. This question must be examined from two points of view. The first is that of the maintenance of a system under which the Scheme is administered by self-governing organisations responsible for their own finance, and all that this implies in regard to additional benefits; or its supersession by a centralised system with a common fund, the benefits being administered, possibly, by local agencies but subject to close control and direction from the central governing body. The second point of view is that of the criticisms which have been directed against the methods and procedure of the Approved Societies as such, and the possibility that if these criticisms are so weighty as to indicate the desirability of abolishing the Societies, some other form of organisation, short of complete centralisation, can be found to take their place.

To the first of these problems we have given careful thought. We feel that if a centralised system were adopted it would compel the dissolution of the Approved Societies, since the reduction of the Societies to mere paying agencies would involve the separation of administrative and financial responsibility, a result which could not, in our opinion, be defended. This is a serious consideration and one involving more than a mere change of method in the administration of the Health Insurance system. We feel that it is to the public advantage that this great Scheme should be administered by the representatives of the insured persons themselves, and that the governing bodies should have that full responsibility for the results of their own activities without which it is as hopeless as it would be unreasonable to look for a high standard of efficiency and vigilance. In this connexion we realise that there are features of the system which must appear to many as defects, and that these cannot be eradicated from it. On the other hand we cannot disregard the consideration that opinion as to faults and defects in a Scheme of this kind is largely a matter of the individual standpoint, and that what amounts in the eyes of some to a flaw will commend itself to others as an element of equity and justice. It is clear that if effect is to be given to the views of one school of thought, acute dissatisfaction will be aroused in the minds of those who hold the contrary opinion and regard the present machinery as equitable in its operation. We do not ourselves think that the best interests either of the State or of the insured population would be served by a vast amalgamation of all the resources of the Scheme in a common fund administered from the centre, and for the reason given we are satisfied that such an amalgamation would create as much discontent as it would allay. From this point of view, therefore, we have come to the conclusion that a system of self-governing bodies is to be preferred and should be retained.

As to the other type of criticisms, the substantive plea behind which is that the system of administration through the Approved Societies is open to so many objections that some new method of administration should be substituted for it, we have to take note of the fact that the Approved Societies are in possession of the field, by the action of Parliament, that they have their organisations widely distributed over the whole of the country and their staffs trained in the details of what, in many respects, is an intricate piece of social administration. The onus of showing that the system, either from causes inherent in itself, or from personal shortcomings of those by whom it is operated, works so imperfectly that it ought to be abolished, rests upon those who take this view. We have considered their evidence with care, and, we trust, without bias. We have also reviewed the evidence given to us by the large number of officials who have appeared before us as representing the Societies, and we have studied their attitude of mind in their relations with the insured person and their work generally as revealed to us by the answers given to the many questions which we have put to them. In the result we have come to the conclusion that no case for the abolition of the Societies can be established on the broad ground of defects and shortcomings in administration. In saying this we are not to be understood as indicating that there are no faults to be remedied. We could wish, for instance, that in some quarters the interests of the insured persons were more fully considered in regard to such matters as expenditure on administration within the prescribed limit or that the rights of the members had been more fully respected when the constitutions of certain of the Societies were framed; and we have had occasional evidence, which must be treated with respect, pointing to shortcomings in the payment of benefits and other dealings between the Societies and their members. But we realise that defects of these kinds spring less from improper motives than from those human weaknesses that in some form or another must reveal themselves in whatever type of organisation may be erected to administer a great scheme such as the one we have under review; and we cannot accept them as amounting, in the whole, to the establishment of such a case against the Societies as to warrant us in recommending that they should be superseded.

It has also seemed to us in the course of our investigation that certain of the Societies may be so large as to make it impossible for the highest degree of administrative efficiency to be attained, regard being had to the limits of human capacity to deal with an intricate piece of administration of which the subjects are not mechanical but human beings with all their idiosyncrasies and weaknesses . . . Taking everything into consideration, however, we conclude that the Approved Societies should be retained as an essential part of the system and on this fundamental question we submit a recommendation to that effect.

From the Royal Commission on National Health Insurance, *Majority Report*, Cmd 2596 (1926)

A15 And Against, 1926

Until . . . the system is taken out of the hands of Approved Societies and placed in the hands of Local Authorities, we hold that the policy which received the general support of our colleagues, and is being urged by the Minister of Health in application to services at present administered by Boards of Guardians, cannot be applied to its full and proper extent.

We take this view because, first, we think that in essence the administration of benefits paid in cash under the National Health Insurance Acts is a health service. These payments are made either

(1) When a woman within the present scope of maternity benefit is confined of a child; or

(2) When an insured person becomes and remains incapable of work owing to illness; or

(3) When an insured person who happens to belong to a Society

which can provide additional benefits, can show that a payment enabling him to get one of these benefits would be likely to improve his health.

If the function of the Approved Society in relation to these types of payment is examined, it will be seen to be as follows:

(1) The interest of the Approved Society in the child-bearing woman begins and ends with handing over to her a lump sum of money. That Local Authorities could make this payment equally well is self-evident. It is scarcely less obvious that much more could be done for child-bearing women who need other services directed to safeguarding the health of mothers and infants by Local Authorities, who already administer such services, than by Approved Societies, who have nothing to do with them.

(2) The interest of the Approved Society in the normal and the additional benefits is less narrow. In relation to the normal benefits they are concerned (*a*) to see that insured persons who are entitled to benefit are promptly paid, and (*b*) to see that no insured person is paid unless he is entitled to payment.

Local Authorities, who deal with people living in their respective areas, could of course pay benefit in proper cases at least as quickly as Approved Societies, whose members may live in any one of the administrative areas of the country.

Whether a payment ought to be made to an insured person depends upon the answer to the question, 'Is this person incapable of work owing to illness?' This question is answered, in practice, by a doctor, subject to the right of the body through whom payment is made to scrutinise the doctor's certificate, to obtain a further medical opinion, and to complain if they think that the doctor has not told the truth.

Now it seems to us that the whole of these proceedings are an integral part of the medical service rendered by insurance practitioners under their contracts.

The Commission are unanimous in recommending that Insurance Committees should be abolished and that their functions should be transferred to Local Authorities, and we cannot resist the further conclusion that Local Authorities could and should take the place of Approved Societies as the Authorities through whom sickness and disablement benefits should be administered.

(3) In relation to the payment of sums enabling an insured person

to get an additional benefit:

   (*a*) so far as the additional benefits consist in increases of the normal benefits, the Approved Society is concerned with the points already dealt with;

   (*b*) so far as the additional benefits are in the nature of medical benefit, the interest of the Approved Society is, or (as our colleagues agree) ought to be, no more extensive. They do not provide the benefits. They merely hand over to some of their members, who, if properly selected, are so selected on medical grounds, money enabling the benefits to be obtained. They are not qualified to assess the value of the services rendered for the money, and we gather that the business of securing a proper return for the sums spent on dental and ophthalmic treatment given by way of additional benefit is, in fact, receiving the attention of the Minister of Health.

   We are convinced that the whole of this work, so far as it is a matter of local administration, could be far better done by the Local Authorities already responsible for other health services.

Secondly, we do not think that the administration of benefits paid in cash, being a health service, is a health service which it is desirable to administer through agencies specially constituted for the purposes of this service alone.

In support of this view we would submit four arguments, one based upon considerations of general policy, and three upon the practical consequences of these considerations.

The first is that the citizenship of insured persons is more important than their insurability. Just as Your Majesty's Government refuse to accept the argument of Boards of Guardians that separate authorities ought to deal with citizens who happen to be destitute, so we hold that any attachment which insured persons may have to their Approved Societies can and should be transferred, with the work of the Societies, to the Local Authorities of the areas in which they live.

The second argument is that the result of this transfer would be to remove the scandal, admitted by our colleagues, that Approved Societies comprising a very large part of the total insured population are administered with complete disregard of the direction of . . . the Act of 1911 that their affairs should be subject to the absolute control of their members.

The Majority Report seems to us to evade that issue in the

statement that most people do not 'maintain that degree of interest in public affairs which good citizenship postulates'.

The fact is that the constitution of the Approved Societies to which we have referred, makes it impossible for the members to take any substantial part in the management.

The third argument is that the transfer to Local Authorities of the administration of benefits paid in cash would result in a greater equalisation of liabilities over the insured population as a whole than is secured under the present system. The present association of insured persons in Approved Societies is inimical to the interest of those persons as a whole, and to the interest of employers and taxpayers who contribute to the cost of the system, because in practice it encourages the process by which the members composing the healthy groups get most (by way of additional benefits) in return for their contributions, and the least healthy least. Under the Approved Society System it is, in our opinion, impossible to use the whole resources of National Health Insurance to the greatest advantage of the insured population as a whole.

The object of a 'national' health insurance system must presumably be, not to supply cream to the fat and skim milk to the lean, but good milk to all insured persons.

It is already an accepted doctrine of local government that the inhabitants of a given town or country have such community of interest with each other that those who are able can properly be called upon to pay for services which others need. A system based upon the historic administrative areas of the country has, therefore, the indefinable but important advantage of enlisting the support of local sentiment and local patriotism.

Where the local community of interest in a public service stops, and the interest of the community as a whole in the efficiency of the service begins, that fact is recognised by the payment of a contribution by the taxpayer in aid of the cost of the service.

The fourth argument is that the transfer of the work of Approved Societies to Local Authorities must, if it had any effect of this kind at all, improve and not weaken the possibility of putting into operation the provisions of the Act of 1911 which were designed to enable the burden of cost resulting from excessive sickness (that is, sickness which could and should have been prevented) to be put upon the right shoulders.

It is clear from Sections 15 (7), 22 and 63 of the Act of 1911 (now Sections 85 and 107 of the 1924 Consolidating Act), and from the statements made in Parliament on the introduction of the Bill, that the framers of the measure intended their scheme to be intimately connected with the other health services, and enquiry and action were to be possible wherever bad environment induced ill-health. Thus action could be taken wherever the conditions or nature of employment, bad housing or sanitation, insufficient water supply, or indeed, neglect on the part of any person or Authority to enforce the law relating to public health or housing was involved.

Yet Section 107 is a dead letter, and that this is so is largely due to the fact that membership of Approved Societies is scattered all over the kingdom instead of being localised, and that in one street, or indeed in one house, every inhabitant may belong to a different Society, each with its headquarters entirely out of reach of the ordinary insured member.

This brings us to another essential point laid down by the framers of the Act. The scheme was to be democratic, controlled by the insured for the insured. Here again the Act is almost a dead letter, and we feel that in this case also the constitution of the Societies renders it inoperative.

The statement of our colleagues that most people do not 'maintain that degree of interest in public affairs which good citizenship postulates' is of general philosophic interest, but it appears to us to have no bearing on the question before us. In every class of life people are interested in matters which affect their pockets, and the fact that insured members are not interested in the management of a scheme which involves deductions from their wages and accruing benefits, suggests something very wrong with the machinery. We believe that different results might be achieved if these Societies came under the control of the Local Authority. This would limit their numbers to about 150 Societies as against 7,876 existing financial units. The best officers already trained in Approved Society work would be available and the varying occupational risks which at present aggravate inequalities would be modified by territorial grouping.

From the Royal Commission on National Health Insurance, *Minority Report*, Cmd 1596 (1926)

A16   Principles of Unemployment Assistance, 1935

A standard scale and rules   The Regulations are based upon a standard scale and rules for the whole country, with power for modification in individual cases.

The large majority of applicants to the Board live in industrial areas. With the exception of rent, there was no sufficient difference in the cost of living as between industrial areas that would have justified a standard of payment based on need for a man with wife and children higher, or lower, in, say, Sunderland or the Rhondda than for a similar family in Newcastle or Lanarkshire. Nor could the Board see why, as a general rule, a son in employment and living at home should contribute a higher or lower proportion of his wages to the support of his unemployed father because he lived in Sheffield, for example, rather than in Liverpool, or in Manchester rather than in Birmingham.

On the other hand, it had to be recognized that the standards of assistance given by the Local Authorities, at their own charges, to able-bodied unemployed persons in their own area showed wide variations.

These variations became more marked during the administration of transitional payments. Upon examination of them it was difficult to discern any principles which could be said to account for the differences in payments and in the methods of assessment adopted; they were the result of a number of local factors, few of which had any recognizable relation to the question of the applicant's need.

After taking careful account of the considerations . . . the Board decided that it would not be justified, as a central department administering central funds, in proceeding on any other principle than that of equality of treatment for households in similar circumstances, wherever they lived. Both as a matter of principle and of practical common sense, therefore, the Board prepared Regulations based upon a standard appropriate to the normal needs of a household, and not upon the local variations of standard which existed in transitional payments and public assistance and were to a large extent accidents of the boundaries of Local Authorities.

Discretion   It has been maintained that a scheme of administration by officials, even with the safeguard of Appeal Tribunals, must necessarily be mechanical and bureaucratic in temper. A centralized system, it was argued, must be out of touch with the realities of the

lives of unemployed persons and would be less sensitive to the variations of their personal needs than administration by a number of
local people on local committees.

This criticism was probably founded upon the belief that all
applicants under the previous schemes had had their cases considered individually and personally by committees. Whatever may
have been true of the administration of the Poor Law in dealing with
the ordinary poor, it is indisputable that where the numbers of
persons on outdoor relief or transitional payments were large, the
committees could not carry out their duty except by the application,
mainly through their officials, of scales of relief, with some attempt
at uniformity of allowance within the areas.

The standard laid down by the Regulations and approved by
Parliament must, of course, be regarded as the normal standard,
capable of application to the generality of cases; otherwise the
Regulations would fail in their purpose and the approval of Parliament would be meaningless. But every applicant is a separate
human being with his own needs and his own environment, and the
Board has throughout encouraged and instructed its officers to take
this view of each case.

The answer to the criticism that administration by officers of a
central board must be mechanical, or that the interest of an officer in
a household under his charge would be limited to an arithmetical
calculation of the allowance to be paid, is . . . that a crude and
uniform mathematical method has not been applied. In not less than
20 per cent of the cases, the officers of the Board have used their
authority to grant allowances above the normal provided for in the
Regulations, and many instances have come to the knowledge of the
Board of personal service given by officers, or secured by them, for
households with which they are in touch.

The Relation Between Relief and Wages

The Board thinks it necessary to call attention to a fundamental
question that arises on any general scale of assistance for
unemployed persons. Reference is made . . . to the difficult
problem of the relation between assistance given during
unemployment on the one hand, and general wage levels and the
normal earnings of applicants when at work on the other. Even with
the rule that no applicant should receive in assistance as much as he
could ordinarily earn, the amount of assistance granted in many
cases may be so little below an applicant's normal net earnings as to

diminish both his eagerness to obtain work and his reluctance to relinquish it.

There are already disquieting signs in individual cases that the close correspondence between wages and allowances is influencing some applicants of the Board. Opportunities of training are provided for unemployed men with a view to the improvement of their physical condition and their chances of employment. The number of younger men, many of whom have never had a regular job since leaving school, who refuse to avail themselves of these opportunities is causing the Board much concern. Similarly, many of the younger women without prospect of employment in their own home area have shown themselves unwilling to take employment elsewhere. Not infrequently also there are cases of married men with families whose allowances are practically the same as the earnings they would normally gain; they find the allowances sufficient for their purpose, with the result that they show little disposition to take work or to hold it when it is given to them. Taken altogether these cases are only a small proportion of the total number of applicants, but they are a significant problem.

The Standstill

By the terms of the Order-in-Council of October 1931, each Local Authority was required to base its allowances by way of transitional payments upon the standard of assistance adopted by it for the relief, at its own charge, of able-bodied unemployed persons in its own area, subject to the provision that the transitional payments allowance was not, in any case, to exceed the amount that would be payable as unemployment benefit. Any supplementation of these allowances in a particular case was at the charge of the Local Authority. It was inevitable, therefore, that there should be considerable differences in the principles adopted for the determination of need and in the amounts paid in the various areas. In the same district amounts paid to households in similar circumstances varied by several shillings merely because the homes of applicants on one side of the street were situated within the boundaries of a Local Authority different from that of the homes on the other side of the street. Uniformity of practice did not always obtain even among the sub-committees of an Authority in the same area. Families might and did receive sums of money that varied according to the views of the different sub-committees. Further variations resulted from the fact that the whole cost of transitional payments was borne by the

Exchequer. From the inception of the transitional payments scheme, Local Authorities applied the Order-in-Council with varying degrees of strictness, and before the date at which the new Regulations took effect, there had been in many areas a progressive relaxation of responsibility. This relaxation in the assessment of need was especially marked in the extent to which the resources of other members of the household were disregarded.

The differences between estimates and results were due in part to a fuller disclosure of resources under the Board's administration than had been made under the administration of transitional payments, in part to an increase in earnings due to improving trade after the estimates were made, and in part to transitional payments being higher in some cases than had been anticipated owing to the deterioration of the local administration in the late months of 1934. The field over which these factors operated was so wide that they were bound to affect the original estimate. But, even if these unexpected differences had not arisen, the distribution of public money in accordance with need as assessed under the Regulations rather than with the past practices of Local Authorities was bound to lead to reductions as well as increases. It was natural that more expression should be given in the House of Commons and in the country to discontent about the former than to appreciation of the latter.

It was urged that the Board had not sufficiently exercised its powers of discretion. The full flexibility of the Board's administration naturally was not attained in the first month of its existence. While the Regulations supplied general rules and a general standard for application to the ordinary case, they contained provision for the exercise of discretion to meet the 'special circumstances' . . . of an individual case. The exercise of this discretion would be progressive and cumulative, as cases of special need and special circumstances came to light, and it could not be expected to show its full results in the first two or three weeks of an administration involving the investigation and determination of 100,000 cases a week. But the Regulations did not authorize, and no honest use of discretionary powers would permit, general departures in ordinary cases at the arbitrary decision of the Board and of its officers, from standards laid down in the Regulations so recently approved by Parliament.

It was in this situation that on 15 February 1935 Parliament passed the Unemployment Assistance (Temporary Provisions) Act, 1935, generally known as the 'standstill' Act. Under this Act it was laid down that an applicant should be paid either an allowance according to the Regulations or such allowance as he would have received if transitional payments under the administration of the Local Authorities had continued, whichever was the higher. The standstill Act also postponed the Second Appointed Day.

The officers of the Board are now administering a complicated double standard, whose results are often not intelligible to the applicants; that of the Regulations and of transitional payments. If the standards of assistance of a Local Authority in relation to the able-bodied unemployed are altered, the Board's officers must follow suit, and in some areas where the number of unemployed chargeable to the Local Authority is negligible in contrast with the number chargeable to he Board, these standards have been raised avowedly in order to produce an immediate influence upon the amount of assistance given by the Board. Further, the standstill Act involves, as a statutory obligation upon the officers of the Board, the continuance of many of the anomalies in the transitional payments position whose abolition was one of the reasons for the creation of the Board. It also requires the Board, in numerous cases to pay allowances to households, ostensibly on the ground of need, which are simply an abuse of public money.

From the *Annual Report of the Unemployment Assistance Board*, Cmd 5177 (1935)

A17   A Comment on the 'Standstill', 1935

There are . . . certain vital social and administrative defects in the present scheme which are just as urgently in need of attention, and it is here that the opinion and advice of experienced social workers should come in. Clearly the new system is much too mechanical in conception. If administration of this poverty service is not to degenerate into something less human and more demoralizing than the public assistance it has superseded, it must cease to make a fetish of uniform scale payments. A centrally determined scale is all very well as a guide, and the Board have shown great skill in 'schematizing' the needs test, but, when all is said and done, there is hardly a single rule which would not be better broken in more than half the cases to which it is meant to apply. Personal circumstances vary too much and are too important, both economically and morally, to justify automatic administration by scale and rule. Discretionary treatment is half the battle. By whatever name it may be called, this service is simply an extension of the Poor Law: it requires the Poor Law technique. Personal character and deserts cannot be wholly left out of account; they may lead to an upward as often as to a downward revision of the scale payment. That may be unfashionable doctrine to-day, but no one who has done Poor Law work or served on one of the Board's Appeals Tribunals can honestly deny its truth. In fact a large proportion of the Board's clients are indistinguishable from the Poor Law type and many thousands of them are already familiar with their local Public Assistance Committee. Over the greater part of England today the Insurance Scheme covers very nearly all the unemployment of the really active and eligible workers. What is left over is a fraction of two or three per cent who, at the best of times, have had only a precarious foothold in the industrial field. This is particularly noticeable in the London area and the South, where the methods of mass relief are totally inapplicable. The depressed areas are in a class by themselves.

How then can a sufficiently wide measure of discretion be injected into this essentially bureaucratic scheme? That question cannot be dogmatically answered at present. In the first place the number of 'discretionary' officers may have to be greatly increased if they are to have time even to think about individual cases. At present the average load of an Area Officer is said to vary between 3,000 and 6,000 applicants. Under the Poor Law in London the load was less than 300 out-relief cases per Relieving Officer, and the latter had an Assistant Relieving Officer to help him. The Public Assistance officials naturally had certain other functions added to them, but they always had the chance of knowing their clients and their district. Under the Board's present system that is certainly not possible.

The next and most vital question is: Can a discretionary service ever work smoothly and acceptably without the aid of local interviewing committees? It is no good waiting for applicants to appeal to Tribunals which are courts of second instance. Only a negligible fraction, not one per cent, appear. Either the personnel obtained by the Board for these Tribunals must sit and hear and interview cases in the first instance, or the help of new interviewing committees must somehow be obtained.

To sum up the position: The Act of 1934 told the Unemployment Assistance Board to supersede all local standards by a uniform national scale. For the time being that principle is in abeyance. Now the Board has to accept local determinations or raise them. Thus, once again, the expenditure of national money according to local standards is the order of the day. But the pendulum swung too far back on 5 February. The wise course now would be to redress the extravagances of the swing, though not to reverse it.

Reproduced, with permission, from R.C. Davison, 'Unemployment Assistance: The Next Move', *Social Service Review* (April 1935), published by the National Council of Social Service (now the National Council for Voluntary Organisations)

Note

1. 'The Turk complex . . . the satisfaction the institution of a dependent family gives to all sorts and conditions of men.'

TESTS OF NEED OR DESERT

A18   Old Age Pensions: The Case for Selectivity and Tests, 1895

. . . We fully recognise that there are many among those who become destitute in old age for whom assistance in some form should be secured independent to the workhouse; and we have specially insisted that where outdoor relief is granted the amount should be adequate to the needs of the recipient. But if we look closely at the statements of the more extreme advocates of extended outdoor relief, it is clear that some of them contemplate its grant as a matter of course to the poorer members of the working classes, provided that they have led decent lives, as soon as they cease to be able to earn the normal wages of their calling. It has been proposed that the relief should not be limited to those who are destitute, that it should be granted to persons whose relatives could provide the reasonable necessities of life, or who could procure them upon their own resources; and that it should not be made conditional on proof in each case of efforts to provide in the earlier years of life for the inevitable wants of old age, it being often assumed that any such provision is impossible for larger classes of the population. We have found many indications of such views in the evidence of witnesses who have come before us as representatives of the working classes . . .

While we fully appreciate the humane motives of those who wish for the general extension of outdoor relief in the case of the aged, we cannot but feel that grave risks would be incurred if no definite tests were imposed dependent on the individual circumstances of each case; such, for example, as the requirement of a clear measure of destitution, and evidence of respectability and a reasonable endeavour on the part of the applicant to make provision for his old age in accordance with his means during working life, and of general independence of the rates until the failure of physical faculties has deprived him of the means of support. We also feel that it would be undesirable to interfere with the discretion at present exercised by the guardians in cases where the applicants have relatives in a position to keep them, who are with-holding the assistance they might fairly be expected to give. We do not advise that persons should be relieved who are not really destitute, but we feel that

evidence of an industrious or independent life is presumptive proof
of thrift, and entitles the applicant to better treatment than the
wastrel or drunkard. In the absence, however, of such safeguards as
we have indicated, the lot of those relying on assistance upon the
rates would be more inviting than that of the independent aged with
the inevitable result that, as with the able bodied under the old Poor
Law, there would be a great increase in that pauperism, the wide
extent of which at present is so much deplored. And we fear that this
increase would not be among those seeking occasional and slight
help, by whom the figures of pauperism are now so largely swelled,
but among those who are in receipt of permanent assistance from the
rates, and who under such a system would have had no motive to
make even partial provision for themselves. Moreover, the cost of
relief so administered would, as we think, prove very heavy, while
there would be a great risk of neglect of that substained supervision
so absolutely necessary, and consequently of a return to the system
of doles with its attendant evils. These latter objections, grave as
they are, are perhaps of secondary importance compared with the
recognition of the principle that dependence on the rates is henceforth to be regarded as the proper condition of the respectable poor
in old age; a principle as it seems to us, fatal to that hope so generally
expressed that pauperism is becoming a constantly diminishing evil,
ultimately to disappear before the continuous progress of thrift and
social well-being . . .

From *The Report of the Royal Commission on the Aged Poor*, 1895,
C. 1684

A19   Charles Booth and the Case for Universality, 1895

Charles Booth: On the scheme that I wish to bring before the
Commission it is intended that every one born in England or Wales
. . . shall, when 65, be entitled to the pension . . . of 5s. a week.
Lord Aberdare (Chairman): The most startling part of your proposition and one, I think, we all find most difficult to explain to ourselves, is why the very large numbers of those who do not want 5s. a
week should have 5s. a week pressed upon them?
Charles Booth: I believe it to be necessary to take from this proposal
the harmful economical effects which do, in my judgement, come
from relief when it depends upon consideration or desert or
necessity . . .

Lord Aberdare: You have made a suggestion, I think, as to how the £24,000,000 [the estimated cost of the scheme for the United Kingdom] should be raised?

Charles Booth: I have stated that there is no difficulty in raising it fairly, if by fairly is meant that everyone should pay in proportion to what he earns, I do feel strongly that for public expenditure it is very desirable that all classes should feel the pressure of taxation . . .

In order to guard against misuse, the claim for a pension to everyone who has had relief during a certain previous period . . . should be made through the guardians; and the money applied at the discretion of the guardians indoors or out for the benefit of the pauper . . . This difference would be keenly felt and I should hope that out-relief under inspection would after a time be tabooed by respectability as much as relief in the house now is. Thus a scheme of general endowment, besides providing equitably and honourably for the needs of all old people, should head towards the total abolition of out-relief. Out-relief has a strong hold on public opinion but is radically bad in its influence on thrift. And I would say that if this scheme is not free from economical objection, my advocacy of it would fall to the ground; my view is that only if it can be fairly held that universal pensions would have no adverse effect on work, wages, thrift, self-respect and energy, and if it can be shown also that besides reducing the existing mass of pauperism, and lightening much poverty outside the whole problem of pauperism and poverty would be simplified, would it be worthwhile to consider whether the financial difficulties could be faced.

From The Examination of Charles Booth, a member of the Commission. *Minutes of Evidence to the Royal Commission on the Aged Poor,* 1895

A20   Groups to be Excluded from Old Age Pensions, 1908

Mr Lloyd-George   There is the thrift and industry test, which will not effect a very substantial diminution in the cost. The two tests that will make a very considerable inroad upon the number of persons over seventy who can claim 10s. are, first, the persons with a 10s. limit of income, and, secondly, the pauper test. Making all necessary deductions in respect of all these tests, the Prime Minister has already told the House that the net pensionables — the number of people who can pass all these tests and claim a pension — aggregate 572,000.

I now come to examine in detail some disqualifications and the objections raised to them. The first is the age limit. Hon. Members have suggested that we ought to reduce the limit from seventy to sixty-five. Of course, if we . . . had put half the charge on the local rates, we could have done it, but that is not quite consistent with the attitude . . . that the charges for the local rates are much too high at the present time . . . That shows that we are not in a position to consider the only scheme which up to the present has been considered feasible with the view of reducing the age limit to sixty-five. The expenditure would be too great to begin with . . . It is because of the fact that it costs more, that is my answer for the moment . . . I come now to the industry test. It is very difficult to find out what the full operation of this test will be. There has been a good deal of misapprehension as to its purpose . . . It is supposed from the use of the word 'misbehaviour' that this implied a character test. It does not; it is an industry test, which is a very different thing . . . It is a test to exclude the loafer and the wastrel. This man, I think, ought to be excluded for two reasons. One reason is applicable to the pensioners themselves. I think it is highly important that the receiver of the pension should be regarded as quite honourable, that there should be nothing in the nature of pauperisation, that the pension should be regarded as the recognition of faithful services to the State; and if every man, without distinction of conduct — if men who have never done an honest day's work in their lives, receive this pension in common with men who have really worked hard, I think that the receiver of the pension will be regarded in the same light as he who is actually known to be of that stamp which we wish ruthlessly to exclude, as they ought to be. In order, therefore, to raise the character of the gift, or, rather, the recognition of faithful service to the State, we eliminate the loafer and the wastrel from among the recipients of the bounty of the State. My second reason is this. I am thinking rather of the effect it will have on men whose sole interest in the scheme is to contribute by means of taxation to the finance of it. If men who are paying heavily for the right, see men of that kind receiving at their expense an honourable pension of £13 a year, depend upon it, although not numerous, they will be multiplied a hundredfold in the imagination of every man who has paid his taxes. He would naturally say: 'I pay so much in income-tax and in a number of ways to the fund, and this is what the money goes for.' I am certain the result would be that you would poison their minds against the whole proposal. It is very important that all classes of the community, not merely those who receive a pension, but also those who contribute towards it, should feel that it is fair, just, and equitable in all its essentials.

Lord R. Cecil It was necessary to inquire what class would obtain the benefits. What were the statutory conditions? It was clear that the very poor would not benefit; that was quite plain. The clauses which provided that those who had received Poor Law relief were not to be eligible was one bar to the poor. It was plain that a very large proportion of the very poorest must have received Poor Law relief at one time or another, and if they continued to receive it after the 1 January this year they would be disqualified. Then there was the provision against all those who had not habitually worked when not physically prevented from doing so. They heard a good deal about unemployment and they often heard that the man who was unemployed for a certain time became quite unemployable. All such men as that would be excluded from the benefits of the Government proposals. Therefore, it would not be the very poor who would be assisted by this scheme, nor would it be those who were sufficiently well off, such as the thrifty artisan who had saved a considerable sum of money.

The Government did not contemplate the assistance of the really admirable artisan who had put by sufficient provision for his old age. The class they proposed to assist was the artisan or worker who was fairly well off, but not very well-to-do, and who had made no provision for his old age. That was a very large and numerous section of the community, and that was the section whom the Government proposed to assist. They were now in a position to state shortly what the real proposal of the Government was. It was to make an enormous gift of money, originally stated to be between £6,000,000 and £7,000,000, to a very large section of the working classes who were possessed of very large electoral power.

From Hansard, *Parliamentary Debates*, House of Commons, 4th Series, vol. 140, Cols 565–586, June 1908

A21   National Health Insurance: Only for the Breadwinner, 1911

Mr Keir Hardie   My object . . . is to bring the women within the scope of this Clause as insured persons . . . The Chancellor of the Exchequer has stated the difficulties in the way; he is himself quite sympathetic with the proposal if it could be done, but first of all he points out the enormous cost, because he says it is admitted that sickness amongst women is much more frequent than sickness amongst men. His second point was the difficulty of checking sickness amongst women who are not industrially employed, and his third point was the difficulty of getting the doctors to agree. I do not know whether the Chancellor meant to say, when speaking about the difficulty of checking sickness amongst women, that the working women in this country are given to malingering. Those who live like myself among the working classes, and know the conditions of working-class life and character and of the wives and mothers of the working classes know that the fault is not that they are given to malingering and pretending sickness, but, on the contrary, that they frequently overwork themselves when their physical condition is not equal to it.

With regard to the financial objection, it is purely a matter of justice. There are several ways as to how the married woman's contribution might be made . . . The married woman's contribution, for example, could be deducted along with the husband's in the office of the employer . . . If that is not desirable a second course would be open, namely, that the married woman could pay her contribution through an approved society, and therefore there need not be any technical difficulties raised as to the matter of contribution. As for the medical men, I presume their hesitation about seeing women brought into the scheme is purely financial. They know as well and better than any section of the community the great need there is for married women receiving more and better medical attention than they possibly can under existing circumstances. The 30s. alternative benefit is good so far as it goes, but it goes a very little way, and what we desire to see is that the medical benefit, and especially the medical benefit, shall be extended to women, with a certain sickness allowance the same as in the case of industrial women.

. . . The relief that is proposed to be given to the breadwinner under this Bill will, to a certain extent, relieve the pressure which inevitably follows a period of sickness. But that pressure is not felt alone in the time when the breadwinner himself is disabled. When the wife is sick, it is nearly always necessary to pay for outside help which has to be brought in. The married woman requires nursing, the housework requires to be done, young children require to be looked after, and it entails extra expenditure, which the wages of the husband makes it impossible for him to adequately meet. As a result the poor woman suffers, the children suffer, and a great deal of discomfort is added to the life of the husband which might easily be obviated.

Mr Lloyd-George   This is a proposal of a very sweeping and far-reaching character. I am sure the Committee has already gathered its full import. It means not that women should be included, but that women should be compulsorily included; that the wives of all the employed people of the country which comes to something like ten or twelve millions should be compulsorily included in the purview of this Bill. What does that mean? . . .Somebody has got to pay that contribution. [The] proposal is that the workman should pay, not 4d. as proposed under the Bill, but that he should pay 8d., that the employer instead of paying 3d. should pay 6d.; that is what it means unless the State comes to the rescue and finds a few more millions. . . . Some time later on, it may be desired to include the whole of the married women within the purview of the scheme, but there is not the same urgency, for the simple reason that we are making provision now for the workman when ill, and for a time when no money at all is coming into his house. That is not the case when the married woman is ill; I do not say there is not a greater burden upon the household when she is ill . . . but there is not the same hardship as when the breadwinner is ill.

Mr Austen Chamberlain   The objections . . . which the Chancellor of the Exchequer has raised are insuperable. You cannot ask the State at this moment to find an additional £6,000,000, and you cannot ask the employers of married men to double his contribution because the workman has a wife. Just consider the proposition. I do not know whether hon. Members have themselves looked into individual cases to see what the charge upon the employer is going to be under this part of the Bill. I confess I think it is a very serious burden in many cases. The highest figure which has been brought to my notice by a gentleman whom I can absolutely trust, shows that it is going to cost 6s. in the £ on the average profits of the last three years in the case of the particular manufacture in which he is concerned. You cannot ask an employer, in addition to the burdens placed upon him, to take an additional burden, not on behalf of the person he is employing, but on behalf of his dependent. If you did it would have a result which I am sure the hon. Member for Merthyr Tydvil would be among the first to regret. It would cause every employer when taking on a man to ask whether he was married or single, and he would reject married men in favour of single men.

From Hansard, *Parliamentary Debates*, House of Commons, 5th Series, vol. 27, Cols 1197–1201, June 1911

A22   The Unemployed and the 'Genuinely Seeking Work' Clause, 1929

. . . Of the evidence received by the Committee, that . . . which requires a claimant to prove that he is genuinely seeking work but unable to obtain suitable employment formed the dominating feature of our enquiry. It was to the first part of the condition requiring a genuine search for work that by far the greater part of the evidence related . . .

From the statistics given by the Ministry of Labour . . . it appears that, for the year ending 6 May 1929, the number of persons who claimed benefit was approximately 4,000,000 whose claims totalled 10,000,000, with an average number of claims current of 1,144,400. During the same period, benefit was refused or stopped, either by Insurance Officers in the first instance or on the recommendations of Courts of Referees on 340,045 claims on the ground 'not genuinely seeking work'. To these should be added 37,568 cases where benefit was refused or stopped on the ground that claimants were not unable to obtain suitable employment.

The National Confederation of Employers' Organisations . . . pointed out that the Blanesburgh Committee had laid down the principle that the Unemployment Insurance scheme is not a scheme automatically to give assistance to every person who is out of work, but that every person who seeks to become a beneficiary must be willing and still able to work, must still remain in the field of employment and must, in a real sense, be genuinely unemployed only from circumstance and in no way from choice . . . To safeguard the funds and to eliminate non-genuine persons they relied on the 'faithful administration' of the condition requiring claimants to be genuinely seeking work.

The Confederation contended that it is common ground that the 'genuinely seeking work' test is an essential of any Unemployment Insurance system. The faithful administration of that test has to be considered, not only from the standpoint of those who at present complain about the method of its operation, but also from the standpoint of all those who are compulsorily required to contribute to the scheme, and in the absence of a definite fixed ratio between benefits and contributions, and, still more, in the absence of any substantial contribution test, any weakening of the 'genuinely seeking work' test must bring the whole of the Unemployment Insurance system into disrepute. They said that on the material furnished in evidence by the Ministry of Labour they were satisfied that the machinery is such as to do justice to all claimants entitled to benefit, and, so far as such claims are concerned, it discloses no ground for amendment of the existing constitution or procedure or the nature of the evidence required.

On the other hand the . . . Condition was strongly criticised both from the point of view of its working and the great difficulty that claimants have in satisfying either Insurance Officers or Courts of Referees that they have fulfilled its terms. Those who gave oral evidence on this aspect of the matter included representatives of the Trades Union Congress General Council and individual Trade Unions, two Members of Parliament and other witnesses. It was represented that the condition itself suggests that a man or woman who is thrown out of work is not making any effort to get back into employment and their genuineness is doubted at the outset. It was strongly urged that the genuineness of the claimant should be taken for granted unless facts were proved showing that a case of doubt has arisen. It was pointed out that if a claimant is refused benefit on the ground that he or she is not genuinely seeking work, there is a stigma on that man or woman which it is difficult to get rid of, and this militates harshly against the chance of securing further employment.

Many cases were cited and instances given to show what the witnesses regarded as the unfairness with which this condition had worked and these were used also in support of the objection taken to the cross-examination of claimants at interviews and before Courts of Referees. It was stated that claimants were worried and harassed by a number of questions asking them what they had done on the previous day, the day before and so on for some period back; and such questions as the number of firms visited, the distances traversed, whether they had sought work outside their own district, the nature and incidence of their interviews, whether they had pursued their enquiries further than the works gates, the types of persons they had seen and whether they had been content with the word of a mate or foreman or had spoken to managers and submanagers.

It was contended that claimants when being interviewed at the Exchanges or on being examined at Court of Referees were apt to become nervous and ill at ease and in their confusion might give contradictory and inconsistent answers. On these answers, however, a decision on the claim for unemployment benefit would depend and whilst a good workman who resented the kind of question addressed to him might give a bad impression, another who was self-possessed or possibly had been carefully coached for the task would be successful.

. . . This evidence as a whole was directed to the contention that the proof of the fourth statutory condition had cast far too great a burden upon the claimant and indeed has taxed very heavily those who have to administer and give decisions upon it.

Considerations

In the course of our consideration we have naturally had much regard to the leading decision of the Umpire (. . . given on 14 July 1926), which deals with the fulfilment of this condition.

The following paragraph appears early in the decision:

> In considering whether a person is genuinely seeking work the most important fact to be ascertained is the state of the applicant's mind. If a person genuinely wants work, i.e., really prefers working for wages to living on benefit, it is probable that she[1] is genuinely seeking it. But if a person prefers benefit to wages, or is content to be without work so long as she receives benefit, it may be presumed that she is not genuinely seeking it. Action is guided by desire, and whilst few people genuinely seek what they do not desire, most people genuinely seek what they really desire.

From these words it follows that so long as a condition in the terms of the first part of the fourth statutory condition remains, no satisfactory decision can be arrived at without knowing the state of the claimant's mind. Cases of the kind postulated by the Umpire would be easy of determination once one had ascertained that fact. But that ascertainment is in the nature of the case a matter of difficulty. It is often the case that on evidence presented a fair inference might have been that a claimant's search for work has not been well directed or he had become a little disheartened but where a decision that his efforts were by way of pretence would not be justified by the evidence. In such a case it could hardly be said that the disallowance meant that the claimant preferred benefit to wages. When it is realised that in over 340,000 claims in one year benefit was refused or stopped on the ground that claimants were not genuinely seeking work, it is understandable that the possibility of such an imputation has caused some indignation.

The state of a man's mind may be a matter of fact, but it is a fact of a kind on which two neutral and unbiassed persons might reach opposite conclusions after the most careful consideration of the evidence available to them for forming a judgment.

We are much impressed by the evidence submitted to us as to the difficulty and the impracticability of claimants adducing satisfactory evidence to prove the condition as now worded. This difficulty is especially accentuated in the case of claimants mainly in the depressed areas who are in receipt of benefit by virtue of the transitional conditions . . .

It follows therefore that the nature of the evidence to be required as to the satisfaction of the condition must necessarily involve a prescription of the evidence as to the state of an applicant's mind. This appears to the Committee to be an impossible task and after considerable discussion, we are forced to the conclusion that it is not possible for us to make a recommendation as to the nature of the evidence which insured contributors should be required to furnish to prove that they satisfy this . . . Condition.

From the *Report of the Committee on Procedure or Evidence for the Determination of Claims for Unemployment Benefit*, [The Morris Report] Cmd 3415 (1929)

Note

1. The decision was stated by the Umpire to apply equally to both sexes.

THE ROLE OF CHARITY AND VOLUNTARY EFFORT

A23   Octavia Hill on the Consequences of Charity, 1888

Lord Balfour: And on what do you found that expression of opinion?

Octavia Hill: On what I see in the homes of the poor of the various systems of relief; and what I shall say about this is common to both Poor Law and Charitable relief. They neither of them can really meet the wants of the poor, and they come in as an uncertain element to discourage thrift. Wherever you have either charity or Poor Law, bringing doles to the poor, you discourage the habit of belonging to clubs, the habit of saving, the habit of purchasing things, and possessing things; you bring side by side the man who has laid by nothing, and who is well cared for at a time when misfortune comes to him, and the man who has sacrificed something through his time of steady work, and on whom the whole burden falls when misfortune comes, he having to spend his savings, whereas the other man is helped from outside.

Lord Balfour: When you are administering money derived from a compulsory rate, do you see any way of discriminating between the provident man and the improvident man?

Octavia Hill: Of course you can discriminate in the first place by offering the house to the one.

Lord Balfour: But as long as you are dealing with public funds, derived from a public rate, is it possible to discriminate between the deserving and the undeserving?

Octavia Hill: No, I do not suppose it is with a compulsory rate.

Lord Balfour: You would regard that as the province of charity?

Octavia Hill: The Poor Law has nothing to do with anything but destitution: character is nothing, or ought to be nothing to the Poor Law. But then even as to the charitable funds, they seem to me a cruel kindness to the poor; one is glad of the sympathy they show, but as to their effects on the poor they are most disastrous.

Lord Balfour: It destroys their independence and self-respect, you mean?

Octavia Hill: Yes and raises hopes in them that cannot be fulfilled. Recipients build so much on the hope of something coming, which probably fails them at the very moment when it is most important to them.

Lord Balfour: Do you know anything of the difficulties which have been experienced by those who have tried to establish provident dispensary and medical relief associations in different parts of the metropolis?

Octavia Hill: I know from experience that it is almost impossible to establish a provident dispensary near our large free hospitals . . . I believe that the farther one goes from the centres of wealth the more independent the people are, the more providence there is and the more energy.

Lord Balfour: All leading you to the belief, which you have already expressed, that the expectation of help without exertion tends to diminish the probability of people exerting themselves.

Octavia Hill: Quite so . . . One feels strongly inclined to urge, on all possible opportunities, that people should keep clear from any danger of holding out to the poor hopes that something can be done for them that cannot be done, even inquiries set on foot by the Government raise very great hopes in the people . . . Again, the Mansion House Relief Fund, in the same way, raised extravagant hopes; and it is all speculated on. The people are exceeding sharp and the more their homes look miserable the more they expect to get; and the drink following the distribution of the Mansion Home Relief Fund was something fearful.

Octavia Hill: I should say, speaking generally about the condition of the poor in London, that, since I can recollect, their condition has markedly improved. They have better rooms, more of them, more appliances in them; better schools, better clothes, better food, even less drink, decidedly less drink; but that their temper is more dissatisfied and more difficult to deal with. I hope it may only be a transition stage, but that is where they seem to me worse. They are more dissatisfied, and they expect a very great deal from other people, and they are rather less thrifty.

Earl of Aberdeen: Do you think that that is owing to the indiscreet methods of relief that have been rather common in recent years?

Octavia Hill: I think, you know, that many more educated people are coming forward to care about them and sympathise with them and so on, and are taking the tone that it is their duty to do it (which is certainly is), and the poor feel it and see it and say it, and they expect help to come in forms in which it does not seem to me that it will really be helpful to them.

From the *Minutes of Evidence taken before the Select Committee of the House of Lords on Poor Law Relief*, 1888

A24   The 'Errors' of the Charity Organisation Society, 1911

Instead of recognizing that the poor law was already obsolete and was bound to become more anomalous with every succeeding measure of social legislation, they accepted it as immutable and made it the corner stone of their system. Their line of argument was very singular. They admitted that the poor law was demoralizing; that its action was merely palliative, not restorative; that at best it could only prevent the worst horrors of destitution, but could not prevent its occurrence and its recurrence; and yet they never proposed any change in the application of public funds! They insisted that private funds should always be expended with a view to prevention and cure, but that public funds should be strictly reserved for those who were already in the last stage of destitution, and therefore already beyond curative measures.

Taking for granted that State action must demoralize, they assigned to private charity the task of preserving from pauperism all those persons or families whose need was only temporary or accidental, or easily remediable, especially where such need was accompanied by good character and record.

It is interesting to find this limitation of State action in a book published in 1868 by Mr Charles Bosanquet . . .

'It would not be difficult', he says, 'to classify cases between the poor law and voluntary charity. The former would take the ordinary chronic cases, the latter, perhaps, some of the more deserving chronic cases, but especially those temporary cases which, it might be hoped, judicious help would save from sinking into pauperism.'[1]

Whether Mr Charles Bosanquet was or was not the first to introduce this system of classification into the COS creed, there is no doubt that he continued to preach it after he became secretary and that it has taken a permanent place .   . .

An authoritative statement of the same view is to be found in the introduction to a recent number of the very valuable Charities Register and Digest which is published annually by the society.

The claim for poor law relief rests, it may be broadly stated, upon the destitution of the claimant . . . On the threshold of the question then we see the boundary lines of charity and the poor law. To charity it is not a question of primary importance whether a person is destitute or not. For it destitution is no test. It has more chance of helping effectually if a person is not destitute. It has to prevent destitution and indigence. It may have to supply actual necessaries, but to place the poor beyond the reach of need or to prevent the recurrence of need is its true vocation. It is unlimited in its scope and gives as a free gift. From the point of view of the poor law the question of destitution is all important. It is the passport to relief. Its administration is tied and bound with restrictions. Its supplies are drawn from a ratepayers' trust fund. Its main purpose is not to prevent or remove distress, but to alleviate it. It is a stern alleviative measure. It helps only when it must; charity always when it wills.[2]

It is singular that in these utterances . . . the charity organizers give no reason (other than the present condition of the law) for this hard and fast distinction between the principles which should guide public and private administrators in dealing with destitution . . . Much might be said for entirely reversing their decision. The prevention of destitution implies that we should search out those who are on the downward road and arrest their progress before they become 'destitute'. Such action demands a many-sided and far-sighted policy, for the roads that lead to destitution are many and gradual. It demands a considerable outlay, producing distant and not always obvious results. Above all, it demands disciplinary powers. Where are we to look for the statesman who will co-ordinate and maintain such a policy, for the Exchequer to supply capital for such a purpose, for the authority to wield such powers, if not the Government of the country? And yet, according to Dr Loch and Dr Bosanquet, this is precisely where we are not to look.

If they wished to lay down a hard and fast rule, one might have expected that it would be that great remedial and preventive measures should be left to the national and local executive, the collective wisdom of the nation, while private charity should concern itself with the pitiable, but apparently hopeless cases, should indeed humbly take up the work of palliation with instruments of love and religion and personal self-sacrifice that the State can with difficulty command, as, in fact, the Salvation Army and the Church Army profess to do. On the contrary, their decision is, as has been shown, exactly the reverse; charity is to be remedial, the State is to confine its action to palliation.

This decision accords perfectly, no doubt, with facts as they are. It is a statement of the theory behind the existing poor law, but in the writings of the charity organizers there is acceptance and approval as well as statement. Dr Bosanquet emphasizes and explains that approval in his essay on 'Socialism and Natural Selection'. 'We should never forget', he says, 'that the system', i.e. State 'interference', 'is a necessary evil, nor ever handle our national initiative, whether through the poor law or through more general legislation, so as to relieve the father of the support of the wife and children or the grown up child of the support of his parents. We should raise no expectation of help or of employment invented ad hoc which may derange the man's organization of life in view of the whole moral responsibilities which as a father he has accepted.'[3]

A good example of the actual mischief wrought by this pernicious doctrine that public action weakens private resource is to be found in the COS attitude towards the agitation for school clinics. The absolute futility of school inspection unless followed by treatment is obvious. At least fifty per cent of the children in our schools are suffering from defects which, if not dealt with, will seriously handicap them in after life. These defects require treatment from a nurse under medical supervision . . . It is perfectly clear that if the men and women of the next generation are to start life with a fairly sound physique, the preventive measures which are taken for the rich man's child in the nursery must be taken for the poor man's child in the school.

Advice, nurses, nursing appliances must be provided collectively, since it is a sheer impossibility that they can be provided in the home. The Education Department, the medical profession, members of care committees, and even county councils outside of London, are beginning to see that the difficulty can be met only by means of medical centres in connection with the schools. One might expect that a society whose aim is 'the improvement of the condition of the poor' would guide public opinion towards such a conclusion. We find instead that the COS has been acting, as usual, not as a pioneer, but as a powerful, though fortunately insufficient, brake.

At this last stage of the controversy (21 March 1911) nothing authoritative has been issued by the society. In default of it we may quote from the Occasional Paper on 'The Relief of School Children' (No. 8, Fourth Series). Such measures 'teach him' (the child) 'to look to outside help for the things he has a right to expect from his parents, a lesson he will not be slow to remember when he himself is a parent. The child needs before all things in the present day to learn the lessons of self-reliance and self-respect.'[4]

And from an essay of Dr Bosanquet's entitled 'The Social Criterion':

Granting a complete system of inspection at schools and of sanitary supervision through the health authorities and advice from health visitors, the normal mode of medical attendance should be for the wage earner as for ourselves, attendance by his family doctor, whom the head of the family chooses, trusts, and pays. On a provident system this is in many places successfully arranged, to the complete satisfaction of the doctor and of the patient. When, however, we should go to the specialist or to expensive nursing homes, the wage earner will be referred by his family doctor to the appropriate hospital or infirmary . . . Thus the division of labor is properly maintained, the all important relation of trust and confidence between the family and the family doctor is not interfered with, the general practitioner's position is secured, and the hospital also is secured in the acquisition of interesting cases and in the fullest exercise of its powers of helpfulness.[5]

With regard to proposals for free medical treatment, Dr Bosanquet says: 'Such a policy is calculated to ruin the medical clubs and provident dispensaries, and to substitute visits of an official who, however good, is not the people's choice for the family doctor whom they like and trust and pay.'[6]

This question of school medical treatment is for the moment, perhaps, more under discussion than any other question of social reform, and for that reason affords the most striking example of the COS policy of obstruction; but that policy is perfectly consistent and perfectly general in character. It erects a barrier in the face of every attempt to lighten that pressure on the wage-earner which results from existing industrial conditions.

Another arbitrary assumption of the charity organizers is that for any man to enjoy any benefits which he has not definitely worked for and earned is injurious to his character. The naïveté with which they take this for granted is really preposterous when one remembers that nearly all the more respectable and refined members of the community are themselves living chiefly on wealth which they have not earned. One begins to wonder how those of us whose income is derived from dividends have any independence of character left. Dr Bosanquet points out that the recipient of charitable help is injured because it comes miraculously and not as the nature result of personal effort,[7] but what effort do I make in connection with my dividends from the North Eastern Railway, and what can be more miraculous than my waking up one morning to find that certain shares that were worth £100 yesterday are now worth £105?

Dr Bosanquet must really find some other reasons for objecting to doles, unless he is prepared to return to the ancient canon law with reference to usury.

The third grave error in COS theory is like the first, in that it arises out of the acceptance of human arrangements as if they were heaven-sent and unchangeable.

Accepting the individual ownership of land and capital and a competitive wage system — all with exactly the same limitations and mitigations that are today in force, and no more — as the inevitable basis of society, the charity organizers are driven to an easy optimism that sees a satisfactory opportunity open to every virtuous worker, and looks forward with composure to a future when the working class, having been taught thrift, industry, and self-control, will do its duty in that state of life to which modern industrial processes shall call it.

Poverty, even extreme poverty, seems to them unavoidable. 'Destitution', says Dr Loch in his last book, 'cannot disappear. Every group of competing men is continually producing it.'[8] Not to abolish destitution, but to improve 'social habit', should be, he thinks, the aim of the philanthropist. It is for this reason that he looks coldly at all recent schemes for social betterment.

'The remarkable and well known investigations of Mr Charles Booth and Mr Seebohm Rowntree, which have stirred public thought in many circles, were, in our judgement', he says, 'faulty from this point of view. They were not analytical of social habit, but of relative poverty and riches. They graded the population according as they were "poor", or "very poor", or above a poverty line. Their authors aimed at marking out such a line of poverty, forgetful, as it seems to us, of the fact that poverty is so entirely relative to use and habit and potential ability of all kinds, that it can never serve as a satisfactory basis of social investigation or social reconstruction. It is not the greater or lesser command of means that makes the material difference in the contentment and efficiency of social life, but the use of means relative to station in life and its possibilities. Nevertheless, in these investigations it was on the possession of means that stress was laid. Hence the suggestion that the issue to be settled by the country — the line of social reform — was the endowment of the class or classes whose resources were considered relatively insufficient.

'But to transfer the wealth of one class to another, by taxation or otherwise, is no solution of social difficulty.'[9]

From Mrs Townsend, *The Case Against the Charity Organisation Society* (Fabian Society, 1911)

A25 Canon Barnett on Charity Up-to-date, 1912

The tender mercies of the thoughtless, as of the wicked, are often cruel, and charity when it ceases to be a blessing is apt to become a curse; A Mansion House fund we used in old days to count among the possible winter horrors of East London. The boldly advertised details of destitution, the publication of the sums collected, the hurried distribution by irresponsible and ignorant agents, and the absence of any policy, stirred up wild expectation and left behind a trail of bitterness and degradation. The people were encouraged in deception, and were led on in the way which ends in wretchedness.

In 1903 a Committee was formed which used a Mansion House fund to initiate a policy of providing honourable and sufficiently paid work which would, at the same time, test the solid intention of unemployed and able-bodied applicants. The report of that Committee has been generally accepted, and has indeed become the basis of subsequent action and recommendations. It seemed to us East Londoners as if the bad time had been passed, and that henceforth charitable funds would flow in channels to increase fruitfulness and not in floods to make devastation.

The hope has been disappointed. Funds inaugurated by newspapers, by agencies, or by private persons have appeared in overwhelming force, and have followed in the old bad ways. The heart of the public has been torn by harrowing descriptions of poverty and suffering, which the poor also read and feel ashamed. The means of relief are often miserably inadequate. A casual dinner eaten in the company of the most degraded cannot help the 'toiling widows and decent working-men', 'waiting in their desolate homes to know whether there is to be an end to their pains and privations'. Two or three hours spent in fields hardly clear of London smoke, after a noisy and crowded ride, is not likely to give children the refreshment and the quiet which they need for a recreative holiday.

Much of the charity of today, it has to be confessed, is mischievous, if not even cruel, and to its charge must be laid some of the poverty, the degradation, and the bitterness which characterize London, where, it is said, eight million sterling are every year given away. Ruskin, forty years ago, when he was asked by an Oxford man proposing to live in Whitechapel what he thought East London most wanted, answered, 'The destruction of West London'. Mr Bernard Shaw has lately, in his own startling way, stated a case against charity, and we all know that the legend on the banner of the unemployed, 'Curse your charity', represents widely spread opinion.

But — practically — what is the safe outlet for the charitable instinct? The discussion of the abolition of charity is not practical. People are bound to give their money to their neighbours. Human nature is solid — individuals are parts of a whole — and the knowledge of a neighbour's distress stirs the desire to give something, as surely as the savour of food stirs appetite. But as in the one case the satisfaction of the appetite is not enough unless the food builds up the body and strength, so in the other case the charity which relieves the feelings of the giver is not enough unless it meets the neighbour's needs.

The charity which does not flow in channels made by thought is the charity which is mischievous. People comfort themselves and encourage their indolence by saying they would rather give wrongly in ten cases than miss one good case. The comfort is deceptive. The gift which does not help, hinders, and it is the gifts of the thoughtless which open the pitfalls into which the innocent fall and threaten the stability of society. Such gifts are temptations to idleness, and widen the breach between rich and poor. When people of good-will, in pursuit of a good object, do good deeds which are followed by cries of distress and by curses there is a tragedy.

Charity up to date, whether it be from person to person or through some society or fund, must be such as is approved by the same close thinking as business men give to their business, or politicians to their policy. The best form of giving must always, I think, be that from person to person. Would that it were more used — would that those whose feelings are stirred by the sight of many sick folk were content to try and heal one! . . . Gifts which pass from person to person are something more than ordinary gifts. 'The gift without the giver is bare', and when the giver's thought makes itself felt, the gift is enriched. The best form of charity, therefore, is personal, and if for some reason this be impossible, then the next best is that which strengthens the hands of persons who are themselves in touch with neighbours in need, such as are the almoners of the Society for the Relief of Distress, the members of the Charity Organization Committees, or the residents in Settlements.

Charities should aim at encouraging growth rather than at giving relief. They should be inspired by hope rather than by pity. They should be a means of education, a means of enabling the recipient to increase in bodily, mental, or spiritual strength. If I spend twenty shillings on giving a dinner or a night's lodging to twenty vagrants, I have done nothing to make them stronger workers or better citizens. I have only kept poverty alive; but if I spend the same sum in sending one person to a convalescent hospital, he will be at any rate a stronger man, and if during his stay at the hospital his mind is interested in some subject — in something not himself — he will probably be a happier man. Societies which devote a large income to providing food and clothing do not in the long run reduce the number of those in want, while Societies which promote the clearing of unhealthy areas, the increase of open space about own dwellings, greater accessibility to books and pictures, gradually raise people above the need of gifts of food and clothing. Hospitals which do much in restoring strength to the sick would do more if they used their reputation and authority to teach people how to avoid sickness, and to make a public opinion which would prevent many diseases and accidents. The distinguished philanthropist who used to say she would rather give a poor man a watch than a coat was, I believe, wiser than another philanthropist who condemned a poor women for spending her money on buying a picture for her room. It is more important to raise self-respect and develop taste than just to meet physical needs.

Charities intruding themselves upon the intimacies of domestic life have by their patronage often dwarfed the best sort of growth. Warnings against patronizing the poor are frequent, but many charities are by their very existence 'patronizing', and many others, by sending people to collect votes, by requiring expressions of their gratitude, and by the attitude of their agents, do push upon the poor reminders of their obligations. They belong to a past age, and have no place in the present age, where they foster only a cringing or rebellious attitude. It has been well said that, 'a new spirit is necessary in dealing with the poor, a spirit of humility and willingness to learn, rather than generosity and anxiety to teach' . . .

Charities should, I think, look to, if not aim at, their own extinction. Their existence, it must be remembered, is due to some defect in the State organization or in the habits of the people. Schools, for instance, were established by the gifts of good-will to meet the ignorance from which people suffered, and when the State itself established schools the gifts have been continued for the sake of methods and experiments to meet further needs which the State has not yet seen its way to meet. Charities, in this case, have looked, or do look, to their own extinction when the State, guided by their example may take up their work. They have been pioneers, original, daring by experiment to lead the way to undiscovered good. Relief societies have, in like manner, shown how the State may help the poor by means which respect their character, by putting work within their reach, by emigrating those fit for colonial life, by giving orphan children more of the conditions of a family home. There are others which have looked, or still look, to their extinction, not in State action, but in co-operation with other societies with which they now compete. Competition may be the strength of commerce, but co-operation is certainly the strength of charity, and wise are those charities which are content to sink themselves in common action and die that they may rise again in another body. The Charity Organization Societies in some of the great cities have in this way lost themselves, to live again in Social Welfare Councils and Civic Leagues. There are, finally, other charities which, by their own action, tend to make themselves unnecessary. The Children's Country Holiday Fund, for instance, by giving country holidays to town children, and by making the parents contribute to the expense, develop at once a new desire for the peace and beauty of the country and a new capacity for satisfying this desire. When parents realize the necessity of such holiday and know how it can be secured, this Fund will cease to have a reason for existence.

Charities are many which fulfil this condition, but charities also are many which do not fulfil it. They seem to wish to establish themselves in permanence, and go on in rivalry with the State and with one another. There is waste of money, which might be used in pioneer work, in doing what is equally well done by others; there is competition which excites greed and imposition, and there is overlapping. Very little thought is wanted to discover many such charities which now receive large incomes from the public.

Charities should keep in line with State activities. The State — either by national or by municipal organization — has taken over many of the duties which meet the needs of the people. Ignorance, poverty, disease and dullness have all been met, and the means by which they are being met are constantly developed. The Church, it may be said, has so far converted the State, and a cheerful payer of rates may perhaps deserve the same Divine commendation as the cheerful giver. But State organizations, however well considered and well administered, will always want the human touch. They will not, like the charities, be fitful because dependent on subscribers and committees, but they will not, like charities, temper their actions to individual peculiarities and feelings. Charities, therefore, I think, do well when they keep in line with State activities. They may, for instance, working in co-operation with the Guardians, undertake the care of the families when the bread-winner is in the infirmary, or superintend the management of industrial colonies to which the unemployed may be sent, or provide enfeebled old people with pensions until the age when they are eligible for the State pension . . .Men and women of good-will may, I believe, find boundless opportunities if they will serve on Municipal bodies or on the Committees appointed by such bodies to complement their work.

It may, indeed, be a further indictment against charities that much of the good-will which might have improved and humanized State action has by them been diverted. If, for instance, the passion of good-will which now finds an outlet in providing free shelters and dinners for the starving, or orphanages for destitute children, had gone to improve Casual Wards and Barrack Schools, many evils would have been prevented. At any rate, it may be said that charities working alongside of the State organizations would become stronger, and State organizations inspired by the charities would become more humane. It costs more, doubtless, to work in co-operation with others, and to subject self-will to the common will as a member of a Board of Guardians, than to be an important member of a charitable committee, but in charity it is cost which counts.

Charity — to sum up my conclusion — represents a very important factor in the making of England of tomorrow. The outbreak of giving, of which there has been ample evidence this Christmas, may represent increased good-will and more vivid reali-zation of responsibility for those afflicted in mind, body, or estate, or it may represent the impatience of light-hearted people anxious to relieve themselves and get on to their pleasures. Society is out of joint because the wealth of the rich and the poverty of the poor have been brought into so great light. It seems intolerable that when wealth has to invent new ways of expenditure, there should be families where the earnings are insufficient for necessary food, where the children cannot enjoy the gaiety of their youth, where the boys and girls pass out through unskilled trades to pick up casual labour and casual doles. The needs are many, but the point I wish to urge is that charity which intends to help may hinder. No gift is without result, and some of the gifts are responsible for the suffering, carelessness, and bitterness of our times. Charity up to date is that which gives thought as well as money and service. The cost is greater, and many who will even deny themselves a pleasure so as to give a generous cheque cannot exercise the greater denial of giving their thought. 'There is no glory', said Napoleon, 'where there is no danger'; and we may add, there is no charity where there is no thought, and thought is very costly.

From Samuel A. Barnett, 'Charity Up to Date', *The Contemporary Review*, February 1912

A26   Weaknesses of the Voluntary Hospitals, 1922

Hospital Abuse

The Voluntary Hospitals, built and endowed by charity for the really necessitous poor, are now utilised to a great extent by the skilled artisan, and to an increasing extent by the lower middle and even the professional classes; this leads to constant disputes as to 'hospital abuse', or the admission of patients other than those for whom hospitals were intended, and to a great increase in the number of out-patients and would-be in-patients.

Under Staffing

The medical and surgical staff is not directly paid for its services, its members looking to the experience, which cannot be gained elsewhere, and to the prestige attached to the appointments for their reward. In other words, an appointment to a hospital staff carries a certain monopoly value, and this being so, the number of appointments is jealously guarded, with the result that all big hospitals are badly under-staffed. The extension of hospital service to other than the necessitous poor and this under-staffing lead to over-crowding of the out-patients' departments. Patients have to wait long hours in crowded waiting-rooms often none too well constructed and ventilated . . . Within the consulting room it entails constant working at high pressure and against time, which, in its turn, leads to hasty diagnosis and often to putting off to a future occasion what should be done at once . . .

Delays

The demand on the existing number of beds and the under-staffing again causes long waiting lists for admission; which in its turn leads to prolonged and unnecessary suffering, to diminished chances of recovery and in many instances to months of idleness, causing loss of production and diminished national wealth, not to mention the straits to which the family may be reduced owing to the loss of the bread-winner's wages.

Appointments

Though there is a monopoly value attaching to an honorary appointment to a hospital staff, it takes many years before a junior member begins to feel its benefits and to reap the rewards of his labours. Consequently, it is very difficult for a man without some private income to venture on the career of a consultant; this greatly limits the choice of men for hospital appointments, and therefore it is not necessarily the best man who gets the post, but frequently the man with money, who can afford to wait.

Nurses

Nurses are grossly under-paid, their work is arduous, involving risks to life and health, and their hours are long; moreover, the accommodation provided for them is very often insufficient and uncomfortable, and these conditions taken in conjunction with an often inadequate and badly prepared dietary render their occupation unhealthy. This is probably a consequence of Voluntary Hospitals being founded as charitable institutions for the necessitous poor. Originally, charitably-minded women were willing to give their services for a minimum return as their share towards the support of these institutions, and in some instances the nursing was undertaken entirely by religious orders. With the advance of medicine and surgery nursing has become a skilled profession, requiring a long training, but salaries and conditions of service have not kept pace with these increased demands.

Patients

. . . In order to get through necessary work with the inadequate staffs at present allowed, even in the best hospitals, it is impossible, even if it were regarded by the hospital authorities as desirable, for nurses to pay regard to the mentality of the individual patient, and a general brisk cheerfulness takes the place of any real sympathy or understanding. All medical instructions are faithfully followed, but any needs or demands of the patient outside of these tend to be ignored, and a cut-and-dried unintelligent course of procedures results, against which a private patient would revolt at once.

The shortage of staff and the consequent pressure on the night nurse to wash and feed the patients before her period of duty comes to an end probably accounts for the custom of starting the hospital day between 2 and 3 a.m. causing a continual state of movement and unrest in the wards from that time until about 9.00 a.m. During this period patients are washed, breakfasts are served, beds are made and ward-cleaning takes place. The need for more consideration of the patient as an individual and a personality, and of more regard for the nerves of highly-strung patients, makes itself more felt with the extension of the hospital service to others than the unfortunate 'downs and outs' of Society.

Choice of Patients

The method of choosing patients for admission to the wards of the hospitals is full of anomalies. There can be no doubt whatever that admission should be solely guided by the nature and severity of the patient's illness and by the prospects of institutional treatment being of real and permanent benefit. In the past, and even now to some extent, this has been of secondary consideration. 'Letters of recommendation' — so many for every guinea subscribed — were in vogue, and carried with them a certain degree of patronage, and gave to the public, ignorant of medical matters, the right of recommendation to the out-patient and in-patient departments at their own discretion. This system, demoralising to both subscribers and patients, is not so common as of old, but still exists at some of the smaller London hospitals and many provincial hospitals. More common now is the custom of large business firms or private people subscribing handsome sums to a hospital and demanding almost as a right the admission of their employees or dependants. The hospital authorities, for fear of losing the subscriptions, yield to their demands often to the exclusion of more urgent or more suitable cases.

From *The Labour Movement and the Hospital Crisis* (Labour Party, 1922)

Notes

1. 'London: Some Account of its Growth, Charitable Agencies, and Wants', by G.B.P. Bosanquet, M.A., Barrister-at-Law, pp. 199–202. Hatchard, 1868.
2. Introduction to Annual Charities Register and Digest, 1909, 'On the Functions of the Poor Law and Charity.' Cf. 'Charity and Social Life,' C.S. Loch, p. 349. Macmillan, 1910.
3. 'Aspects of the Social Problem': XVI. 'Socialism and Natural Selection', Dr B. Bosanquet, p. 304.
4. Occasional Paper COS No. 8, Fourth Series.
5. 'The Social Criterion', a paper read by B. Bosanquet, M.A., LL.D, 15 November 1907, before the Edinburgh COS, p. 23.
6. Ibid., p. 24.
7. 'The point of private property is that things should not come miraculously and be unaffected by your dealings with them, but that you should be in contact with something which in the external world is the definite material representation of yourself.' 'Aspects of the Social Problem', p. 313.
8. 'Charity and Social Life', C.S. Loch, p. 393. Macmillan, 1910.
9. Ibid., pp. 386–7.

A27   The Unemployed: The Chamberlain Circular, 1886

The inquiries which have been recently undertaken by the Local Government Board unfortunately confirm the prevailing impression as to the existence of exceptional distress amongst the working classes. This distress is partial as to its locality and is, no doubt, due in some measure to the long-continued severity of the weather.

The returns of pauperism show an increase, but it is not yet considerable; and the numbers of persons in receipt of relief are greatly below those of previous periods of exceptional distress.

The Local Government Board have, however, thought it their duty to go beyond the returns of actual pauperism, which are all that come under their notice in ordinary times, and they have made some investigation into the condition of the working classes generally.

They are convinced that in the ranks of those who do not ordinarily seek Poor Law relief there is evidence of much and increasing privation, and if the depression in trade continues it is to be feared that large numbers of persons usually in regular employment will be reduced to the greatest straits.

Such a condition of things is a subject for deep regret and very serious consideration.

The spirit of independence which leads so many of the working classes to make great personal sacrifices rather than incur the stigma of pauperism is one which deserves the greatest sympathy and respect, and which it is the duty and interest of the community to maintain by all the means at its disposal.

Any relaxation of the general rule at present obtaining which requires, as a condition of relief to able-bodied male persons on the grounds of their being out of employment, the acceptance of an order for admission to the workhouse or the performance of an adequate task of work as a labour test, would be most disastrous, as tending directly to restore the condition of things which, before the reform of the Poor Laws, destroyed the independence of the labouring classes, and increased the poor rate until it because an almost insupportable burden.

It is not desirable that the working classes should be familiarised with Poor Law relief, and if once the honourable sentiment which now leads them to avoid it is broken down it is probable that recourse will be had to this provision on the slightest occasion.

The Local Government Board have no doubt that the powers which the guardians possess are fully sufficient to enable them to deal with ordinary pauperism, and to meet the demand for relief from the classes who usually seek it.

When the workhouse is full, or when the circumstances are so exceptional that it is desirable to give out-door relief to the able-bodied poor on the ground of want of work, the guardians in the unions which are the great centres of population are authorised to provide a labour test, on the performance of which grants in money and kind may be made, according to the discretion of the guardians. In other unions, where the guardians have not already this power, the necessary order is given whenever the circumstances appear to require it.

But these provisions do not in all cases meet the emergency. The labour test is usually stone breaking or oakum picking. The work, which is selected as offering the least competition with other labour, presses hardly upon the skilled artisans, and, in some cases, their proficiency in their special trades may be prejudiced by such employment. Spade husbandry is less open to objection, and when facilities offer for adopting work of this character as a labour test, the Board will be glad to assist the guardians by authorising the hiring of land for the purpose, when this is necessary. In any case, however, the receipt of relief upon the guardians, although accompanied by a task of work, entails the disqualification which by statute attaches to pauperism.

What is required in the endeavour to relieve artisans and others who have hitherto avoided Poor Law assistance, and who are temporarily deprived of employment, is,

1. Work which will not involve the stigma of pauperism;
2. Work which all can perform, whatever may have been their previous avocations;
3. Work which does not compete with that of other labourers at present in employment;

and, lastly, work which is not likely to interfere with the resumption of regular employment in their own trades by those that seek it.

In districts in which exceptional distress prevails the Board recommends that the guardians should confer with the local authorities, and endeavour to arrange with the latter for the execution of works on which unskilled labour may be immediately employed.

It may be observed that spade labour is a class of work which has special advantages in the case of able-bodied persons out of employment. Every able-bodied man can dig, although some can do more than others, and it is work which is in no way degrading, and need not interfere with existing employment.

In all cases in which special works are undertaken to meet exceptional distress it would appear to be necessary, first, that the men employed should be engaged on the recommendation of the guardians as persons whom, owing to previous condition and circumstances, it is undesirable to send to the workhouse, or to treat as subjects for pauper relief, and, second, that the wages paid should be something less than the wages ordinarily paid for similar work, in order to prevent imposture, and to leave the strongest temptation to those who avail themselves of this opportunity to return as soon as possible to their previous occupations.

From *Circular Addressed by the President of the Local Government Board to the Several Boards of Guardians*, 1886

A28   The 'Cab-Horse Charter', 1890

What, then, is Darkest England? For whom do we claim that 'urgency' which gives their case priority over that of all other sections of their countrymen and countrywomen?

I claim it for the Lost, for the Outcast, for the Disinherited of the World.

These, it may be said, are but phrases. Who are the Lost? I reply, not in a religious, but in a social sense, the lost are those who have gone under, who have lost their foothold in Society, those to whom the prayer to our Heavenly Father, 'Give us day by day our daily bread', is either unfulfilled, or only fulfilled by the Devil's agency: by the earnings of vice, the proceeds of crime, or the contribution enforced by the threat of the law.

But I will be more precise. The denizens in Darkest England, for whom I appeal, are (1) those who, having no capital or income of their own, would in a month be dead from sheer starvation were they exclusively dependent upon the money earned by their own work; and (2) those who by their utmost exertions are unable to attain the regulation allowance of food which the law prescribes as indispensable even for the worst criminals in our gaols.

I sorrowfully admit that it would be Utopian in our present social arrangements to dream of attaining for every honest Englishman a gaol standard of all the necessaries of life. Some time, perhaps, we may venture to hope that every honest worker on English soil will always be as warmly clad, as healthily housed, and as regularly fed as our criminal convicts — but that is not yet.

Neither is it possible to hope for many years to come that human beings generally will be as well cared for as horses. Mr Carlyle long ago remarked that the four-footed worker has already got all that this two-handed one is clamouring for: 'There are not many horses in England, able and willing to work, which have not due food and lodging and go about sleek coated, satisfied in heart.' You say it is impossible; but, said Carlyle, 'The human brain, looking at these sleek English horses, refuses to believe in such impossibility for English men.' Nevertheless, forty years have passed since Carlyle said that, and we seem to be no nearer the attainment of the four-footed standard for the two-handed worker. 'Perhaps it might be nearer realisation', growls the cynic, 'if we could only produce men according to demand, as we do horses, and promptly send them to the slaughter-house when past their prime' — which, of course, is not to be thought of.

What, then, is the standard towards which we may venture to aim with some prospect of realisation in our time? It is a very humble one, but if realised it would solve the worst problems of modern Society.

It is the standard of the London Cab Horse.

When in the streets of London a Cab Horse, weary or careless or stupid, trips and falls and lies stretched out in the midst of the traffic, there is no question of debating how he came to stumble before we try to get him on his legs again. The Cab Horse is a very real illustration of poor broken-down humanity; he usually falls down because of overwork and underfeeding. If you put him on his feet without altering his conditions, it would only be to give him another dose of agony; but first of all you'll have to pick him up again. It may have been through overwork or underfeeding, or it may have been all his own fault that he has broken his knees and smashed the shafts, but that does not matter. If not for his own sake, then merely in order to prevent an obstruction of the traffic, all attention is concentrated upon the question of how we are to get him on his legs again.

The load is taken off, the harness is unbuckled, or, if need be, cut, and everything is done to help him up. Then he is put in the shafts again and once more restored to his regular round of work. That is the first point. The second is that every Cab Horse in London has three things; a shelter for the night, food for its stomach, and work allotted to it by which it can earn its corn.

These are the two points of the Cab Horse's Charter. When he is down he is helped up, and while he lives he has food, shelter and work. That, although a humble standard, is at present absolutely unattainable by millions — literally by millions — of our fellow-men and women in this country. Can the Cab Horse Charter be gained for human beings? I answer, yes. The Cab Horse standard can be attained on the Cab Horse terms. If you get your fallen fellow on his feet again, Docility and Discipline will enable you to reach the Cab Horse ideal, otherwise it will remain unattainable. But Docility seldom fails where Discipline is intelligently maintained. Intelligence is more frequently lacking to direct, than obedience to follow direction. At any rate it is not for those who possess the intelligence to despair of obedience, until they have done their part.

From William Booth, *In Darkest England and the Way Out* (Salvation Army, 1890)

A29   Rowntree on Working-class Living Standards in 1899

Immediate Cause of Poverty: Lowness of Wage

Comprising 51.96 per cent of the total population living in 'primary' poverty.

Total number of persons	3756
Number of families	640
Average size of family	5.86
Average family earnings	18s. 9d.
Average rent	3s. 6½d.

This section comprises more than half of the persons who are living in 'primary' poverty.

The total weekly earnings of this section amount to £600, which is contributed by householders and supplementary workers in the following proportions:

	Total Sum			Per Family	
	£	s.	d.	s.	d.
Contributed by householders	586	14	0	18	4
Contributed by supplementary					
workers	13	6	0	0	5[1]
	£600	0	0	18	9

The occupations of the heads of households in this section are as follows:

469 general labourers[2]	8 postal service, etc.
47 carters, cabmen, grooms, etc.	3 watermen
21 painters' labourers	3 furniture removers
19 railway employees	2 porters
12 small shopkeepers	2 packers
12 cobblers	8—one each tanner, milkman,
9 clerks	waiter, lamp-lighter, teacher of
8 chimney sweeps	music, barman, hairdresser, and
7 gardeners	bookbinder
5 butchers	
5 tailoring trade	640

The following statement shows the income and estimated necessary expenditure of [this] Section

Income				Expenditure			
	£	s.	d.		£	s.	d.
Weekly income of							
640 families	600	0	0	Weekly rent	112	15	5
Weekly balance—				Weekly minimum cost of			
Deficiency	160	17	5	food and sundries neces-			
(= 5s. 0¼ d. per family)				sary to maintain 1376 adults			
				and 2380 children in a state			
				of physical efficiency	648	2	0
	£760	17	5		£760	17	5

It will have been noticed that [this Section] consists of unskilled workers of various grades, 73 per cent being general labourers; whilst the others holding the lower posts in their respective occupations are employed upon work which is scarcely more difficult or responsible than that of the general labourer, and whose wages are consequently only slightly, if at all, in excess of those paid to the latter . . . Allowing for broken time, the average wage for a labourer in York is from 18s. to 21s.; whereas, according to the figures given earlier in this chapter, the minimum expenditure necessary to maintain in a state of physical efficiency a family of two adults and three children is 21s. 8d.[3] or, if there are four children, the sum required would be 26s.

It is thus seen that *the wages paid for unskilled labour in York are insufficient to provide food, shelter, and clothing adequate to maintain a family of moderate size in a state of bare physical efficiency* . . . The above estimates of necessary minimum expenditure are based upon the assumption that the diet is even less generous than that allowed to able-bodied paupers in the York Workhouse, and that *no allowance is made for any expenditure other than that absolutely required for the maintenance of merely physical efficiency.*

And let us clearly understand what 'merely physical efficiency' means. A family living upon the scale allowed for in this estimate must never spend a penny on railway fare or omnibus. They must never go into the country unless they walk. They must never purchase a halfpenny newspaper or spend a penny to buy a ticket for a popular concert. They must write no letters to absent children, for they cannot afford to pay the postage. They must never contribute anything to their church or chapel, or give any help to a neighbour which costs them money. They cannot save, nor can they join sick club or Trade Union, because they cannot pay the necessary subscriptions. The children must have no pocket money for dolls, marbles, or sweets. The father must smoke no tobacco, and must drink no beer. The mother must never buy any pretty clothes for herself or for her children, the character of the family wardrobe as for the family diet being governed by the regulation, 'Nothing must be bought but that which is absolutely necessary for the maintenance of physical health, and what is bought must be of the plainest and most economical description.' Should a child fall ill, it must be attended by the parish doctor; should it die, it must be buried by the parish. Finally, the wage-earner must never be absent from his work for a single day.

If any of these conditions are broken, the extra expenditure involved is met, *and can only be met*, by limiting the diet; or, in other words, by sacrificing physical efficiency.

That few York labourers receiving 20s. or 21s. per week submit to these iron conditions in order to maintain physical efficiency is obvious. And even were they to submit, physical efficiency would be unattainable for those who had three or more children dependent upon them. It cannot therefore be too clearly understood, nor too emphatically repeated, *that whenever a worker having three children dependent on him, and receiving not more than 21s. 8d. per week,*

indulges in any expenditure beyond that required for the barest
physical needs, he can do so only at the cost of his own physical
efficiency, or of that of some members of his family.

If a labourer has but two children, these conditions will be better
to the extent of 2s. 10d.; and if he has but one, they will be better to
the extent of 5s. 8d. And, again, as soon as his children begin to
work, their earnings will raise the family above the poverty line. But
the fact remains that every labourer who has as many as three
children must pass through a time, probably lasting for about ten
years, when he will be in a state of 'primary' poverty; in other words,
when he and his family will be *underfed*.

The life of a labourer is marked by five alternating periods of want
and comparative plenty. During early childhood, unless his father is
a skilled worker, he probably will be in poverty; this will last until he,
or some of his brothers or sisters, begin to earn money and thus
augment their father's wage sufficiently to raise the family above the
poverty line. Then follows the period during which he is earning
money and living under his parents' roof; for some portion of this
period he will be earning more money than is required for lodging,
food, and clothes. This is his chance to save money. If he has saved
enough to pay for furnishing a cottage, this period of comparative
prosperity may continue after marriage until he has two or three
children, when poverty will again overtake him. This period of
poverty will last perhaps for ten years, i.e. until the first child is
fourteen years old and begins to earn wages; but if there are more
than three children it may last longer.[4] While the children are
earning, and before they leave the home to marry, the man enjoys
another period of prosperity — possibly, however, only to sink back
again into poverty when his children have married and left him, and
he himself is too old to work, for his income has never permitted his
saving enough for him and his wife to live upon for more than a very
short time.

A labourer is thus in poverty, and therefore underfed —

(a) In childhood — when his constitution is being built up.

(b) In early middle life — when he should be in his prime.

(c) In old age.

The accompanying diagram may serve to illustrate this:

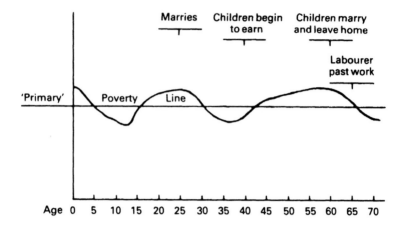

It should be noted that the women are in poverty during the greater part of the period that they are bearing children.

We thus see that the 7,230 persons shown by this inquiry to be in a state of 'primary' poverty, *represent merely that section who happened to be in one of these poverty periods at the time the inquiry was made.* Many of these will, in course of time, pass on into a period of comparative prosperity; this will take place as soon as the children, now dependent, begin to earn. But their places below the poverty line will be taken by others who are at present living in that prosperous period previous to, or shortly after, marriage. Again, many now classed as above the poverty line were below it until the children began to earn. The proportion of the community who at one period or other of their lives suffer from poverty to the point of physical privation is therefore much greater, and the injurious effects of such a condition are much more widespread than would appear from a consideration of the number who can be shown to be below the poverty line at any given moment.

From B.S. Rowntree, *Poverty, A Study of Town Life* (Longman, 1901)

A30   Rowntree on Working-class Living Standards in 1936

I have taken the standard of living attainable by a family of man, wife and three dependent children, with an available income of 43s. 6d.[5]

a week after paying rent, as the minimum. Families whose incomes do not enable them to live up to this standard are classified as below the poverty line. This poverty line has no relation whatever to the primary poverty line adopted in the 1899 survey, which only provided 30s. 7d. (at 1936 prices) for a family of five persons. A family of five with 43s. 6d. after paying rent can, if they lay out their money with great economy, buy food sufficient for physical efficiency and clothing sufficient for warmth and respectability, pay for necessary heating, lighting, household sundries and essential items such as Trade Union subscriptions and compulsory insurance, sick clubs, and transport to and from work, and if they are very careful they will have left over 4s. 11d. a week for the whole family to cover all other expenditure, including a daily newspaper, 6d. a week for a wireless set, all transport other than that of the wage-earner to and from work, holidays, cinemas and recreation of all kinds, beer, tobacco and so on.

Our inquiry showed that 31.1 per cent of the working-class population were in receipt of insufficient income to enable them to live in accordance with the above standard, and so are classified as living under the poverty line; 18.9 per cent belong to families with incomes of less than 10s. a week above the minimum figure; 13.9 per cent to those with incomes between 10s. to 20s. above it, and 36.1 per cent to families with incomes of not less than 20s. a week above it.

The Immediate Causes of Poverty

Three-quarters of the poverty is due to three causes: 28.6 per cent is due to unemployment, 32.8 per cent to the fact that workers in regular work are not receiving wages sufficiently high to enable them to live above the poverty line, and 14.7 per cent are in poverty on account of old age. Of the income of the families whose poverty is due to unemployment 80 per cent is derived from social services, and 66 per cent is so derived in the case of those whose poverty is due to old age. On the other hand, families whose poverty is due to inadequate wages only derive 1.7 per cent of their total income from social services.

Unemployment

Clearly the only way to overcome poverty in the case of the unemployed is either to find them work or to increase the benefit. Our investigation pointed to the fact that probably about 76 per cent of the unemployed were eagerly seeking for work and capable of working; 12 per cent would need to have their morale restored and their physical condition built up before they were fit for work, while the remainder were people getting on in years, many of whom could only do light work. Some of them were almost past work. If work cannot be found for the unemployed, then, if they are to be raised above the poverty line, the only alternative is to increase benefits . . . If any increase is given it should be given in the form of increased benefits per child rather than increased benefits to the parents. It is the unemployed families with a number of dependent children that are most liable to be in poverty, and therefore any increase in benefits given to children is most likely to go to families who stand in most urgent need of it. Adequate help to raise families with many children above the poverty line would, in the case of low-paid workers, involve paying a man more when unemployed than he gets when working. This difficulty would be overcome if a scheme of family allowances were made general.

Inadequate Wages

Turning now to the families which are in poverty owing to inadequate wages of the chief wage-earner, notwithstanding the fact that he is in regular work, this is in part due to low wages, in part to large families, and in part to high rents. By 'low wages' I here mean wages under 53s. a week, by 'large families' I mean families with more than three children, and by 'high rents' I mean rents over 9s. 6d.

Of the 1,338 heads of households whose poverty is classified as being due to inadequate wages, 1,157 earned less than 53s. The others were in poverty because wages, although not under 53s., did not suffice to raise them above the poverty line, either because their families were 'large' or their rents were 'high'.

The remedies usually proposed for dealing with poverty due to low wages are statutory minimum wages and family allowances . . . To get rid of it altogether would involve a minimum wage of 53s. a week for an adult male and an allowance of 5s. a week for all dependent children.

Old Age

The only way of dealing with poverty due to old age is by increasing the pension, legislation for which is being considered as I write these lines.[6] It is interesting to note that of the 3,268 old age pensioners covered by our schedules only 50 per cent are in poverty. The others either have other sources of income, such as children who are earning money and living at home, or they are themselves living with families who are above the poverty line.

In addition to the old age pensioners covered by our schedules there are probably about 1,700 living with families which are better off than those we investigated, so that probably only 33 per cent of all the old age pensioners in York are living below the poverty line.

The 1899 'Poverty Line' Quite Different from that of 1936

Before concluding this account of the economic condition of the workers, I must again warn the reader against drawing a completely false deduction from the fact that in 1899 I concluded that 33 per cent of the working-class population were living in poverty, and as a result of the present investigation I conclude that 31.1 per cent are living in poverty through inadequate income, and suggest that perhaps a further 7 to 10 per cent may be possibly be in this state through expenditure on non-essentials.

In 1899 I estimated that 17.93 per cent of the population were living in 'secondary poverty', which I defined as 'families whose total earnings would be sufficient for the maintenance of merely physical efficiency were it not that some portion of it is absorbed by other expenditure, either useful or wasteful.' I explained in the following words how I arrived at the number of families in 'secondary' poverty:

> The number of persons living in 'secondary' poverty was ascertained in the following way. The investigator, in the course of his house-to-house visitation, noted down the households where there were evidences of poverty, i.e., obvious want and squalor. Direct information was often obtained from neighbours, or from a member of the household concerned, to the effect that the father or mother was a heavy drinker; in other cases the pinched faces of the ragged children told their own tale of poverty and privation.
>
> Judging in this way, partly by appearance and partly from information given, I have been able to arrive at a fair estimate of the total number of persons living in poverty in York. From this total number I subtracted the number of those ascertained to be living in 'primary' poverty; the difference represents those living in 'secondary' poverty.

In this survey I have made no attempt to measure the amount of 'secondary' poverty by direct observation, partly because the methods of doing this adopted in 1899 appear to me now as being too rough to give reliable results, and also because even had I done so the results would not have rendered possible a comparison with 1899, for ideas of what constitutes 'obvious want and squalor' have changed profoundly since then. There is no doubt that in 1899 investigators would not have regarded as 'obvious want and squalor' conditions which would have been so regarded in 1936, and on the other hand a large proportion of the families living below the 1936 poverty line would not in 1899 have been regarded as 'showing signs of poverty'.

The facts that in 1899 only 33.39 per cent of the working class was regarded as living in poverty, either primary or secondary, whereas in 1936 31.1 per cent are living below the minimum through lack of income, and an unknown further proportion, possibly 7 or 10 per cent, are living in 'secondary' poverty, have therefore no relation to each other.

The only figures that are absolutely comparable are those for primary poverty and as we have seen the proportion of the working-class population living in primary poverty in 1936 was 6.8 per cent, whereas in 1899 it was 15.46 per cent.

There is not the least doubt that the economic condition of the workers is immensely better than in 1899, possibly by as much as 30 per cent, but the satisfaction which we may rightly feel at this great improvement must be qualified by a serious sense of concern that so large a proportion of the workers are living below a poverty line which few, if any, will regard as having been fixed at too high a level.

From B.S. Rowntree, *Poverty and Progress* (Longman, Green, 1941)

A31   Providing School Meals, 1904

With scarcely an exception, there was a general consensus of opinion that the time has come when the State should realize the necessity of ensuring adequate nourishment to children in attendance at school; it was said to be the height of cruelty to subject half-starved children to the processes of education, besides being a short-sighted policy, in that the progress of such children is inadequate and disappointing; and it was, further, the subject of general agreement that, as a rule, no purely voluntary association could successfully cope with the full extent of the evil. Even those witnesses who were inclined to think that its magnitude had been much exaggerated, did not question the advisability of feeding, by some means or other, those children who are underfed, provided it could be done quietly and without impairing parental responsibility. The only witness who appeared absolutely to dissent from that view was the Bishop of Ross, who, while admitting an enormous number of underfed children in Ireland, deprecated any steps being taken to remedy the evil, on the ground that it would weaken the sense of self-respect and self-reliance both of parent and child.

The purely medical view was well put forward by Dr Robert Hutchison, a well-known authority on nutrition, nominated to give evidence by the Royal College of Physicians. He said, 'looking at it purely scientifically, it would be an extremely important thing to ensure to every child at school a sufficient and proper sort of meal'; and again, 'I feel certain that the provision of meals would do a great deal to improve the health and growth and development of the children of the poorer classes.' . . . This witness further gave the Committee to understand, that a child ought to have a certain amount of nourishment during the twenty-four hours, but that it does not very much matter how you divide it up; except that it is more important to have a meal before physical exercise than before mental; and, therefore, mid-day dinner is more important than breakfast. This view is interesting, as differing from a very general opinion that no child should be allowed to come to school without sufficient breakfast . . . He spoke entirely from the medical point of view, and refused to discuss the economic question.

The general trend of opinion is in favour of some sort of regularised feeding in school, or at centres, exacting payment from the parents where they are in a position to pay, but giving the meal free where they are not. Thus, Mr Charles Booth is in favour of some sort of school restaurant in every school, or connected with every school, where food could be obtained at a minimum cost, but with no intention of giving it away; though he admitted that 'in some cases it might be a mere charitable assistance'.

Sir Lauder Brunton thought it might be necessary to provide food at schools, and 'in cases where the parents are absolutely unable to pay, food might be provided out of the poor rates'; but 'every effort must be made to force the parents to pay properly for the food.'

Mr Atkins said, 'We have got to the point where we must face the question whether the logical culmination of free education is not free meals in some form or other, it being cruelty to force a child to go and learn what it has not strength to learn.'

But he agreed that the parents should be made to pay, if possible.

Dr Collie thought that underfed children should be fed by means of school kitchens, and that the parents should be prosecuted for neglect; a few prosecutions would have a salutary effect. Mr Seebohm Rowntree advocated the judicious feeding of school children, so as not to pauperise the parents . . .

The opinion of Mr C.S. Loch is worthy of consideration, as being presumably the official view of the Charity Organisation Society. He found fault with the existing systems of voluntary feeding, as 'purely a movement against destitution without regard to education'; he stated his belief that no child should ever be fed without thorough investigation into the circumstances of its family, and no free meal given except in special cases, and then only as secretly as possible; but he admitted the necessity in special cases. The feeding should not be at the school, though it does not appear from his evidence where it ought to be. He instanced the difficulty in former days, before the Free Education Act of 1891, of getting educational fees out of parents, and argued there would be similar difficulty in getting feeding fees. Mr Loch . . . thought that in cases of real destitution the Poor Law Administration should always be brought into play, and not kept out by any system of free feeding.

Dr Niven propounded a definite scheme for ascertaining the fact of malnutrition, for feeding the child, and enforcing parental responsibility. The teacher would be taught to note all children obviously suffering or undersized, and to report them, if diseased, to a medical officer; if underfed, to the educational authority. The director would then instruct the attendance officer to ascertain the circumstances of the family; and the subsequent feeding of the child would depend upon the facts thereby elicited. It is worth noting that any such system would in the first instance be rendered easier by an organised medical inspection of schools, a proposal, as it has been seen, very widely and generally advocated.

The most uncompromising advocacy of public responsibility came from Sir John Gorst and Dr Macnamara, and as the first-named appealed to the authority of the other, it is fair to treat his proposals as put forward in the name of the two. Dr Macnamara has based his recommendations on the following proposals of a Committee of the London School Board in 1898, which, however, do not appear to have commended themselves to the School Board of the day:

Children attending School unfit for School work

(i) It should be deemed to be part of the duty of any authority by law responsible for the compulsory attendance of children at school to ascertain what children, if any, come to school in a state unfit to get normal profit by the school work — whether by reason of under-feeding, physical disability, or otherwise — and that there should be the necessary inspection for that purpose.

Provision for Children sent to School 'Underfed'

(ii) That where it is ascertained that children are sent to school 'underfed,' (in the sense defined above), it should be part of the duty of the authority to see that they are provided, under proper conditions, with the necessary food, subject to the provision contained in Clause (vi).

Supervision of Voluntary Organisations by Authority

(iii) That existing or future voluntary efforts to that end should be supervised by the authority.

Voluntary Effort to be Supplemented if Inadequate

(iv) That in so far as such voluntary efforts fail to cover the ground, the authority should have the power and the duty to supplement them.

School Dinners available for all Children, and Method of Payment

(v) That where dinners are provided it is desirable that they should be open to all children, and should be paid for by tickets previously obtained, which parents should pay for, unless they are reported by the Board's officers to be unable by misfortune to find the money; but in no case should any visible distinction be made between paying and non-paying children.

Prosecution of Parent for culpable Neglect

(vi) That where the Board's officers report that the underfed condition of any child is due to the culpable neglect of a parent (whether by reason of drunkenness or other gross misconduct) the Board should have the power and the duty to prosecute the parent for cruelty, and that, in case the offence is persisted in, there should be power to deal with the child under the Industrial Schools Act.

Dr Macnamara was good enough to explain to the Committee how a scheme on these lines could be brought into practical application, and gave interesting evidence as to the success claimed for similar schemes in Brussels, Vienna and Paris. Upon the plan followed in the last-named city he estimated the outside cost of its application to London to amount to £120,000. He did not believe that any serious difficulty would arise in determining what children should be fed without paying, as 'the attendance officer and the teacher together could bring you very near to the actual state of facts', and he was prepared to press the case against the parents who neglected their children with all the force at the disposal of the law. He advocated dealing with them by an extension of the Prevention of Cruelty to Children Act, or under the Education Acts by enabling the school authority to recover the cost of food in the same way as fines for non-attendance are recovered. The permission to parents to have their children fed at school, if they desired it, would, it was believed, greatly facilitate the operation of such a scheme, and Dr Macnamara agreed that where parents made use of it as a convenience it would be fair to make them pay something in excess of cost price, which would to some extent diminish the charge that would in the last resort fall upon the community. The weak point in the system was admitted to be the difficulty of maintaining voluntary effort and providing public help at the same moment. Sir John Gorst, it is true, said the British public is very fond of doing some part of the work of the Government for them, instancing the lifeboat service, and thought private benevolence would still come in, though the school authority should be responsible for its efficient working; but Dr Macnamara was obliged to acknowledge that in those towns abroad where the municipality had stepped in, the flow of charity had been arrested, and he was not prepared to think his scheme could be adopted without a substantial public charge . . .

On a general survey of the evidence, . . . the Committee think that a large number of children habitually attend school ill-fed, but this number varies locally with the time of year and with the conditions of employment, and is not likely to increase — indeed they look, as they have said, with confidence to the operation of many causes towards its diminution.

It seems, further, that in a large number of cases voluntary organisations with the support and oversight of the Local Authority are sufficient for the purpose, and as long as this is so the Committee would strongly deprecate recourse being had to direct municipal assistance.

Circumstances, however, do arise which call for more immediate aid, and in which the School Authority, taking into account the difficulty in the way of home provision of suitable food, and the number of children who attend school habitually underfed, are willing to provide regular and sufficient meals, and in such cases the Committee agree with the opinion of the Royal Commission on Physical Training (Scotland), that 'the preparation and cooking of these meals, where it is found necessary to provide them, ought to be regarded as one of the charges incident to school management.'

By a differentiation of function on these terms — the School Authority to supply and organise the machinery, the benevolent to furnish the material — a working adjustment between the privileges of charity and the obligations of the community might be reached.

In some districts it still may be the case that such an arrangement would prove inadequate, the extent or the concentration of poverty might be too great for the resources of local charity, and in these, subject to the consent of the Board of Education, it might be expedient to permit the application of municipal aid on a larger scale. As a corollary to the exercise of such powers — which should be by scheme sanctioned by the Board — the law, would have to be altered so as to furnish means, as was suggested in evidence, to compel the neglectful parent to take his full share of responsibility, and the Committee are sanguine that a few prosecutions to this end would have a most salutary and stimulating effect . . .

The Committee, moreover, do not think that children should be made the subject of . . . experiment without the concurrence of the Poor Law Authorities, and the funds should be found through the machinery of the Poor Law, with all due precaution against affixing any unnecessary stigma upon the deserving parent.

The Committee deem that by these means the community may be protected from the consequences of the somewhat dangerous doctrine that free meals are the necessary concomitant of free education. Education is a great social need, which individual citizens are, as a rule, not able to provide for their children on a sufficient scale, but food, like clothing and lodging, is a personal necessity, which in a well-ordered society it is not inherently impossible for parents to provide; and the effort to supplement their deficiencies, and to correct the effects of their neglect, should aim, in the first instance, at the restoration of self respect and the enforcement of parental duty.

From the *Report of the Select Inter-Departmental Committee on Physical Deterioration*, C.2175 (1904)

A32 Beveridge on Unemployment, 1909

The problem of unemployment lies, in a very special sense, at the root of most other social problems. Society is built up on labour; it lays upon its members responsibilities which in the vast majority of cases can be met only from the reward of labour; it imprisons for beggary and brands for pauperism; its ideal unit is the household of man, wife and children maintained by the earnings of the first alone. The household should have at all times sufficient room and air according to its size — but how, if the income is too irregular always to pay the rent? The children, till they themselves can work, should be supported by the parents — but how, unless the father has employment? The wife, so long at least as she is bearing and bringing up children, should have no other task — but how, if the husband's earnings fail and she has to go out to work? Everywhere the same difficulty recurs. Reasonable security of employment for the bread-winner is the basis of all private duties and all sound social action.

At one time this reasonable security was assumed as axiomatic. The great majority of people were people who had obtained employment. The great majority argued from their own cases that any man who really wanted employment could always obtain it. Only now and again came exceptional circumstances . . . to be met by emergency measures of relief . . . Now that this optimism is shaken, as it certainly is, there is danger that it may give place to a pessimism as unreasoning and as harmful.

There has been a steady, if gradual, growth of the sense of public responsibility for the case of the unemployed. If this sense of respon-sibility is to issue in further action, it is before all things necessary that that case should be fully understood. In a matter of the first importance there is room for mistakes of the first importance. A community may treat its criminals or its lunatics unwisely without more than local inconvenience; it will touch in any case but an insig-nificant percentage of its members. It cannot treat the question of employment unwisely without the risk of grave harm in every quarter; its policy there is a policy affecting the great majority of citizens. Fortunately, with the growth of a sense of public responsibility in regard to this problem, there has been a growth of knowledge and understanding. The administration of the Unemployed Workmen Act in particular has afforded a mass of new experience and of discussion. If much, with regard to unemployment, remains obscure, yet much has been done to lighten the past obscurity; many crude ideas are in process of dispersal; it is even possible to suggest the outlines of a general theory of causes and principles for treatment. This is the attempt which will be made in the following pages. The manner of that attempt is governed by two general considerations. First, the inquiry must be essentially an economic one. The evil to be analysed is, in technical language, that of maladjustment between the supply of and the demand for labour. Second, the inquiry must be one as to unemployment rather than as to the unemployed.

The inquiry must be essentially an economic one. The object in view is not the framing of palliatives for present distress, but the discovery of causes and the suggestion, if possible, of preventive measures and final remedies. With this in view the problem must be approached, not from the standpoint of the Poor Law or of charitable administration, but from that of industry. The first question must be, not what is to be done with the unemployed individual, but why he is thus unemployed. His involuntary idleness indicates excess of the supply of labour over the demand for labour. To what extent, under what circumstances, and in what forms is such an excess observable in the industry of today? To what economic and social causes may it be attributed? How is the action of the social and economic causes complicated by the influence of personal character? How, if at all, can they be rendered harmless or eliminated? How far, if at all, can this be done without risk of graver harm in other directions?

The inquiry must be one into unemployment rather than into the unemployed. It will appear at once, indeed it is manifest from the start, that any one unemployed individual may represent, and commonly does represent, the concurrence of many different forces, some industrial, some personal. A riverside labourer in Wapping during February 1908 might be suffering at one and the same time from chronic irregularity of employment, from seasonal depression of his trade, from exceptional or cyclical depression of trade generally, from the permanent shifting of work lower down the river, and from his own deficiencies of character or education. His distress could not be attributed to any one of these factors alone. Classification of men according to the causes of their unemployment is, strictly speaking, an impossibility. The only possible course is to classify the causes or types of unemployment themselves.

From W. Beveridge, *Unemployment, A Problem of Industry* (Longman, 1909) reproduced as Part One of *Unemployment* (Longman, 1930)

A33   Beveridge on Unemployment, 1930

The record of the past twenty years of dealing with unemployment is depressing. Those parts of the policies of 1909 which were aimed at the reduction of unemployment — de-casualisation and the evening out of the demand for labour — have failed most completely of adoption; the Labour Exchanges, indispensable as they have become, have had a limited and inadequate success; the disorganisation of the labour market continues. That part of the policies which was designed mainly, though not wholly, for relief of unemployment has grown portentously and grown always in the direction of becoming relief and nothing else.

Yet the failures of these twenty years must not be taken too hardly. After all, what a twenty years they have been! One may dream that but for the war there would be no failure to record. And the main result of the fresh examination here made of unemployment should not be discouraging . . . The policies then proposed were . . . making the supply of labour more capable of following and waiting for the demand — of following the demand through labour market organisation, of waiting for it through insurance. To these policies another must now be added — that of adjusting production to standards of living or standards of living to production. But, with this addition, unemployment remains, in 1930 as in 1909, a problem of industry, not an Act of God.

Some things in Britain's destiny are beyond management by its governments and its leaders; the slow vast forces shaping and re-shaping the economic structure of the world and the swift changes of personal desire that determine future numbers work uncontrollably, outside their reach or beneath their feet. But unemployment is not of these. It is no mysterious visitation, but in the main the consequence of our own choices, the measure of how our industry adjusts itself to the changing world. For one great industry the changes have been too catastrophic for adjustment and have left a disaster for which there is no full remedy. The problem of the ruined mining areas stands by itself — an ill to make the best of till time ends it, by moving one by one all who can move, by expenditure in organising such work as is possible for those who cannot move. Apart from this acute but limited problem, we know what to do if we wish to get back to the level of unemployment that ruled before the war; we must either lower our standards of life or bring production up to justify them. We know also what to do if we wish to bring unemployment below that level; carry out the main preventive policy of 1909 and organise completely the labour market, abolishing the hawking of labour and casual under-employment and the anarchic recruiting of trades and the blind choice of careers. These things cannot be done in a day, but with time they can be done. They cannot be done by wishing for them but, by fixed purpose, by willing means as well as ends, by counting and deciding to pay the price, they can be done. If we prefer not to do them, if we think the cost of curing unemployment too high, we may continue instead to pay for unemployment; the post-war situation puts frankly the question, how much unemployment we are prepared to carry in order to avoid surrender of standards of life once gained.

Solution of the problem of unemployment is thus practicable today as it was practicable twenty years ago. The price of a solution is perhaps higher but it is payable in the same coin. '"Practicability" is never anything but a relative term — dependent upon the urgency with which an object is desired and upon the inconveniences which men are prepared to undergo in its pursuit . . . So it is not practicable for a nation to get a mastery of unemployment without being prepared to submit to some change of industrial methods and customs. The problem of unemployment — this is a point that cannot be too strongly emphasised — is insoluble by any mere expenditure of public money. It represents not a want to be satisfied but a disease to be eradicated. It needs not money so much as thought and organisation.' The repeated lesson of twenty-one years since those words were penned is how much more abundant is money than thought, how much harder it is, for the cure of social ills, to change men's habits and open their minds than to slit their purses — how much harder and how much more important.

From W. Beveridge, *Unemployment* (Longman, 1930)

A34   The Housing Shortage and the State, 1917

On no subject — not even that of demobilisation — is it so urgent that Parliament and the Government should come to a decision of policy as on housing . . . But houses do not become instantly ready for occupation on the Government giving the order. Many months must necessarily elapse between the decision to provide dwellings and the entry of the families into these new homes. It is emphatically a matter for the present War Cabinet within the next few weeks . . . to return to.

The Extent of the Shortage

What creates the urgency is . . . the appalling shortage of houses for the wage earners, and the consequent overcrowding, notwithstanding the temporary absence of 5,000,000 men in the Army and Navy. This shortage is due to three causes —

(a) We were already overcrowded ten years ago. No family, large or small ought anywhere to be living more than two persons to a room — yet the census of 1901 showed that in England and Wales alone, there were then no fewer than 2,667,500 persons living (in tenements of one to four rooms) more than two to a room.

There was thus already in 1901, a shortage of many hundred thousand rooms, and the 80,000 new working-class dwellings that were then being put up annually did no more than keep pace with the increase of population.

(b) The speculative builder gradually gave up the building of working-class cottages and tenements: and from 1907 onward the number of new houses built to let at less than 10s. per week rapidly declined, and (including all municipal, rural, landlord, and philanthropic building) it has latterly, taking the country as a whole, year by year fallen far short of the annual increase in population.

(c) During the three years of war all such building (except in about a dozen 'munition areas' especially subsidised by the Government) has ceased — it has, in fact, been prohibited.

The result is that, in nearly all the towns of Great Britain, as also in Dublin and Belfast, in all the mining districts and in nearly all the agricultural areas of England and Wales, and in parts of Scotland the over-crowding has become intensified . . . Including Scotland and Ireland, at least 1,000,000 new dwellings, to be let at not more than a few shillings a week, according to size, are urgently required.

Who is to Build the New Cottages?

The times will be bad for speculative building; all materials will continue dear for years to come; loans of capital will be hard to get, and the rate of interest will remain high. If speculative builders found no profit in putting up working-class dwellings before the war, it is plain that they will be quite unable to do so under the more adverse conditions that will now prevail. We cannot possibly allow grants of public money to private builders. Co-operative societies will find it equally impossible to build without loss. We cannot rely on philanthropic landowners and charitable trusts for more than a trifling proportion of the need. What are called 'public utility societies' (in which the shareholders content themselves with 5 per cent dividends) cannot now operate without subsidies from public funds.

It seems clear that no one but the municipalities and the National Government can possibly shoulder the task of building 1,000,000 new rural and urban dwellings — 5,000,000 additional rooms — which may cost at the high prices that will prevail, at least £250,000,000.

The Cost

To build, properly and healthily, 1,000,000 new working-class dwellings in all parts of the United Kingdom in both rural and urban areas may probably cost at the high prices that will prevail £250,000,000 (the cost of five or six weeks of the war). But even charging no more than the rents customary in each locality, probably £200,000,000 of this cost would be no more than a sound financial investment, covering not only repairs, management and interest, but also a sinking fund to repay the whole debt within 60 years. The real expense, would be represented by [a] Free Grant from the Exchequer to enable the several housing schemes to pay their way. If the Government were to lend the whole capital free of interest (thus permitting an actual reduction of rent) this would involve a cost to the Exchequer in the first year (assuming that the Government borrows at 5 per cent) of £12,500,000. If the Government, as an alternative, makes the same sort of Free Grant as it has done in a dozen 'munition areas', just sufficient to enable the local authorities to avoid any charge on the rates at rents not exceeding those heretofore customary (putting this Free Grant at an average of 20 per cent), we get a total expense once for all of no more than £50,000,000 — less than ten days cost of the war; less even than would be covered by a continuation for three months of the excess profits tax! The nation cannot afford not to do it.

From *The Housing Problem After the War* (The Labour Party, 1917)

A35   Tawney on Secondary Education for All, 1922

It is still true that, as far as more than ninety per cent of the children are concerned, the primary school is like the rope which the Indian juggler throws into the air to end in vacancy; that while in the United States some twenty-eight per cent of the children entering the primary schools pass to high schools, in England the percentage passing from elementary to secondary schools is less than ten, and that of those who do, the majority have hitherto left at, or soon after, their fifteenth birthday and after a school course of less than three years.

Nor can it be said that there is at present any clear conviction in England as to the part which secondary education should play in the life of the community or as to the lines upon which it should develop in the future. There are some signs, indeed, as we point out below, that the policy advocated in this pamphlet has commended itself to certain of the more progressive Local Education Authorities, several of whom — we need mention only the West Riding and Durham among the counties, and Darlington and West Ham among the county boroughs — appear to envisage as their goal the development of full-time secondary education to such a point that the majority of children may be transferred to a secondary school at eleven, and remain in it to the age of sixteen. But the earlier tradition, which subordinated educational to social and economic considerations, dies hard. Apart from the children of the well-to-do, who receive secondary education almost as a matter of course, and whose parents appear usually, though quite mistakenly, to believe that they pay the whole cost of it, secondary education is still commonly regarded as a 'privilege' to be conceded only to the exceptionally brilliant or fortunate. It is still possible for an association of manufacturers to protest against any wide extension of it for the

rank and file of children on the ground that it is likely to be
'unsuitable for the employment which they eventually enter'.[7] It is
still possible for the largest education authority in the country to
propose to erect inequality of educational opportunity into a
principle of public policy by solemnly suggesting, with much parade
of philosophical arguments, that the interests of the community
require that the children of well-to-do parents, who pay fees, should
be admitted to public secondary schools on easier intellectual terms
than the children of poor parents who can enter them only with free
places, and that the children who are so contemptible as to be unable
to afford secondary education without assistance in the form of
maintenance allowances shall not be admitted unless they reach a
higher intellectual standard still![8]

These survivals from the doctrines of 1870 have their significance.
But they need not disturb us overmuch. It would be a grave injustice
to employers to assume that the pronouncement of the Federation
of British Industries represents the views of a majority even of its
own members: as a matter of fact, indeed, it was immediately
repudiated by a considerable proportion of them. Against the
special pleading of the London County Council can be set the educational theorists, the policy of twenty other Local Education
Authorities, the policy of Parliament itself. For, whatever the
shortcomings of the Education Act of 1918, it did two things of
capital importance. For the first time in English history it imposed
on Local Education Authorities the duty of organising higher education; for the first time it declared that no child capable of profiting by
higher education should be prevented from obtaining it by inability
to pay fees. But in effect this last provision concedes in principle the
very demand for universal secondary education which is urged by
the educationalists and which has been for a generation the policy of
the Labour movement. For what the most recent expert inquiry tells
us is that seventy-five per cent of the children in the primary schools
are intellectually capable of profiting by full-time education up to
sixteen.[9] If secondary education is to be so organised that three-
quarters of the children are to pass from the primary school to one
type or another of secondary school, then clearly the old conception
both of 'elementary' and of secondary education vanishes for good
and all. The latter becomes the education of all normal children
during the years of adolescence from eleven to sixteen; the former
the preparatory education of children of whom three out of four will
continue it in a secondary school. The doctrine of the parallel

systems with links between them disappears. The doctrine of the single system, with two stages embracing various types of institution, takes its place.

In pressing for a general system of full-time education up, at least, to sixteen, Labour can claim with some confidence that it is both voicing the demands of nearly all enlightened educationalists and working for the only organisation of education which will enable the community to make the best use of the most precious of its natural resources — the endowments of its children.

We are far, indeed, from making the best use of it today. 'The fact to bear in mind at present', *The Times* has truly said, 'is that the highway which Mr Fisher himself helped to construct is effectively blocked . . . Our educational system is not economical because of the waste of power in the elementary schools. The whole "elementary system" imposes a wrong upon the 2,000,000 children who are ripe for secondary education and are denied it. Mr Fisher, at Romford, talked of there being no need for an official definition of elementary and secondary education. We entirely agree; but in fact there is in existence "elementary" education whether it is defined or not, a type of education which is not secondary, which does not supply an outfit for life, a truncated type of instruction which is condemned on all hands and is responsible for a truncated type of training for teachers. The whole system is wrong and cannot be made right by waiving aside definitions. The country wants no definitions, it wants to be rid, once and for all, of "elementary" education. Every child in this country who is intellectually fit for secondary education is entitled to it under the express provisions of the Act of 1918, and yet 2,000,000 children are clamouring for it only to meet with a blank refusal, not really on the ground of economy at all but because — we insist on maintaining an "elementary" system supplemented by a totally inadequate number of so-called secondary schools, containing a large percentage of children who have no capacity for secondary education at all. The whole system is wrong, costly and inefficient.'

From R.H. Tawney, *Secondary Education for All* (The Labour Party, 1922, and later published by Allen & Unwin)

Notes

1. It will be noted that the average sum earned by the supplementary earners is much smaller than in the other sections. The explanation of this is to be found in the fact, that in this section the chief wage-earner is in every case in receipt of a regular income, and as soon as the earnings of the children become considerable the family rises above the 'primary' poverty line. The families below it are therefore chiefly those with young children who are not earning wages.
2. Many of these are engaged in factories or on the railway.
3. This estimate is arrived at thus

	s.	d.
Food — two adults at 3s.	6	0
three children at 2s. 3d.	6	9
Rent — say	4	0
Clothes — two adults at 6d	1	0
three children at 5d.	1	3
Fuel	1	10
All else — five persons at 2d.	0	10
Total	21	8

4. It is to be noted that the family are in poverty, and consequently are underfed, during the first ten or more years of the children's lives.
5. In fixing the figure of 43s. 6d. for a family of five, it is assumed that the house has been furnished. In the case of young married couples without children or with one child, the sum of 5s. was included in the minimum cost of living, a nd 3s. in the case of young married couples with two children. Compulsory insurance has been taken into account in fixing the minimum standard.
6. In 1940 supplementary pensions up to a maximum of 9s. a week were granted to oid people who could prove need.
7. Federation of British Industries Memorandum on Education (January 1918), p. 4.
8. Scheme of the London County Council (July 21,1920) pp. 81–8.
9. Report of the Departmental Committee on Scholarships and Free Places.

SECTION B: 1940–85

Introduction

In writing about social policy in the 1940s, one always risks lapsing into cliché. Thus it could be held that these years saw a clear change in direction from previous practice as, under Beveridge, public opinion came to recognise the wisdom of a coherent social policy which succeeded in reconciling the state's obligation to guarantee a subsistence level of living to all its citizens as of right with the preservation of a largely free-market economy in which profit and work incentives were recognised as central and crucial by all parties. Driven on by the social cohesion generated in the first instance by the exigencies of total war, the coalition government entered into a commitment that there would be no return to inter-war normalcy. A society distinguished by universality in social service provision, underpinned by Keynesian economic theory, could hardly be less like one characterised by the selective degradation of the household means test and neo-classical economic dogmatism.

It is tempting in retrospect to conclude that the forging of this new dominant orthodoxy was inevitable, that there were no serious alternatives to social insurance, and that the liberalism and Liberalism of Beveridge and Keynes enjoyed a relatively uncontested triumph. That there was opposition, though, is attested to by the unease of some Conservatives during the three-day debate on the Beveridge Report held in February 1943, especially by Conservative members of the government, while a small though not insignificant minority within the Labour Party felt that flat-rate social insurance and managed capitalism hardly constituted the dawn of the socialist millennium.

Space does not allow us to illustrate these contrary opinions and the extracts included under the heading 'The 1940s', with one exception, illustrate the historical triumph of this new world view. The single exception is Evan Durbin's warning to his fellow socialists that the economic base had to be given first priority (*B1*). Of the extracts included under this heading, a strong argument can be advanced that the most significant are *B2* and *B3*, which outline the principles and assumptions on which Beveridge's entire schema were based, and *B5*, the announcement of the government's plans for the creation and maintenance of a high and stable level of employment. Children's Allowances both attacked family poverty and allowed for the preservation and augmentation of work incentives. A National Health Service would reduce claims on the insurance fund and make a major contribution to effective labour supply. The commitment to full employment would guarantee economic growth and prevent the benefit system from buckling under the strain of mass, chronic, involuntary unemployment as its predecessors had in the inter-war period. Beveridge and Keynes made the world safe for social democracy but only for so long as the conditions they prescribed continued to obtain.

The institutional structure of the modern welfare state was established by the 1944 Education Act, based on the Educational Reconstruction White Paper (*B4*), the Family Allowances Act of 1945, the National Insurance Acts of 1946, the National Health Service Act of 1946 (see *B7*) and the National Assistance Act of 1948. The Simon extract (*B6*) indicates the importance of housing provision as an element of policy. Legislation here, however, was more obviously a continuation of pre-war policy. Since 1948, each service has experienced a number of changes in administration, nature and structure but, in spite of these changes, the model itself remains. Developments have tended to be of an *ad hoc*, incremental nature. Until the return of the Conservative Government headed by Margaret Thatcher in 1979 there has been little evidence of a determined attempt to implement an overall vision of social policy of the same order of magnitude as that engendered by Beveridge and the social reformers of the 1940s.

The changes that have occurred have been born out of a growing awareness by governments of all parties of the constraints within which they operate. The most fundamental of these constraints is that of scarce resources and this is the dominant theme of those extracts included under the heading 'General Issues in Social Policy'. The first two of these were produced by the Central Policy Review Staff, the 'think tank' established by Edward Heath in 1971 as part of his attempt to reform the machinery of government and, in the process, to set up an organisation free of departmental pressures and capable of offering reasonably objective advice on any issue submitted to it. *A Joint Framework for Social Policies* (*B8*) remains one of the most interesting and important documents in post-war social policy because of its plea for the creation of a rational and coherent framework for the analysis of public policy, capable of taking into account resource availability and the whole range of government commitments. Sadly, its influence has been minimal. The observations on population and the social services (*B9*) highlight one of the most fundamental factors in policy development and, ironically, one of the most ignored. Anyone concerned about rationality and the long-term view in the making of social policy cannot but be saddened by the Thatcher Government's abolition of the CPRS.

Social policy is now more than ever dominated by whatever happens to be the prevailing Treasury view. 'Public Expenditure: Future Prospects, 1984' (*B11*) is a clear manifestation of this reality. It is essential reading if we are to understand the probable future development of social policy, certainly for as long as the present government remains in office wedded to its current philosophy, and perhaps for even longer. The identification of what is regarded as excessive public expenditure and of consequential high rates of direct taxation as the most important causes of Britain's economic decline has profound implications for the Welfare State. The Green Paper published in June 1985 'Reform of Social Security', from the first volume of which (Cmnd 9517) extracts *B10* and *B37* are taken, can be seen as a product of this conviction.

Governments have always been sensitive to the public expenditure requirements of a complex and comprehensive system of social provision. This is one of the persistent themes to emerge from the extracts included in the section 'Politics and Social Policy'. The Conservative Party has made the cost of welfare a major concern from the earliest days of the post-war settlement as can be seen in *The Right Road for Britain* (*B12*) and *One Nation* (*B13*). The Labour Party was also clearly aware of the potential conflict inherent in the struggle between competing claimants for scarce resources. *The Welfare State* (*B14*) makes the need for a clear and conscious prioritisation a major requirement. The document also identifies certain characteristics of public social policy as potentially unattractive to large numbers of citizens. The presence of an impersonal bureaucracy, standardisation, the need to preserve an element of localism and democratic accountability are features which have a modern ring about them.

The substance of the political consensus surrounding the Welfare State until the early 1970s is described in the articles by Sir Richard Clarke (*B18*) and by Gould and Roweth (*B19*).

In a number of ways, the Conservative Party's approach to

welfare issues is of more interest than that of Labour during this period. Several extracts demonstrate the omnipresent tensions within the party between more or less official pronouncements and those relatively independent ones from influential individuals and groupings. This conflict is clearly evident in the different positions adopted in two almost contemporary publications. *The Right Road for Britain* (*B12*) is an official source and *One Nation* (*B13*) represents the collective thoughts of spokesmen of what has been called 'opportunity state Conservatism'. Some members of the latter group, including Heath, Powell and Macleod, were to become major figures in the political life of the party and the nation. The growth of liberal Conservatism is demonstrated further in the extracts from Goldman (*B16*) and Powell (*B17*).

In the early post-war years, one of the clear divisions between Conservative and Labour Parties centred around the conditions on which services were to be provided. In general, the Labour Party followed Beveridge in his advocacy of universality as the proper philosophical and administrative basis of service delivery while the Conservative Party was largely convinced that universality wasted scarce resources by providing benefit for those who did not need them. The extracts under the heading 'Principles and Techniques of Resource Allocation' give some indication of the nature of the debate. One of the key figures is Richard Titmuss, who did so much to shape social policy and administration as an intellectual discipline and who exercised a major influence on the development of the Labour Party's social philosophy in the post-war period. In his official history of social policy during the Second World War, *Problems of Social Policy* (HMSO, 1950), Titmuss appeared a committed universalist, but over the years his position changed considerably. In *B21*, he calls for a fusion of the best elements of both the universalist and selectivist approaches and, in so doing, leaves himself open to scathing rebuke from Arthur Seldon (*B22*). Seldon is the most persistent and influential writer from the selectivist camp and was very active in the creation of the Institute of Economic Affairs in 1957, an organisation which has done much to advance the virtues of the market and consumer choice. Pinker appears as an ideologue of the 'common sensical' centre (*B23*). For him the debate at best is a reminder that issues of principle are at stake in social provision, whilst at worst the two positions are oversimplified irrelevancies with no place in the modern world. The public record would seem to indicate that on this issue the Labour

Party has moved much closer to the traditional position of the Conservative Party.

As we noted earlier, universality was a key feature of the Beveridge Report. The giant 'want' was to be attacked by a system of social insurance providing subsistence level benefits as of right. Social assistance was to be a residual, vestigial element designed to fade away as the insurance scheme matured. One of the great tragedies of modern British social security has been the failure to translate this intent into reality. The combined value of means-tested social assistance payments and the allowance for actual housing costs has always exceeded insurance scale rates. Successive governments have failed to treat poverty via the approved medium, universal, subsistence level social insurance benefits.

The depth and extent of this failure is demonstrated in the extracts presented under the heading 'Social Policy and Poverty'. Full employment, economic growth, rising real personal disposable income and the achievement of the Welfare State provided a context within which an understandable complacency took root. It was difficult to dispel this complacency, supported as it seemed to be by empirical evidence from investigations such as Rowntree's third survey of York, *Poverty and the Welfare State*, but eventually a more critical perspective did begin to emerge. Pivotal figures in this reassessment were Titmuss, Townsend and Abel-Smith. Titmuss's book *Income Distribution and Social Change* (*B24*) has been described as one of the most important texts to have emerged from the study of the British Welfare State largely because of the systematic way he undermined the statistical and methodological basis of the traditional view that poverty had ceased to be a major social problem. The appearance of the book *The Poor and the Poorest* in 1965 (*B25*) finally shattered the illusion of Britain as a prosperous society in which all were sharing. The evidence deployed by Abel-Smith and Townsend has never been seriously challenged and their definition of a 'poverty line' as 140 per cent of the basic assistance scale rates has become a model for a host of subsequent investigations. More than any other British social scientist, Townsend has developed the concept of poverty as relative deprivation and although his approach (*B27*) has been challenged by some (*B29*) it remains a classic example of an attempt to marry political commitment with scholarly objectivity. Townsend's political commitment is at least matched by Sir Keith Joseph's, whose espousal of the idea of transmitted deprivation was tested by a series of research projects funded by the Social Science Research Council (at Sir Keith's behest). Madge and Rutter's observations (*B26*) are an interesting assessment of the status of this controversial and influential concept. The conclusions from the Royal Commission on the Distribution of Income and Wealth (*B28*) provide some insights into the relationship between poverty and certain contingency experiences.

The modern Welfare State grew to maturity in an environment of full employment, economic growth and rising real incomes. In what were arguably the most successful three decades in Britain's economic history, the issues which had been so intractable during the inter-war years seemed to have faded from the political scene. In so far as Britain had an economic problem, it was the apparent inability to match the growth rates of our major industrial competitors. The Welfare State itself was secure and governments' only real concern lay in meeting the population's expectation of rising standards of provision. The political economy of social democracy formed the dominant intellectual paradigm within which debate was conducted.

However, what had seemed so secure for so long was proved to be resting on shallow foundations as the economies of the Western industrial world, and that of Britain in particular, reeled under the shock of the energy crisis of the early 1970s. As the previously unknown combination of rapid inflation and rising levels of unemployment came to form the backcloth of political discussion, social democracy's hegemony was shattered and replaced by a modern reformulation of old ideas, the recrudescence of liberal conservatism. Advocates of neo-classical political economy and the minimal state had never completely disappeared (as the Institute of Economic Affairs, Enoch Powell and Hayek exemplify) but their position in political life had been marginal at best. At first sight, the relatively easy advance, in recent years, of these ideas is surprising but it becomes more understandable if one accepts that the devotees of collective social provision had grown lazy and intellectually flabby. They rarely, if ever, asked what would happen to the Welfare State if the economic growth they took for granted disappeared. The harsher economic climate of the last ten years has caught defenders of the Welfare State totally unprepared to meet the onslaught of the so-called 'New Right' of which 'Thatcherism' is a particularly vivid example. Social democracy's classical political text is Anthony Crosland's *The Future of Socialism* (*B20*) which first appeared in 1956; nothing of the same quality has appeared from the labour movement since then. Indeed, the Left's record is appalling. No representative of the Labour Party's left wing has produced anything remotely comparable to Crosland's work, while Marxist socialists have only rarely descended from the Olympian heights of social theory to consider the complex reality of the Welfare State. For them it remained a crude form of social control through which the ruling class maintained its dominance. In recent years, the position has begun to change and the extracts under the heading 'Political Economy and Social Welfare' contain examples of this ideological debate.

Social Security: the New Priorities (B30) is an early manifestation of Sir Keith Joseph's developing disenchantment with the then current position in social provision. The public burden of welfare is neatly expressed in Geiger's words *(B31)*, an economic approach that is shared by Ian Gough *(B34)* although, as a Marxist, Gough is at a different point in the political spectrum from Geiger. Gough's identification of the contradictory nature of the Welfare State is in the best traditions of classical Marxism while his description of the ideological component of 'Thatcherism' is typical of the best of recent Marxist writing on the Welfare State. Since 1981, the Social Affairs Unit has produced a series of reports attacking public social provision from a liberal, individualistic perspective. *Breaking the Spell of the Welfare State (B33)* is one of the earliest and best examples of its work. Completely opposed to the Social Affairs Unit's world view is Bob Deacon's attempt to delineate what ought to be the major characteristics of communist and socialist social policy *(B35)*. Throughout its existence, the Welfare State has been caught up in the debate about distributional principles (e.g. *B15*). Joseph and Sumption's defence of inequality *(B32)* is powerfully contested by Raymond Plant's statement of the case for democratic equality *(B36)*. Plant's pamphlet is an important example of the way in which Fabian Socialists as well as Marxists have responded, no matter how belatedly, to the challenge of resurgent individualism.

B1   A Programme for a Democratic Socialist Party, 1940

The first of these is a self-denying ordinance: that they should be willing *to place further ameliorative measures in their order of priority after, and not before, the socialization of industry* — or, to put the same point in a more extreme form, that they should be willing to reduce their social service proposals to the minimum consistent with the retention of political power in order to pursue more actively the transfer of industrial ownership.

To take this principle seriously, and to act upon it, will require considerable courage and self-denial on the part of the Left wing electorate and the working class as a whole. It means abandoning the hope of rapid social betterment for some considerable time. It means placing power before benefits — the pill before the jam, of social legislation. It means preaching an unpopular gospel to an electorate that, as a whole, is deeply stirred by the hope of, and instinctively determined to possess, further substantial benefits from the public chest. The legislative trend of a generation must be reversed, and the people at large must be made to think about, and care for, something less immediate than better housing and family allowances. It may well be that practical politicians will feel that this is an impossible task, and that the 'man in the street' is too determined in his intention to be diverted from his perfectly proper appetite for minimum standards of safety and comfort. And many influential groups of wise persons, particularly the specialized advocates of this or that social need — the educational specialists, the family allowance experts, those who care for the unemployed — will claim that the immediate needs for which they speak are so urgent that all more distant aims and more Utopian projects must wait upon the relief of shameful and urgent distress.

Indeed it is certain that a political Party like the Labour Party, grounded in the life of the people and financed by the coppers of the poor, will always be committed to certain improvements in the social services on which it would be political suicide to default.

Yet I feel sure that the price of socialism is the reduction of these advances to the necessary minimum, and a determination on the part of the party and the electorate that it represents, to concentrate its main energies upon other fields of policy and achievement.

I feel sure of this for two reasons. The *first* of these is the one that I have already mentioned. The continuous extension of the social services, and the steady rise in the proportion of the national income that is taken in taxation, imposes a strain upon the capitalist system that has already reduced its potential pace of development and will reduce it still further. Despite the plausible arguments of the apologists for the social services, and of the older type of socialist, there must be some limit to the height that taxation can wisely be allowed to reach. We may not have come up to that level yet, only there must be such a level somewhere ahead of us; and I feel sure that it is far short of one that would produce, by itself, substantial social equality or even finance the major ameliorative provisions that the enthusiast for the social services always has in mind. It is not sensible, in the last resort, to tax property incomes to the limit and at the same time to leave the decisions about investment, employment, the rate of social accumulation and the volume of production in the hands of persons who look primarily to that source of revenue for their maintenance and guidance. It is not wise in the long run to expect to live upon golden eggs and slowly to strangle the goose that lays them. At a certain point economic power must be placed before social betterment if social betterment is to be secured.

The *second* reason is even simpler — though scarcely less important. The time and energies of any party or any Government are limited, and there is a low maximum to the amount of legislation that any group of men can press through Parliament or subsequently administer. They cannot concentrate all their forces on all fronts at once. The laws of arithmetic, let alone those of psychology, make it impossible to proceed equally rapidly and forcibly in all directions at the same time. Particularly this is true of a large Party whose machinery for taking decisions, even in its Parliamentary section, has become too 'democratic' and cumbersome to permit of great speed in legislation. If therefore the energies of Party and Government are concentrated too exclusively upon the improvement of the social services, all other types of action will fall into the background, and in the end cease altogether. It is only if the main enthusiasm of the Party, the main determination of the Government, and the clearest mandate from the electorate, all lie in other fields, that any substantial advance in the reorganization of the national economy will, in fact, be completed. Only if the 'power programme' is put first in the priorities of Government, Party, and electorate alike, will the slow moving and easily bored mind of elector and elected ever pull itself out of the well-worn rut of social service legislation. The Government will relapse into the comfortable and valuable, but in the last resort self-limiting, course of spending more money for the benefit of the relatively poor. There is nothing more conservative than an old reforming party, and particularly one that has repeatedly achieved political success by pressing for a programme of social improvement.

From E. Durbin, *The Politics of Democratic Socialism* (Routledge & Kegan Paul, 1940)

B2   Beveridge: Principles of Recommendations, 1942

7. The first principle is that any proposals for the future, while they should use to the full the experience gathered in the past, should not be restricted by consideration of sectional interests established in the obtaining of that experience. Now, when the war is abolishing landmarks of every kind, is the opportunity for using experience in a clear field. A revolutionary moment in the world's history is a time for revolutions, not for patching.

8. The second principle is that organisation of social insurance should be treated as one part only of a comprehensive policy of social progress. Social insurance fully developed may provide income security; it is an attack upon Want. But Want is only one of five giants on the road of reconstruction and in some ways the easiest to attack. The others are Disease, Ignorance, Squalor and Idleness.

9. The third principle is that social security must be achieved by co-operation between the State and the individual. The State should offer security for service and contribution. The State in organising security should not stifle incentive, opportunity and responsibility; in establishing a national minimum, it should leave room and encouragement for voluntary action by each individual to provide more than that minimum for himself and his family.

10. The Plan for Social Security set out in this Report is built upon these principles. It uses experience but is not tied by experience. It is put forward as a limited contribution to a wider social policy, though as something that could be achieved now without waiting for the whole of that policy. It is, first and foremost, a plan of insurance — of giving in return for contributions benefits up to subsistence level,

as of right and without means test, so that individuals may build freely upon it.

Summary of Plan for Social Security

17. The main feature of the Plan for Social Security is a scheme of social insurance against interruption and destruction of earning power and for special expenditure arising at birth, marriage or death. The scheme embodies six fundamental principles: flat rate of subsistence benefit; flat rate of contribution; unification of administrative responsibility; adequacy of benefit; comprehensiveness; and classification. Based on them and in combination with national assistance and voluntary insurance as subsidiary methods, the aim of the Plan for Social Security is to make want under any circumstances unnecessary.

19. The main provisions of the plan may be summarised as follows:

(i) The plan covers all citizens without upper income limit, but has regard to their different ways of life; it is all-embracing in scope of persons and of needs, but is classified in application.

(ii) In relation to social security, the population falls into four main classes of working age and two others below and above working age respectively, as follows:

I   Employees, that is persons whose normal occupation is employment under contract of service.

II   Others gainfully occupied, including employers, traders and independent workers of all kinds.

III Housewives, that is married women of working age.

IV Others of working age not gainfully employed.

V   Below working age.

VI Retired above working age.

(iii) The sixth of these classes will receive retirement pensions and the fifth will be covered by children's allowances, which will be paid from the National Exchequer in respect of all children when the responsible parent is in receipt of insurance benefit or pension; and in respect of all children except one in other cases. The four other cases will be insured for security appropriate to their circumstances. All classes will be covered for comprehensive medical treatment and rehabilitation and for funeral expenses.

(iv) Every person in Class I, II or IV will pay a single security contribution by a stamp on a single insurance document each week or combination of weeks. In Class I the employer will also contribute, affixing the insurance stamp and deducting the employee's share from wages or salary. The contribution will differ from one class to another, according to the benefits provided, and will be higher for men than for women, so as to secure benefits for Class III.

(v) Subject to simple contribution conditions, every person in Class I will receive benefit for unemployment and disability, pension on retirement, medical treatment and funeral expenses. Persons in Class II will receive all these except unemployment benefit and disability benefit during the first thirteen weeks of disability. Persons in Class IV will receive all these except unemployment and disability benefit. As a substitute for unemployment benefit, training benefit will be available to persons in all classes other than Class I, to assist them to find new livelihoods if their present ones fail. Maternity grant, provision for widowhood and separation and qualification for retirement pensions will be secured to all persons in Class III by virtue of their husbands' contributions; in addition to maternity grant, housewives who take paid work will receive maternity benefit for thirteen weeks to enable them to give up working before and after childbirth.

(vi) Unemployment benefit, disability benefit, basic retirement pension after a transition period, and training benefit will be at the same rate irrespective of previous earnings. This rate will provide by itself the income necessary for subsistence in all normal cases. There will be a joint rate for a man and wife who is not gainfully occupied. Where there is no wife or she is gainfully occupied, there will be a lower single rate; where there is no wife but a dependant above the age for children's allowance, there will be a dependant allowance. Maternity benefit for housewives who work for gain will be at a higher rate than the single rate in unemployment or disability, while their unemployment and disability benefit will be at a lower rate; there are special rates also for widowhood as described below. With these exceptions, all rates of benefit will be the same for men and for women. Disability due to industrial accident or disease will be treated like all other disability for the first thirteen weeks; if disability continues thereafter, disability benefit at a flat rate will be replaced by an industrial pension related to the earnings of the individual subject to a minimum and a maximum.

(vii) Unemployment benefit will continue at the same rate without means test so long as unemployment lasts, but will normally be subject to a condition of attendance at a work or training centre after a certain period. Disability benefit will continue at the same rate without means test, so long as disability lasts or till it is replaced by industrial pension subject to acceptance of suitable medical treatment or vocational training.

(viii) Pensions (other than industrial) will be paid only on retirement from work. They may be claimed at any time after the minimum age of retirement, that is 65 for men and 60 for women. The rate of pension will be increased above the basic rate if retirement is postponed. Contributory pensions as of right will be raised to the full basic rate gradually during a transition period of twenty years, in which adequate pensions according to needs will be paid to all persons requiring them. The position of existing pensioners will be safeguarded.

(ix) While permanent pensions will no longer be granted to widows of working age without dependent children, there will be for all widows a temporary benefit at a higher rate than unemployment or disability benefit, followed by training benefit where necessary. For widows with the care of dependent children there will be guardian benefit, in addition to the children's allowances, adequate for subsistence without other means. The position of existing widows on pension will be safeguarded.

(x) For the limited number of cases of need not covered by insurance, national assistance subject to a uniform means test will be available.

(xi) Medical treatment covering all requirements will be provided for all citizens by a national health service organised under the health departments and post-medical rehabilitation treatment will be provided for all persons capable of profiting by it.

(xii) A Ministry of Social Security will be established, responsible for social insurance, national assistance and encouragement and supervision of voluntary insurance and will take over, so far as necessary for these purposes, the present work of other Government Departments and of Local Authorities in these fields.

The Nature of Social Insurance

20. Under the scheme of social insurance, which forms the main feature of this plan, every citizen of working age will contribute in his appropriate class according to the security that he needs, or as a married woman will have contributions made by the husband. Each

will be covered for all his needs by a single weekly contribution on one insurance document. All the principal cash payments — for unemployment, disability and retirement will continue so long as the need lasts, without means test, and will be paid from a Social Insurance Fund built up by contributions from the insured persons, from their employers, if any, and from the State. This is in accord with two views as to the lines on which the problem of income maintenance should be approached.

21. The first view is that benefit in return for contributions, rather than free allowances from the State, is what the people of Britain desire. This desire is shown both by the established popularity of compulsory insurance, and by the phenomenal growth of voluntary insurance against sickness, against death and for endowment, and most recently for hospital treatment. It is shown in another way by the strength of popular objection to any kind of means test. This objection springs not so much from a desire to get everything for nothing, as from resentment at a provision which appears to penalise what people have come to regard as the duty and pleasure of thrift, of putting pennies away for a rainy day. Management of one's income is an essential element of a citizen's freedom. Payment of a substantial part of the cost of benefit as a contribution irrespective of the means of the contributor is the firm basis of a claim to benefit irrespective of means.

22. The second view is that whatever money is required for provision of insurance benefits, so long as they are needed, should come from a Fund to which the recipients have contributed and to which they may be required to make larger contributions if the Fund proves inadequate. The plan adopted since 1930 in regard to prolonged unemployment and sometimes suggested for prolonged disability, that the State should take this burden off insurance, in order to keep the contribution down, is wrong in principle. The insured persons should not feel that income for idleness, however caused, can come from a bottomless purse. The Government should not feel that by paying doles it can avoid the major responsibility of seeing that unemployment and disease are reduced to the minimum. The place for direct expenditure and organisation by the State is in maintaining employment of the labour and other productive resources of the country, and in preventing and combating disease, not in patching an incomplete scheme of insurance.

23. The State cannot be excluded altogether from giving direct assistance to individuals in need, after examination of their means.

However comprehensive an insurance scheme, some, through physical infirmity, can never contribute at all and some will fall through the meshes of any insurance. The making of insurance benefit without means test unlimited in duration involves of itself that conditions must be imposed at some stage or another as to how men in receipt of benefit shall use their time, so as to fit themselves or to keep themselves fit for service; imposition of any conditions means that the condition may not be fulfilled and that a case of assistance may arise. Moreover for one of the main purposes of social insurance — provision for old age or retirement — the contributory principle implies contribution for a substantial number of years; in the introduction of adequate contributory pensions there must be a period of transition during which those who have not qualified for pension by contribution but are in need have their needs met by assistance pensions. National assistance is an essential subsidiary method in the whole Plan for Social Security, and the work of the Assistance Board shows that assistance subject to means test can be administered with sympathetic justice and discretion taking full account of individual circumstances. But the scope of assistance will be narrowed from the beginning and will diminish throughout the transition period for pensions. The scheme of social insurance is designed of itself when in full operation to guarantee the income needed for subsistence in all normal cases.

24. The scheme is described as a scheme of insurance, because it preserves the contributory principle. It is described as social insurance to mark important distinctions from voluntary insurance. In the first place, while adjustment of premiums to risks is of the essence of voluntary insurance, since without this individuals would not of their own will insure, this adjustment is not essential in insurance which is made compulsory by the power of the State. In the second place, in providing for actuarial risks such as those of death, old age or sickness, it is necessary in voluntary insurance to fund contributions paid in early life in order to provide for the increasing risks of later life and to accumulate reserves against individual liabilities. The State with its power of compelling successive generations of citizens to become insured and its power of taxation is not under the necessity of accumulating reserves for actuarial risks and has not, in fact, adopted this method in the past. The second of these two distinctions is one of financial practice only: the first raises important questions of policy and equity. Though the State, in conducting compulsory insurance, is not under the

necessity of varying the premium according to the risk, it may decide as a matter of policy to do so.

25. When State insurance began in Britain, it was felt that compulsory insurance should be like voluntary insurance in adjusting premiums to risks. This was secured in health insurance by the system of Approved Societies. It was intended to be secured in unemployment insurance by variation of contribution rates between industries as soon as accurate valuation became possible, by encouragement of special schemes of insurance by industry, and by return of contributions to individuals who made no claims. In the still earlier institution of workmen's compensation, adjustment of premiums to industrial risks was a necessary consequence of the form in which provision for industrial accidents was made, by placing liability on employers individually and leaving them to insure voluntarily against their liability. In the thirty years since 1912, there has been an unmistakable movement of public opinion away from these original ideas, that is to say, away from the principle of adjusting premiums to risks in compulsory insurance and in favour of pooling risks. This change has been most marked and most complete in regard to unemployment, where, in the general scheme, insurance by industry, in place of covering a large part of the field, has been reduced to historical exceptions; today the common argument is that the volume of unemployment in an industry is not to any effective extent within its control; that all industries depend upon one another, and that those which are fortunate in being regular should share the cost of unemployment in those which are less regular. The same tendency of opinion in favour of pooling of social risks has shown itself in the views expressed by the great majority of witnesses to the present Committee in regard to health insurance. In regard to workmen's compensation, the same argument has been put by the Mineworkers' Federation to the Royal Commission on Workmen's Compensation; as other industries cannot exist without coalmining, they have proposed that employers in all industries should bear equally the cost of industrial accidents and disease, in coalmining as elsewhere.

26. There is here an issue of principle and practice on which strong arguments can be advanced on each side by reasonable men. But the general tendency of public opinion seems clear. After trial of a different principle, it has been found to accord best with the sentiments of the British people that in insurance organised by the community by use of compulsory powers each individual should

stand in on the same terms; none should claim to pay less because he is healthier or has more regular employment. In accord with that view, the proposals of the Report mark another step forward to the development of State insurance as a new type of human institution, differing both from the former methods of preventing or alleviating distress and from voluntary insurance. The term 'social insurance' to describe this institution implies both that it is compulsory and that men stand together with their fellows. The term implies a pooling of risks except so far as separation of risks serves a social purpose. There may be reasons of social policy for adjusting premiums to risks, in order to give a stimulus for avoidance of danger, as in the case of industrial accident and disease. There is no longer an admitted claim of the individual citizen to share in national insurance and yet to stand outside it, keeping the advantage of his individual lower risk whether of unemployment or of disease or accident . . .

303. *Six Principles of Social Insurance*: The social insurance scheme set out below as the chief method of social security embodies six fundamental principles:

Flat rate of subsistence benefit
Flat rate of contribution
Unification of administrative responsibility
Adequacy of benefit
Comprehensiveness
Classification

304. *Flat Rate of Subsistence Benefit*: The first fundamental principle of the social insurance scheme is provision of a flat rate of insurance benefit, irrespective of the amount of the earnings which have been interrupted by unemployment or disability or ended by retirement; exception is made only where prolonged disability has resulted from an industrial accident or disease. This principle follows from the recognition of the place and importance of voluntary insurance in social security and distinguishes the scheme proposed for Britain from the security schemes of Germany, the Soviet Union, the United States and most other countries with the exception of New Zealand. The flat rate is the same for all the principal forms of cessation of earning — unemployment, disability, retirement; for maternity and for widowhood there is a temporary benefit at a higher rate.

305. *Flat Rate of Contribution*: The second fundamental principle of the scheme is that the compulsory contribution required of each

insured person or his employer is at a flat rate, irrespective of his means. All insured persons, rich or poor, will pay the same contributions for the same security; those with larger means will pay more only to the extent that as tax-payers they pay more to the National Exchequer and so to the State share of the Social Insurance Fund. This feature distinguishes the scheme proposed for Britain from the scheme recently established in New Zealand under which the contributions are graduated by income, and are in effect an income-tax assigned to a particular service. Subject moreover to one exception, the contribution will be the same irrespective of the assumed degree of risk affecting particular individuals or forms of employment. The exception is the raising of a proportion of the special cost of benefits and pensions for industrial disability in occupations of high risk by a levy on employers proportionate to risk and pay-roll (paras. 86–90 and 360).

306. *Unification of Administrative Responsibility*: The third fundamental principle is unification of administrative responsibility in the interests of efficiency and economy. For each insured person there will be a single weekly contribution, in respect of all his benefits. There will be in each locality a Security Office able to deal with claims of every kind and all sides of security. The methods of paying different kinds of cash benefit will be different and will take account of the circumstances of insured persons, providing for payment at the home or elsewhere, as is necessary. All contributions will be paid into a single Social Insurance Fund and all benefits and other insurance payments will be paid from that fund.

307. *Adequacy of Benefit*: The fourth fundamental principle is adequacy of benefit in amount and in time. The flat rate of benefit proposed is intended in itself to be sufficient without further resources to provide the minimum income needed for subsistence in all normal cases. It gives room and a basis for additional voluntary provision, but does not assume that in any case. The benefits are adequate also in time, that is to say except for contingencies of a temporary nature, they will continue indefinitely without means test, so long as the need continues, though subject to any change of conditions and treatment required by prolongation of the interruption in earning and occupation.

308. *Comprehensiveness*: The fifth fundamental principle is that social insurance should be comprehensive, in respect both of the persons covered and of their needs. It should not leave either to national assistance or to voluntary insurance any risk so general or

so uniform that social insurance can be justified. For national assistance involves a means test which may discourage voluntary insurance or personal saving. And voluntary insurance can never be sure of covering the ground. For any need moreover which, like direct funeral expenses, is so general and so uniform as to be a fit subject for insurance by compulsion, social insurance is much cheaper to administer than voluntary insurance.

309. *Classification*: The sixth fundamental principle is that social insurance, while unified and comprehensive, must take account of the different ways of life of different sections of the community; of those dependent on earnings by employment under contract of service, of those earning in other ways, of those rendering vital unpaid service as housewives, of those not yet of age to earn and of those past earning. The term 'classification' is used here to denote adjustment of insurance to the differing circumstances of each of these classes and to many varieties of need and circumstances within each insurance class. But the insurance classes are not economic or social classes in the ordinary sense; the insurance scheme is one for all citizens irrespective of their means.

From the *Report of the Committee on Social Insurance and Allied Services*, Cmd 6404 (1942)

B3   Beveridge: Social Security and Social Policy, 1942

409. Social security as used in this Report means assurance of a certain income. The Plan for Social Security set out in the Report is a plan to win freedom from want by maintaining incomes. But sufficiency of income is not sufficient in itself. Freedom from want is only one of the essential freedoms of mankind. Any Plan for Social Security in the narrow sense assumes a concerted social policy in many fields, most of which it would be inappropriate to discuss in this Report. The plan proposed here involves three particular assumptions so closely related to it that brief discussion is essential for understanding of the plan itself. These are the assumptions of children's allowances, of comprehensive health and rehabilitation services and of maintenance of employment.

Assumption A. Children's Allowances

410. The first of three assumptions underlying the Plan for Social

Security is a general scheme of children's allowances. This means that direct provision for the maintenance of dependent children will be made by payment of allowances to those responsible for the care of those children. The assumption rests on two connected arguments.

411. First, it is unreasonable to seek to guarantee an income sufficient for subsistence, while earnings are interrupted by unemployment or disability, without ensuring sufficient income during earning. Social insurance should be part of a policy of a national minimum. But a national minimum for families of every size cannot in practice be secured by a wage system, which must be based on the product of a man's labour and not on the size of his family. The social surveys of Britain between the two wars show that in the first thirty years of this century real wages rose by about one-third without reducing want to insignificance, and that the want which remained was almost wholly due to two causes — interruption or loss of earning power and large families.

412. Second, it is dangerous to allow benefit during unemployment or disability to equal or exceed earnings during work. But, without allowances for children, during earning and non-earning alike, this danger cannot be avoided. It has been experienced in an appreciable number of cases under unemployment benefit and unemployment assistance in the past. The maintenance of employment — last and most important of the three assumptions of social security — will be impossible without greater fluidity of labour and other resources in the aftermath of war than has been achieved in the past. To secure this, the gap between income during earning and during interruption of earning should be as large as possible for every man. It cannot be kept large for men with large families, except either by making their benefit in unemployment and disability inadequate, or by giving allowances for children in time of earning and not-earning alike.

413. In addition to these two arguments, arising directly from considerations of social security, there are arguments arising from consideration of numbers of population and care of children. With its present rate of reproduction, the British race cannot continue; means of reversing the recent course of the birth rate must be found. It is not likely that allowances for children or any other economic incentives will, by themselves, provide that means and lead parents who do not desire children to rear children for gain. But children's allowances can help to restore the birth rate, both by making it

possible for parents who desire more children to bring them into the world without damaging the chances of those already born, and as a signal of the national interest in children, setting the tone of public opinion. As regards care of children, whatever possibilities the future may hold of larger families than now, the small families of today make it necessary that every living child should receive the best care that can be given to it. The foundations of a healthy life must be laid in childhood. Children's allowances should be regarded both as a help to parents in meeting their responsibilities, and as an acceptance of new responsibilities by the community.

414. The general principle of children's allowances can by now be taken as accepted. But it is desirable to make suggestions as to the practical form of such allowances from the standpoint of social security. The main points to be settled relate to the source from which allowances should be paid, to the scale of allowances, to the children in respect of whom they should be paid, and to the authority which should administer them.

415. As to the source of children's allowances, the view taken here is that they should be non-contributory, provided wholly out of taxation, and not to any extent out of insurance contributions. The considerations leading to this view are practical. First, the flat rate of contribution required for purposes which should be contributory is about as high as it seems right to propose; flat insurance contributions are either a poll-tax or a tax on employment, justifiable up to certain limits, but not capable of indefinite expansion. Second, the provision for children should clearly be made to some extent in kind. Though, on the view taken here, children's allowances should be given mainly in cash, the amount of cash at any time must be adjusted to the provision in kind and this adjustment can probably be made more easily, if the cost of allowances is provided from the State than if it forms part of a contributory system. Both these are practical grounds. On principle, it is possible to argue either way. It can be said, on the one hand, that children's allowances should be regarded as an expression of the community's direct interest in children; it can be argued on the the hand that children are a contingency for which all men should prepare by contributions to an insurance fund. As it is possible to argue on each side in principle, it might be provided in practice that the cost of allowances should be shared. It is in fact proposed below that the first child in each family should be omitted from allowances, while the responsible parent is earning, so that the financial burden of every family is shared

between the State and the parents. This involves providing an allowance for the first child whenever the responsible parent is not earning, that is to say providing an allowance for the first child, to be added to unemployment, disability and guardian benefits. Even if the other allowances are provided wholly by the State, the cost of allowances for the first child might well be charged to the Social Insurance Fund, as the cost of the children's allowances now given in unemployment insurance are charged to the Unemployment Fund. On the whole, it appears better to put the whole cost of children's allowances, both when the parent is earning and when he is not earning, upon the National Exchequer, that is to say to make children's allowances non-contributory. The allowances, though non-contributory, may be administered by the Ministry of Social Security. The cost of them should be provided, not from the Social Insurance Fund, but by special Exchequer grant.

Assumption B. Comprehensive Health and Rehabilitation Services

426. The second of the three assumptions has two sides to it. It covers a national health service for prevention and for cure of disease and disability by medical treatment; it covers rehabilitation and fitting for employment by treatment which will be both medical and post-medical . . . The case for regarding Assumption B as necessary for a satisfactory system of social security needs little emphasis. It is a logical corollary to the payment of high benefits in disability that determined efforts should be made by the State to reduce the number of cases for which benefit is needed. It is a logical corollary to the receipt of high benefits in disability that the individual should recognise the duty to be well and to co-operate in all steps which may lead to diagnosis of disease in early stages when it can be prevented. Disease and accidents must be paid for in any case, in lessened power of production and in idleness, if not directly by insurance benefits. One of the reasons why it is preferable to pay for disease and accident openly and directly in the form of insurance benefits, rather than indirectly, is that this emphasises the cost and should give a stimulus to prevention. As to the methods of realising Assumption B, the main problems naturally arise under the first head of medical treatment. Rehabilitation is a new field of remedial activity with great possibilities, but requiring expenditure of a different order of magnitude from that involved in the medical treatment of the nation.

427. The first part of Assumption B is that a comprehensive

national health service will ensure that for every citizen there is available whatever medical treatment he requires, in whatever form he requires it, domicilliary or institutional, general, specialist or consultant, and will ensure also the provision of dental, ophthalmic and surgical appliances, nursing and midwifery and rehabilitation after accidents. Whether or not payment towards the cost of the health service is included in the social insurance contribution, the service itself should

(i) be organised, not by the Ministry concerned with social insurance, but by Departments responsible for the health of the people and for positive and preventive as well as curative measures;

(ii) be provided where needed without contribution conditions in any individual case.

Restoration of a sick person to health is a duty of the State and the sick person, prior to any other consideration. The assumption made here is in accord with the definition of the objects of medical service as proposed in the Draft Interim Report of the Medical Planning Commission of the British Medical Association:

(*a*) to provide a system of medical service directed towards the achievement of positive health, of the prevention of disease, and the relief of sickness;

(b) to render available to every individual all necessary medical services, both general and specialist, and both domiciliary and institutional.

Assumption C. Maintenance of Employment

440. There are five reasons for saying that a satisfactory scheme of social insurance assumes the maintenance of employment and the prevention of mass unemployment. Three reasons are concerned with the details of social insurance; the fourth and most important is concerned with its principle; the fifth is concerned with the possibility of meeting its cost.

First, payment of unconditional cash benefits as of right during unemployment is satisfactory provision only for short periods of unemployment; after that, complete idleness even on an income demoralises. The proposal of the Report accordingly is to make unemployment benefit after a certain period conditional upon attendance at a work or training centre. But this proposal is impracticable, if it has to be applied to men by the million or the hundred thousand.

Second, the only satisfactory test of unemployment is an offer of work. This test breakes down in mass unemployment and makes necessary recourse to elaborate contribution conditions, and such devices as the Anomalies Regulations, all of which should be avoided in a satisfactory scheme of unemployment insurance.

Third, the state of the labour market has a direct bearing on rehabilitation and recovery of injured and sick persons and upon the possibility of giving to those suffering from partial infirmities, such as deafness, the chance of a happy and useful career. In time of mass unemployment those who are in receipt of compensation feel no urge to get well for idleness. On the other hand, in time of active demand for labour, as in war, the sick and the maimed are encouraged to recover, so that they may be useful.

Fourth, and most important, income security which is all that can be given by social insurance is so inadequate a provision for human happiness that to put it forward by itself as a sole or principal measure of reconstruction hardly seems worth doing. It should be accompanied by an announced determination to use the powers of the State to whatever extent may prove necessary to ensure for all, not indeed absolute continuity of work, but a reasonable chance of productive employment.

Fifth, though it should be within the power of the community to bear the cost of the whole Plan for Social Security, the cost is heavy and, if to the necessary cost waste is added, it may become insupportable. Unemployment, both through increasing expenditure on benefit and through reducing the income to bear those costs, is the worst form of waste.

From the *Report of the Committee on Social Insurance and Allied Services*, Cmd 6404 (1942)

B4   Educational Reconstruction, 1943

1. The Government's purpose in putting forward the reforms described in this Paper is to secure for children a happier childhood and a better start in life; to ensure a fuller measure of education and opportunity for young people and to provide means for all of developing the various talents with which they are endowed and so enriching the inheritance of the country whose citizens they are. The new educational opportunities must not, therefore, be of a single

pattern. It is just as important to achieve diversity as it is to ensure equality of educational opportunity. But such diversity must not impair the social unity within the educational system which will open the way to a more closely knit society and give us strength to face the tasks ahead. The war has revealed afresh the resources and character of the British people — an enduring possession that will survive all the material losses inevitable in the present struggle. In the youth of the nation we have our greatest national asset. Even on a basis of mere expediency, we cannot afford not to develop this asset to the greatest advantage. It is the object of the present proposals to strengthen and inspire the younger generation. For it is as true today, as when it was first said, that 'the bulwarks of a city are its men'.

2. With these ends in view the Government propose to recast the national education service. The new layout is based on a recognition of the principle that education is a continuous process conducted in successive stages. For children below the compulsory school age of 5 there must be a sufficient supply of nursery schools. The period of compulsory school attendance will be extended to 15 without exemptions and with provision for its subsequent extension to 16 as soon as circumstances permit. The period from 5 to the leaving age will be divided into two stages, the first, to be known as primary, covering the years up to about 11. After 11 secondary education, of diversified types but on equal standing, will be provided for all children. At the primary stage the large classes and bad conditions which at present are a reproach to many elementary schools will be systematically eliminated; at the secondary stage the standard of accommodation and amenities will be steadily raised to the level of the best examples. The provision of school meals and milk will be made obligatory.

3. When the period of full-time compulsory schooling ends the young person will continue under educational influences up to 18 years of age either by remaining in full-time attendance at a secondary school, or by part-time day attendance at a young people's college. Throughout all the foregoing stages the benefits of medical inspection and treatment will be available without charge. Opportunities for technical and adult education will be increased.

4. Among other important features of the plan are an effective system of inspection and registration of schools outside the public system; new financial and administrative arrangements for the voluntary schools, and the recognition of the special place of religious instruction in school life.

5. It will be appreciated that these . . . other changes . . . cannot be achieved at once. The introduction of each portion of the plan will be related to an Appointed Day. In this way it will be possible to fit the schemes for educational reform into the general picture of social reconstruction and to introduce the various portions of the plan as and when the necessary buildings, the equipment and the teachers become available.

6. The reforms proposed involve a steady increase over a series of years in the expenditure which will fall on the taxpayer and the ratepayer . . . The rate at which it will be possible to proceed will depend not only on the factors mentioned in the preceding paragraph, but on the financial resources available, having regard to our existing commitments, to the new claims we may have to meet and to such orders of priority as may have to be laid down. The rate of development of the proposals will therefore have to be determined from time to time in the light of these considerations. The Prime Minister, in a recent pronouncement, foreshadowed in relation to general social advancement a four years plan to be undertaken immediately after the War. In that period and within that conception, it should be possible to complete the initial design of the future structure of a reorganised statutory scheme of full-time education, and to take the first steps in the programme of raising the school-leaving age, and of establishing a system of compulsory part-time education for young persons up to the age of 18. The future rate of progress at the end of this period could again be examined in the light of the conditions then obtaining.

From *Educational Reconstruction*, Cmd 6458 (1943)

B5   General Conditions of a High and Stable Level of Employment, 1944

In the transition period, employment policy will be primarily concerned with the transfer of men and women to peacetime jobs. But however smoothly this transition can be made, and however rapid may be the return to normal conditions, there will still remain for treatment those long-term problems connected with the maintenance of an adequate and steady volume of employment which eluded solution before the war.

If the features which have afflicted our economic life in the past are to be banished, as it is our resolve to banish them, from the future, three essential conditions must be satisfied:

(a) Total expenditure on goods and services must be prevented from falling to a level where general unemployment appears.

(b) The level of prices and wages must be kept reasonably stable.

(c) There must be sufficient mobility of workers between occupations and localities.

(a) The Maintenance of Total Expenditure

Assuming a given level of wages and prices, and full mobility of labour, workers will lose or fail to find employment because there is not a sufficiently large expenditure on the goods and services which they might produce. If more money is spent on goods and services, then more money will be paid out as wages and more people will be employed. Thus the first step in maintaining a policy of general employment must be to prevent total expenditure from falling away. Once it is allowed to do so, a minor decline may rapidly gather momentum and take on the proportions of a major depression. If, for example, there is a decline in the demand for steel for the erection of new buildings, unemployment will first appear among steel workers. The steel workers, in consequence, will have less to spend on food and other consumer goods, so that the demand for consumer goods will fall. This leads to unemployment among the workers in the consumer goods industries who, in turn, find their purchasing power reduced. As a result of this general loss of purchasing power in the community, the demand for new building is still further reduced and the demand for constructional steel falls once again. The original decline in expenditure produces secondary reactions which themselves aggravate the source of the trouble. This is an over-simplified illustration but it is sufficient to make it clear that the crucial moment for intervention is at the first onset of the depression. A corrective applied then may arrest the whole decline; once the decline has spread and gathered momentum, interventions on a much greater scale would be required — and at that stage might not be effective.

The Government are prepared to accept in future the responsibility for taking action at the earliest possible stage to arrest a threatened slump. This involves a new approach and a new responsibility for the State. It was at one time believed that every trade depression would automatically bring its own corrective, since prices and wages would fall, the fall in prices would bring about an increase in demand, and employment would thus be restored. Experience has shown, however, that under modern conditions this process of self-recovery, if effective at all, is likely to be extremely prolonged and to be accompanied by widespread distress, particularly in a complex industrial society like our own.

The guiding principles of the Government's policy in maintaining total expenditure will be as follows:

(a) To avoid an unfavourable foreign balance, we must export much more than we did before the war.

(b) Everything possible must be done to limit dangerous swings in expenditure on private investment — though success in this field may be particularly difficult to achieve.

(c) Public investment, both in timing and in volume, must be carefully planned to offset unavoidable fluctuations in private investment.

(d) We must be ready to check and reverse the decline in expenditure on consumers' goods which normally follows as a secondary reaction to a falling off in private investment.

From *Employment Policy*, Cmd 6527 (1944)

B6   Rebuilding Britain: The Long-term Programme, 1945

For a hundred years or more the number of houses built in Britain failed to keep pace with the increasing number of families who wanted separate houses. Undoubtedly the high rate of building in the thirties substantially reduced the shortage, but the Minister of Health estimates that we still need one and a half million houses to give each family a separate dwelling.

The first thing we must do in examining the post-war housing situation is to consider the three aspects of the housing programme:

How many houses do we need?
At what rate shall they be built?
For what classes of families?

All sorts of elaborate calculations have been made in this matter. These estimates proceed on the basis of dividing up the demand into a number of categories and then trying to estimate the numbers under each heading.

The categories are broadly as follows:

1. Houses destroyed by bombing.
2. Houses needed to reduce overcrowding.
3. Houses to meet future increase in the number of families.
4. A reserve of empties for flexibility.
5. Additional houses in certain areas to meet any redistribution of the population.
6. Houses needed for slum clearance.
7. Houses needed to replace sub-standard houses which are yet not of so low a standard as to be officially condemned as unfit for human habitation.

Unfortunately, while it is possible to form a reliable estimate of the number required to replace bombed houses, and perhaps of the reserve of empties required for flexibility, most of the other estimates can be nothing better than intelligent guesses, since they depend on the judgment of the public and of Parliament as to standards of overcrowding and of the quality of houses, or on the future size of the family, which again depends partly on the birth rate and partly on the decision of various groups as to whether they will live separately or together.

For these reasons, elaborate research into the future requirements of housing is of little useful value. The only practical solution is undoubtedly the one adopted by the Government: to study the problem in all its aspects, to give full consideration to the urgency of housing, to other demands for labour, to the financial situation, and to other relevant factors, then to fix the number of houses to be built over a period sufficiently long to render it possible for the building industry to be adjusted to the necessary size, and for town and country planners to know at what speed the new houses will be built. The Government's decision was announced by the Minister of Health in the following terms:

The generally accepted estimate of 3,000,000 to 4,000,000 houses is a broad indication of the probable housing need during the first 10 to 12 years of the peace, and has been arrived at not so much by the combination of a series of detailed estimates, which could not be precise, as by reference to the two overriding considerations, namely, the number of dwellings required to replace slum dwellings and dwellings in a poor condition or grossly deficient in modern amenities and the number required to give each family a separate dwelling and so eliminate overcrowding. 1,500,000 to 2,500,000 dwellings are included for the former purpose and 1,500,000 for the latter. Compared with these figures the number of houses destroyed or damaged beyond repair is, I am glad to say, not material.

Under these conditions, I estimate that the number of permanent houses completed each year after the war, if the whole matter is vigorously tackled, is likely to be about as follows:

1st year	50,000
2nd year	100,000
3rd year	250,000
4th and every succeeding year	400,000

This programme would give four million houses in twelve years.

At the end of the twelve-year period the building industry should have settled down to a high degree of efficiency and should be in a position to continue to build 400,000 houses a year, as well as all the other necessary buildings. It is to be hoped that we shall continue building houses at about the same speed for a second programme of, say, three million houses in eight years, which would in that case be completed twenty years after the armistice.

At the date of the armistice there will be in Great Britain about $12\frac{1}{2}$ million houses. Of these, $8\frac{1}{2}$ million will be pre-1914 houses and 4 million inter-war houses. Assuming that the total number of houses needed is likely to be $13\frac{1}{2}$ million, the following table shows how these will be made up after twelve years and after twenty years respectively.

Estimated Number of Houses in Great Britain

	At date of armistice. Say 1945	After first 12-year programme of 4 million. Say 1957.	After second 8-year programme of 3 million. Say 1965.
	Millions.	Millions.	Millions.
Total number	$12\frac{1}{2}$	$13\frac{1}{2}$	$13\frac{1}{2}$
Pre-1914	$8\frac{1}{2}$	$5\frac{1}{2}$	$2\frac{1}{2}$
Inter-war	4	4	4
Post-war	0	4	7

This means that if we carry out the programme, we shall in twenty years have only $2\frac{1}{2}$ million pre-1914 houses left. Since there are probably $2\frac{1}{2}$ million of those houses which will still be as good as the inter-war houses, this will complete the process of giving every family in the country a house at least up to inter-war standard level.

From E.D. Simon, *Rebuilding Britain — A Twenty Year Plan* (Gollancz, 1945)

B7   Bevan on the National Health Service, 1946

Mr Bevan   The first reason why a health scheme of this sort is necessary at all is because it has been the firm conclusion of all parties that money ought not to be permitted to stand in the way of obtaining an efficient health service. Although it is true that the national health insurance system provides a general practitioner service and caters for something like 21 million of the population, the rest of the population have to pay whenever they desire the services of a doctor. It is cardinal to a proper health organisation that a person ought not to be financially deterred from seeking medical assistance at the earliest possible stage. It is one of the evils of having to buy medical advice that, in addition to the natural anxiety that may arise because people do not like to hear unpleasant things about themselves, and therefore tend to postpone consultation as long as possible, there is the financial anxiety caused by having to pay doctors' bills. Therefore, the first evil that we must deal with is that which exists as a consequence of the fact that the whole thing is the wrong way round. A person ought to be able to receive medical and hospital help without being involved in financial anxiety.

In the second place, the national health insurance scheme does not provide for the self-employed, nor, of course, for the families of dependants. It depends on insurance qualification, and no matter how ill you are, if you cease to be insured you cease to have free doctoring. Furthermore, it gives no backing to the doctor in the form of specialist services. The doctor has to provide himself, he has to use his own discretion and his own personal connections, in order to obtain hospital treatment for his patients and in order to get them specialists, and in very many cases, of course — in an overwhelming number of cases — the services of a specialist are not available to poor people.

Not only is this the case, but our hospital organisation has grown up with no plan, with no system; it is unevenly distributed over the country and indeed it is one of the tragedies of the situation that very often the best hospital facilities are available where they are least needed. In the older industrial districts of Great Britain hospital facilities are inadequate. Many of the hospitals are too small — very much too small. About 70 per cent have less than 100 beds, and over 30 per cent have less than 30. No one can possibly pretend that hospitals so small can provide general hospital treatment. There is a tendency in some quarters to defend the very small hospital on the ground of its localism and intimacy, and for other rather imponderable reasons of that sort, but everybody knows today that if a hospital is to be efficient it must provide a number of specialised services. Although I am not myself a devotee of bigness for bigness sake, I would rather be kept alive in the efficient if cold altruism of a large hospital than expire in a gush of warm sympathy in a small one.

In addition to these defects, the health of the people of Britain is not properly looked after in one or two other respects. The condition of the teeth of the people of Britain is a national reproach. As a consequence of dental treatment having to be bought, it has not been demanded on a scale to stimulate the creation of sufficient dentists, and in consequence there is a woeful shortage of dentists at the present time. Furthermore, about 25 per cent of the people of Great Britain can obtain their spectacles and get their eyes tested and seen to by means of the assistance given by the approved societies, but the general mass of the people have no such facilities. Another of the evils from which this country suffers is the fact that sufficient attention has not been given to deafness, and hardly any attention has been given so far to the provision of cheap hearing aids and their proper maintenance. I hope to be able to make very shortly a welcome announcement on this question.

One added disability from which our health system suffers is the isolation of mental health from the rest of the health services. Although the present Bill does not rewrite the Lunacy Acts — we shall have to come to that later on — nevertheless, it does, for the first time, bring mental health into the general system of health services. It ought to be possible, and this should be one of the objectives of any civilised health service, for a person who feels mental distress, or who fears that he is liable to become unbalanced in any way to go to a general hospital to get advice and assistance, so that the condition may not develop into a more serious stage. All these disabilities our health system suffers from at the present time, and one of the first merits of this Bill is that it provides a universal health service without any insurance qualifications of any sort. It is available to the whole population, and not only is it available to the whole population freely, but it is intended, through the health service, to generalise the best health advice and treatment. It is intended that there shall be no limitation on the kind of assistance given — the general practitioner service, the specialist, the hospitals, eye treatment, spectacles, dental treatment, hearing facilities, all these are to be made available free.

From Hansard, *Parliamentary Debates*, House of Commons, 5th Series, vol. 422, Cols 43–5 (April 1946)

GENERAL ISSUES IN SOCIAL POLICY

B8   A Joint Framework for Social Policies, 1975

2. It is in practice hard to translate the political aspirations and objectives of a manifesto into a coherent strategy for social policies which a Government can effectively implement. Resources are always scarce. Economic constraints and the constraints of the legislative programme limit the speed at which things can be done. There are limits to how fast the institutions both of central and local government can respond to change. Many of the most intractable problems affect more than one department, and involve central government, local authorities and other bodies. There is a serious lack of information about many social problems, and thus no reliable basis for assessing need or the effectiveness of provision. There is no effective mechanism for determining coherent and consistent priorities in the field of social policy generally.

3. All this suggests that a new and more coherent framework is required for the making and execution of social policies. In developing this the general aims must be to try to ensure that social problems, including the problem of poverty, are dealt with effectively; and that resources are concentrated where Ministers and Parliament judge they are most needed to meet objectives.

4. This is necessary not only for reasons of social justice, but also in the light of the current and prospective economic situation. Public expenditure has been growing faster than production as a whole, and expenditure on social programmes has been growing faster than the rest of public expenditure. This has to some extent spared governments the task of cutting out low priority programmes in the social field, or indeed of having to decide which programmes should be given low priority. It has led to unrealistic expectations about the scope for improvements and extensions. It has also reduced the incentive to increase the efficiency of existing policies and programmes.

5. This cannot go on. The economic situation over the next few years imposes new constraints on public spending. This will mean cutting back on some plans in the social field, as elsewhere. The present Government, which has taken or promised some major new social initiatives, now needs to consider how these and existing

policies can be accommodated within some more coherent whole. If the structure of social expenditure is not to become increasingly arbitrary, some better basis is needed for defining priorities. This will still be necessary even if public expenditure constraints are eased somewhat in the longer term. Ministers also need to ensure that their priorities are adequately reflected in policies which are actually being carried out; and that in practice these policies are having the effects intended.

Defects in Social Policy-making

12. Our consultations have suggested that the main defects seen in the present situation are:

(*a*) it would obviously be impracticable for all social policies to be handled by one huge department performing the functions of all present departments and other bodies. Responsibilities are bound to be divided — for example, between agencies providing social security, job placement, personal social services, housing and health services. But these divisions can make it hard for central government to see and deal with people 'in the round';

(*b*) the treatment of social issues should, in principle, be related to some broad framework of social policy. In practice, there is an inevitable tendency for them to be dealt with individually as they come to the forefront. This can allow different departments to put different emphases on different major policy instruments — for example means testing, or helping the worst-off through 'positive discrimination', rather than through general improvements in programmes;

(*c*) Government needs better analysed and monitored information about the relative social needs of different groups, about the distributional effects of social programmes and policies and about the connections between the two. The links between policy-makers, social statisticians and other professionals could be closer. The part that research can play in policy-making is not always fully understood: existing research could be more effectively exploited;

(*d*) the Layfield Committee on Local Government Finance and the new Consultative Council on the same subject should lead to important improvements in the financial aspects of local government. But the Government should be able to respond rapidly to any proposals which they may make for improving the working relationship between central government and local authorities, who are the main agents in providing social services. For example:

(i) the division of responsibilities within Whitehall should not impede the effective co-ordination of services at local level. This will become more important as local authorities improve the co-ordination of their own services by developing corporate management and other techniques;

(ii) the trend towards giving greater discretion to local authorities, at least on questions of detail, is not easily reconciled with continuing attempts by central government to ensure that specific social problems are given high priority;

(iii) there are wide variations not only in local standards of service, but in Whitehall's knowledge of these variations. If variations are to be kept within acceptable limits there may well be a case for at least doing more to monitor standards;

(e) even the best-conceived policies sometimes fall short at the point of delivery to their clients. An example is low rates of take-up of benefits or services. The reasons for this might include the attitudes of the intended beneficiaries, the behaviour of local officials or inadequate co-ordination with other services (cf. the multiplicity of overlapping local catchment areas for different services);

(f) many programmes lack adequate operational yardsticks. Without such information it can be hard to make proper comparisons between programmes and objectives, or to take informed decisions about priorities and phasing.

A 'Strategic' Forum for Ministers

16. A longer-term and more coherent approach to social policy should help Ministers to operate more effectively and constructively. They need to be able to assess, more thoroughly than now, the varying needs, problems and opportunities in the social affairs field, and the likely effectiveness of different policies. They should meet from time to time to think about the strategy of social policy and not simply to deal — often at short notice — with a series of separate and probably unrelated issues.

17. A group of senior Ministers most closely concerned could meet in this way, say, every six months. The aim of these meetings would be not to reach executive decisions but to give an opportunity for broad discussions from which guidelines on priorities might

develop. The background material for these discussions could include:

(*a*) the material which would be produced by improved social monitoring arrangements, including regular reviews of developments in the social field . . .

(*b*) the results of the periodic 'forward look' exercise, surveying likely forthcoming developments in social policy . . .

Social Monitoring

19. A lot of work has been done in departments and elsewhere on improving social monitoring. Some aspects — especially evaluating the outputs and effectiveness of programmes — raise problems of measurement which in some cases may be insoluble. Nevertheless, there is clearly a need for a better transdepartmental information base for social policy. This would be an essential tool for regular Ministerial reviews of social policy, and would provide a better basis for determining priorities. It would also help in developing the concept of the 'social wage'.

22. In the longer term, the need will be to develop better and more detailed data on problems of concern to policy-makers. In addition, work of the kind outlined elsewhere in this paper will both require and generate new types of information about social problems and about processes and trends at work in society. Policy-makers, statisticians and social scientists should all be involved. The links between policy and research will need to be stronger than at present.

From *A Joint Framework for Social Policies* (Central Policy Review Staff, HMSO, 1975)

B9   Population and the Social Services, 1977

The Relationship between Demography, Demographic Projections and Social Policies and Social Planning in the Recent Past

How have actual or projected population changes in practice impinged on social policies and planning in the recent past? The answers to this question provide a starting point for examining the extent to which future policy and planning is likely to be, or should be, sensitive to population change . . .

    Some of the main conclusions are

(*a*) Demography is a relevant factor in the planning and policy development of most social programmes, but its influence has been much more direct in some areas, e.g. education (especially teacher supply policy) and regional planning (including new towns), than in others, e.g. housing (where growth in the number of households has been more important, and faster, than growth in population), or law and order programmes (where police cautioning, sentencing practice and crime trends have been more important).

(b) Where allocation of resources at a regional or sub-regional level is involved (e.g. the school or hospital building programmes, and local authority structure plans) changes in population in the country as a whole are often less important than local needs and demands which are themselves likely to have been influenced by changes in the distribution of population and in patterns of internal migration.

(c) Changes in society, social attitudes, social demands and other social policies can often be as important as, or more important than, demographic change, e.g. changing patterns of household formation (housing), the incidence of crime and sentencing policy (law and order), hospitalisation of births (health), children and elderly 'at risk' as a result of changed family patterns (personal social services) and changes in female activity rates in the labour market (employment).

(d) In some areas projections of massive population growth which were subsequently falsified had a significant effect on policy (especially regional planning, new towns, and teacher supply). There were time lags in adjusting, and subsequently readjusting, policies to assumed changes in trend.

General Conclusions

Over the next 25 years numbers in different age groups in the population will change significantly — both absolutely and relatively. These changes have major implications for the social services. Some increase the pressures on particular services, others reduce them. Ministers will be confronted with both the need and the opportunity to change the balance of social expenditure.

Some important changes can be clearly foreseen now, regardless of what happens to the birth rate:

(a) There will be very many fewer children of compulsory school age in the 1980s.

(b) Higher and further education will come under increasing

pressure up to the mid-1980s (provided participation rates do not fall); thereafter and through the 1990s the pressure will be reduced and, unless participation rates were to rise a good deal faster than currently predicted, numbers, particularly in higher education, would decline.

(c) Probation and after care services are likely to face increased demands in the 1980s in view of the increase in the 16–24 age group.

(d) The population of working age will increase quite fast over the next 10 years (whereas it was declining over the last 10). This provides opportunities for a faster rate of economic growth of output given macro-economic policies that will substain high levels of employment, but, in their absence, could add to employment problems (especially in the assisted area regions). From the mid-1980s to the mid-1990s the number and proportion of young people in the working age population will be declining. This is likely to have implications both for the training of the labour force and its adaptability to technological change.

(e) Over the next 25 years the increase in the number of people of retirement age will be quite small (in contrast to the rapid rise in numbers over the last 25 years). In consequence, the pressure of increasing numbers on the pensions bill will be much less.

(f) But the number of the *more* elderly (the over 75s and over 85s) will increase over the next 25 years, and the rate of increase will be fastest over the next 10 years. This means increased pressure on health services, personal social services, and special housing for the elderly.

Generally demographic shifts — whether they are firmly predictable . . . or contingent . . . — are clearly relevant to decisions on priorities for the social services in the medium to longer term. Given the extent to which many of the social services are specially concerned with dependent groups, it should be noted that the dependency ratio (i.e. the ratio of children under 16 plus people of retirement age to the population of working age) is due to decrease on the 'central' projections from 72:100 (1974) to 65:100 (1986) over the next decade, and remain at a level lower than currently up to the end of the century. The decrease would be rather more on the lower projections. This compares with the last 40 or so years during which the ratio has steadily increased from just over 50:100 in 1930 to its recent peak. The ratio is a crude one, and its significance has to be qualified in many ways (many people of working age are nevertheless 'dependent'). But it does indicate in the most general way that, in contrast to the last 40 years, dependence defined in demographic terms is a factor which overall will be easing pressures over the rest of the century rather than the reverse.

Conclusions and Recommendations

This study has left us with two main conclusions. The first is that public expenditure planning for the social services takes insufficient account of demographic change. Increases in the numbers making calls on a particular service are regarded as good reasons for increasing expenditure. Reductions (relatively or absolutely) in a particular client group, on the other hand, are not expected to yield equivalent savings. It is also our impression that where Departments acknowledge the importance of changes in population size and structure for their programmes, their response is often slower than it should be.

The second main impression is the virtual insatiability of 'needs' in the social services. In the past 15 years education and the social services have received more than their proportionate share in increased public expenditure. And public expenditure has risen considerably faster than national output. In part the growth in expenditure in education and social services reflected demographic pressures but in large part they went to provide real improvements in standards. Yet 'needs' were far from satisfied. Indeed, public expectation of yet further improvements seemed to grow with increased provision. It is clear that resources can never be provided on a scale which will meet to the full the hopes of professional practitioners, the ambitions of pressure groups or perhaps even the expectations of the public. There is no reason to expect that in the foreseeable future Governments will be able to finance the rates of increase of social services we saw in the recent past, certainly not to exceed them, and public expectations will need to accommodate this. But needs will change and priorities with them. Resources will have to be provided in part by switching from one programme to another. The room for such switching will be affected to an important extent by the responsiveness of programmes to demographic change. Constraints on social programmes are tight. Ministers' ability to ensure better room for manoeuvre in the period beyond will depend to an important extent on their willingness to take a hard look at the implications of demographic trends and take early decisions.

We therefore recommend:

(*a*) that foreseeable demographic trends . . . should be taken fully into account by Ministers in decisions on priorities for the social services in the medium to longer term;

(*b*) that these trends should be given full weight in decisions on resources allocation at all levels, taking account of the general considerations summarised in paragraph 15.6, including in particular the risks of misallocation by default;

(*c*) that the various specific policy options . . . should be further considered in detail both by the immediately responsible departments in developing their own priorities and policies for the immediate and medium term, and by Ministers collectively in relation to the Public Expenditure Survey and major policy reviews;

(*d*) that this report should be given as wide a circulation as possible with the aim of improving awareness of demographic trends and factors, and their relevance in the development of social policies and planning.

From *Population and Social Policy* (Central Policy Review Staff, HMSO, 1977)

B10 Demography and Social Security: The Next Forty Years, 1985

5.2 . . . Whatever uncertainties there may be about the future some facts about changes in the structure of the population are clear. The number of elderly people in the population has increased substantially in recent years and will begin to increase rapidly again at the start of the next century. The reason for this is clear. The higher number of births from the mid-1950s and during the 1960s inevitably leads to a higher number of pensioners sixty years on. If account is taken of the expected improvements in medical science and thus life expectancy then the result must be a substantially increased number of pensioners. The Government Actuary has estimated the growth in the number of pensioners as follows:

1985 —	9.3 million	2015 —	11.1 million
1995 —	9.8 million	2025 —	12.3 million
2005 —	10.0 million	2035 —	13.2 million

The best evidence therefore shows that the first part of the next century will see a growth in the number of pensioners of over three million.

5.3 During the same period, however, the number of contributors paying for the state part of the pension cost will hardly change. The estimate of the Government Actuary is that over the next fifty years the number of contributors will increase by only 370,000 — on the assumptions of six per cent unemployment compared with thirteen per cent now and an increased fertility rate of 2.1 children per family compared with 1.7 now. So the position here is that the ratio of contributors to pensioners worsens in the first part of the next century.

5.4 The Government Actuary estimates the ratio of contributors to pensioners to change in the following way:

1985 — 2.3 contributors to each pensioner
1995 — 2.2 contributors to each pensioner
2005 — 2.2 contributors to each pensioner
2015 — 2.0 contributors to each pensioner
2025 — 1.8 contributors to each pensioner
2035 — 1.6 contributors to each pensioner

The trends, therefore, are in an unmistakeably difficult direction for a state pension scheme that relies entirely on contributions made at the time. Even if there were no more than the basic state pension, costs would rise. The Government Actuary's central assumption shows that if the basic pension was uprated by prices then the cost would rise from £15 billion now to £22 billion in 2033/4. If it was uprated in line with earnings then it would increase to £43.5 billion by the same year, but of course the existence of the second tier state scheme means that SERPS adds an additional £23 billion to this cost. On the basis of estimates set out in the Government Actuary's note, *total* pension costs will increase in the following way:

	Basic pension uprated in line with prices (1984/5 prices)	Basic pension uprated in line with earnings (1984/5 prices)
1988/9	£16.9 bn	£17.8 bn
1993/4	£17.9 bn	£20.0 bn
2003/4	£21.0 bn	£25.9 bn
2013/4	£27.7 bn	£36.4 bn
2023/4	£35.7 bn	£49.8 bn

5.5 There is a danger in seeing the picture of emerging cost increases simply in terms of pensions. The increased numbers of elderly people will have other effects. They will place an additional strain on the health service and on personal social services. Estimates of cost are difficult, but in the health service it is estimated that the retired population account for slightly over 40 per cent of the cost of the hospital and community health service. An additional three million pensioners will have an inevitable result. Without allowing for any improvements in service or the costs of advances in technology, health service costs could increase by 30 per cent in real terms simply to meet the needs of the extra pensioners.

5.6 Nor should it be thought that the question of costs is for the remote future. In the next twenty years the cost of the social security programme is projected to increase by between £5 billion and £8 billion in real terms on present policies. The range of increases is accounted for by different assumptions about the course of unemployment. The lower figure would result if unemployment fell to half its present level over the next ten years. The higher figure assumes that unemployment falls from the current 13 per cent to 10 per cent. Equally important is the assumption that benefits are uprated in line with prices. This would maintain present living standards for those dependent on state benefits, but over the last forty years benefit rates have in fact increased by more than this and have broadly kept pace with increases in earnings. If benefits were to be uprated by, say, one and a half per cent a year ahead of prices, the range of extra social security costs to be borne by the working population in twenty years' time would be between £16 billion and £20 billion. These figures would represent an increase in total social security spending of between 45 and 55 per cent after allowing for inflation.

5.7 Clearly there are uncertainties in forecasting what will happen in the future, particularly where factors such as unemployment and economic growth are concerned. The same applies to projections of population size where this is influenced by changes in the birth rate. But the basis of forecasts of the future number of pensioners is the existing population on which we have very accurate data; and forecasts of likely patterns of mortality are also subject to much narrower margins of error. Thus, while we may regard forecasts of the future size of the employed population and of growth in the economy as speculative over even quite short periods of time, the current growth of the elderly population and the resumption of that growth at the beginning of the next century are certainties. So too is the growth in expenditure from the build up of entitlements to earnings-related pensions. As the Government Actuary reported:

> while estimates for over forty years ahead must contain uncertainties, the general pattern of a substantial increase in emerging pension payments during the first quarter of the next century is secure.

From *Reform of Social Security*, vol. 1, Cmnd 9517 (HMSO, 1985)

B11   Public Expenditure: Future Prospects, 1984

Longer-term pressures

It is necessary . . . to decide first what can and should be afforded, then to set expenditure plans for individual programmes consistently with that decision. This Green Paper is primarily concerned with this major issue. It does not, accordingly, attempt to make detailed projections of individual expenditure programmes so far ahead in the future. But it is possible now to discern some of the pressures for still higher public spending.

26. It is in the nature of the public services that demands are literally limitless, because they are not restrained by the price mechanism which forces those making demands to balance them against costs. Wherever it is possible and sensible to do so, the government is seeking to transfer the provision of services into the market sector. In other areas it may be possible to use charges as a more direct way of testing demand, even within the public sector. There may, too, be a case for hypothecating revenues to individual expenditure programmes, particularly in the social field, in order to bring home the costs. But over a wide range of services the only means of controlling the cost is for the government to limit the supply.

27. Over the next decade there are reasons to expect continuing pressures for more spending, and insistent demands for improvements. One such pressure is demography — especially the effect of increasing numbers of the very elderly. Demographic projections for the United Kingdom are set out below. Another is rising expectations, as incomes of the working population increase. In those services which depend on personal contact, there may be less scope

for reducing costs by the use of new technology, so that the relative cost of providing these services will tend to increase over time. In other areas technological advance will yield substantial cost savings; but it can also open up new possibilities for improved levels of service, and therefore new demands.

Demographic Projections for the United Kingdom

	1981	1984	1991	millions 1994
Under 15	11.6	11.0	11.1	11.7
(as % total)	(20.6)	(19.5)	(19.5)	(20.4)
15 to pensionable age	34.6	35.1	35.3	35.2
(as % total)	(61.6)	(62.4)	(62.0)	(61.5)
Pensionable age	10.1	10.2	10.5	10.4
(as % total)	(17.9)	(18.1)	(18.4)	(18.1)
Total	56.3	56.3	56.9	57.3
of which over 75	3.3	3.5	3.9	3.8
(as % total)	(5.8)	(6.3)	(6.9)	(6.7)

Source: Office of Population. Censuses and Surveys (OPCS).

28. The following paragraphs indicate the main pressures on individual expenditure programmes.

29. Since there is no clear 'right' level for any particular social security benefit, there are constant demands both for real increases in the level of benefits and for extension of benefit coverage to those who do not at present qualify.

30. The main factor affecting the social security programme is the provision which has to be made for the elderly. About half of present expenditure goes on this group; to provide the basic state pension costs about £160 million for each 100,000 pensioners. The proportion of the programme going to the elderly is likely to increase, in particular because of demographic pressures. The total number of people above pension age will show very little increase between now and 1994 — from about 10.2 million to 10.4 million. But after the turn of the century numbers will rise rapidly as those born during the baby boom of the 1950s and early 1960s reach retirement age. The latest projections suggest a total of 12.6 million by 2025.

31. But before the turn of the century other factors will have a major impact on the costs of provision for retirement. Although the elderly population will not increase much, the number of pensioners

Total Percentage Change in Programmes between 1978–9 and 1983–4 (in real terms)

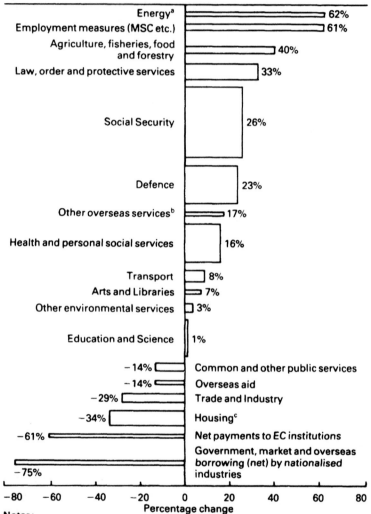

Notes:

The width of each bar on the vertical axis is proportional to expenditure on the programme concerned in 1983–4

Expenditure in Scotland, Wales and Northern Ireland has been allocated to functional programmes

[a] Largely assistance to the coal industry.

[b] Includes a wide variety of items: the Diplomatic Service is about 40 per cent and has not grown in real terms.

[c] Housing figures are calculated before any deduction for council house sales.

will increase by some 600,000 — largely because more people, particularly married women, will be entitled to a pension in their own right. More significantly, the earnings-related element of the State Earnings Related Pension Scheme (SERPS) established under the 1975 Social Security Act is now beginning to increase expenditure. By the time SERPS reached maturity, most people without a private occupational pension would be entitled to a full earnings-related pension in addition to the basic state pension — and hence to a better standard of living. But the costs of the state pension would be building up to a peak at the time when the number of elderly people again begins to increase more rapidly.

32. The cost of provision for the elderly both before and after the turn of the century depends on the interaction of many factors, including demography; the balance between private and state pension provision; the level of additional support available through supplementary pension and housing benefit; and the policy adopted on the uprating of benefits. The Government is committed to raising the basic state pension in line with inflation. But as the recovery progresses, there is likely to be pressure for pensions to rise faster than this. The implications of the present state pension scheme and related pensions issues are under study in the Government's Inquiry into Provision for Retirement; they remain the major source of future pressures on social security expenditure.

33. However, pressures on the programme are not confined to expenditure on the elderly . . . Expenditure on disability benefits has been growing rapidly. To meet the calls for a comprehensive disability benefit would cost about £3 billion a year. Increases in child benefit are often advocated not only to alleviate family poverty, but also to reduce the poverty and unemployment traps. But significant increases in this universal benefit are very expensive; each £1 on child benefit costs £500 million in a full year.

34. Nevertheless, as the economic recovery continues and the number of those unemployed falls, the pressures on the social security programmes will abate. For each 100,000 fewer unemployed there should be a fall in the cost of benefits to the unemployed of around £185 million.

36. As with social security, demographic changes constitute a major influence on this programme. Health care costs are dependent on age. At present the costs in the 0–4 age group are about twice as much per head as for those of working age; for the 65–75 age group about four times as much, and for the 75 and over age

group about nine times as much. Until the early 1990s, and again from the early years of the next century, the proportion of the elderly and very elderly in the population is forecast to rise. In particular the numbers of those over 75 are forecast to rise from 3.5 million in 1984 to 3.8 million in 1994. If current levels of spending on the hospital and community health services per head of population in different age groups were to remain constant over time, spending would need to rise somewhat under 1 per cent a year between 1983–84 and 1993–94 simply to keep pace with demographic changes.

37. Medical advances may prove a major further pressure. Where these lead to simpler or non-hospital treatments, they may in fact reduce costs. But where they involve expensive equipment, expensive surgical techniques or new drugs they can lead to powerful demands for increased funds. Even where unit costs have been reduced, widespread demand for such treatment may strain the resources available.

38. Changes in social attitudes and patterns of treatment may also pose problems for expenditure control in this programme. Increasingly, on both medical and social grounds, the aim is to keep the elderly and the mentally ill and mentally handicapped in the community. Although treatment in hospital is expensive, keeping people in the community requires heavy investment in support services — the medical professions, social workers and domiciliary support. This affects both the family practitioner services and the local authority personal social services, both of which are highly labour-intensive.

39. Finally, evidence from other countries suggests that increased affluence will lead to pressures for higher spending on health care. Within the United Kingdom such spending is largely financed from general taxation although there is a role for charges for those able to pay them. Here as elsewhere, demographic pressures and increasing demands are not the whole story. The Health Service needs to achieve continuing efficiency improvements, from higher productivity and better management, following the example of private industry in recent years. Many people have chosen to make provision for some of their health needs outside the State system, whilst continuing to contribute towards Health Service costs through their taxes. As living standards continue to rise, some further increase may be expected in the numbers who so choose. These developments will moderate the pressures for an increased contribution from the taxpayer, but such pressures will continue.

40. Demographic changes affecting education over the next decade are such that, if current levels of provision per pupil and per student were broadly maintained, education's share of GDP could be expected to decline significantly. The number of pupils in maintained schools is expected to fall from over 8.9 million in 1984 to some 8 million in 1991. If the cost per pupil were maintained at existing levels every 100,000 fewer pupils would lead on average to savings of around £90 million a year. The latest projection, currently under review, of the number of full-time and sandwich home students in higher education shows a fall from over 500,000 now to well under 450,000 in the early 1990s, with the decline in the size of the relevant age-groups more than outweighing a continued increase in the age participation rate. This would yield savings in student grants even without a further reduction in the dependence of students on public funds for their maintenance, and also in expenditure on universities, polytechnics and colleges.

41. A number of factors are however likely to work in the opposite direction. In addition to inescapable diseconomies of scale as pupil and student numbers fall, there is a case for a better as well as a smaller teaching force (see Cmnd 8336) and better in-servicing training. There will be pressure for a further increase in the participation rate of under fives, though it is currently at a record level of 40 per cent. Technological advance in industry should result, in the national interest, in extra demand for relatively expensive courses in science and technology within further and higher education — although there may be scope for involving employers and employees in the financing of some such courses.

Conclusion

61. Public expenditure, in Britain as in other countries, has risen over many years, both in real terms and as a share of national income. It is difficult to escape the conclusion that there is an inbuilt tendency for spending to rise; and an inbuilt resistance to expenditure reductions. The inevitable consequence has been that the taxes required to pay for this spending — taxes on people and on the firms they work for — have risen broadly in step, except for limited periods, when governments increased their borrowing. Such borrowing, however, has to be repaid by a tax on future generations.

62. These increases in taxation have, in the government's view, had a serious impact on Britain's economic performance over many years. Since lower growth has not led to lower demands for public

services, the outcome, year after year, has been still higher taxation to finance ever higher public expenditure.

63. As public spending takes a larger and larger share of GDP, so the public sector steadily encroaches on the rest of the economy. This is a process which could not be allowed to go on indefinitely. Last month's Public Expenditure White Paper confirmed the government's determination to hold its spending at broadly its present level in real terms for the next three years.

65. This Green Paper shows that without firm control over public spending there can be no prospect of bringing the burden of tax back to tolerable levels. On the illustrative framework set out in this Paper the tax burden will be reduced to the levels of the early 1970s only if public expenditure is held broadly at its present level in real terms right up to 1993–94.

66. If, on the other hand, we assume what by historical standards is a very modest rate of public expenditure growth — 1 per cent a year in real terms after 1988–89, compared with the average 3 per cent growth of the last twenty years — the tax burden would be only just below its 1978–79 level even after ten years of growth in the economy at about 2 per cent a year; and it would still be some way above its level in the early 1960s.

67. In order to underline the inescapable connection — so often overlooked in public debate on these issues — between public spending and the taxes required to finance it, the projections in this Green Paper have concentrated upon quantifying the reduction in the tax burden which different combinations of circumstances might produce. But it would, of course, always be open to the government to decide, once the virtuous circle of lower taxes and higher growth had been established, to devote some of these resources to improved public services rather than reduced taxation. There should, however, be no general presumption that higher public spending is inevitable if provision in these areas is to be improved, given the scope for switching from public to private sectors, and for improved efficiency within the public sector.

68. All these projections are, of course, subject to a wide range of uncertainty. But on one issue there can be no room for doubt: the government and parliament must reach their judgement about what public expenditure in total can be afforded, then contain individual programmes within that total. If the public discussion of these important issues leads to a wider understanding of this fact — that finance must determine expenditure, not expenditure finance — the

discussion will have served a useful purpose.

69. The government looks forward to a continuing debate on the fiscal prospects in the longer term. There will, no doubt, be much discussion of the validity and realism of the broad economic assumptions made in this Green Paper; of the conclusions to be drawn for individual programmes from the consideration of future pressures on public spending; and of whether the additional resources created by continuing economic growth should go to reducing the present, historically high, level of taxation, or to further improvements in the public services, or to both in some degree. But the government hopes that the main theme of this Green Paper will remain at the centre of the debate: that to break away from the debilitating pattern of the past in which public spending and taxation took an ever-larger share of our national product, we must establish a clear view of what can be afforded; set our spending plans accordingly; then stick to those plans.

From *Public Expenditure and Taxation into the 1990s*, Cmnd 9189 (HM Treasury, 1984)

POLITICS AND SOCIAL POLICY

B12   The Right Road for Britain, 1949

Government Spending

Of every £ earned in Britain today, Government takes and spends 8s. Conservatives think that this is far too much. Most of the taxes come from the earnings of private persons. They are discouraged from additional effort. The amount they are able to spend and save is reduced and their choice is limited. Much comes from those earnings of industry which should be set aside for renewing machinery to reduce future costs and prices. Some, in the form of indirect taxation, directly increases prices. The heavy burden of taxation and Mr Dalton's methods of rigging the rate of interest have virtually destroyed new private savings. The Government has had to use taxation to finance investment where formerly the stream of voluntary savings sufficed.

We shall curb Government expenditure. We shall cut out the extravagance and waste which has been allowed to run through the whole administration. It should be a first principle of good Government to ensure that every penny is wisely and carefully spent. The country is not getting value for money.

By changes in Government spending, a Conservative Government will seek to make corresponding reductions in taxation. The first reductions must be devoted to encouraging more production at lower cost and to giving incentives to save. Nothing has discouraged thrift and enterprise more than the high level of direct taxation. Income tax on earned incomes discourages extra effort and saving. Industry has not been able to set aside adequate sums for modernising plant. Personal savings have been reduced to a trickle. A reduction in direct taxation must, therefore, be the first object of relief.

Social Services

Mainly during the twentieth century a new conception of Social Services has grown up and Britain has led the world in a vast experiment in social organisation. This has been the work of the Conservative and Liberal parties, mostly in fact of Parliaments with Conservative majorities . . . The Socialists in the last four years have carried out in a partisan spirit the plans prepared by the National Coalition Government with its large Conservative majority. They have no claim to any achievement of their own.

The Social Services are no longer even in theory a form of poor relief. They are a co-operative system of mutual aid and self-help provided by the whole nation and designed to give to all the basic minimum of security, of housing, of opportunity, of employment and of living standards below which our duty to one another forbids us to permit anyone to fall.

This new conception was further developed in 1944 in the legislation and White Papers of the Coalition Government with its majority of Conservative Ministers and the full approval of the Conservative majority in the House of Commons. They passed the Education Act. They set up the Beveridge Committee and produced and approved White Papers based on it setting out the principles for the schemes of pensions, sickness and unemployment benefit, industrial injuries benefit and a national health scheme. They laid the foundations of the post-war housing policy. The subsequent Conservative Government passed the Family Allowances Act.

The Socialist Government has in the main only completed the work which the Coalition had begun and in some cases had only to bring forward Bills already drawn up.

Despite the spirit of class-war with which the Minister of Health in particular has sought to disrupt national unity, the Conservative Party has welcomed the new Social Services which it has done much to create. We regard them as mainly our own handiwork. We shall endeavour faithfully to maintain the range and scope of these Services, and the rates of benefits.

The grave threat to the Social Services is the continued pursuit by our present rulers of policies which may prevent Britain from earning her independent liberty and from surmounting her present crisis. Such policies have already, by raising prices, inflated the cost of the Social Services and reduced the value of the cash benefits and pensions. It is, therefore, in the interest of all citizens, who both receive the benefits and pay for the services, to cut out shameful waste and to insist upon value for their money spent. This the Conservative Party will do.

The Family

Conservatives regard the family as the foundation of a healthy society. Material circumstances should be made to help and not to hinder family life. In our review of Income Tax, reliefs for parents will have a large part to play. Better housing must help the mother whose domestic tasks should be lightened by improved labour-saving appliances and amenities. The children's well-being depends on a happy home as much as on the provision of adequate opportunities through the educational system.

Education

Work for a generation lies ahead in bringing into force all the provisions of the 1944 Education Act. Yet we believe that no task is more important for the future greatness of the nation. We must thus equip our people to withstand the onslaught of materialist ideologies and to bend science to the aid of mankind. Nothing is more important for securing equality of opportunity than to ensure that the education received by each boy and girl gives the fullest scope for their abilities.

There are certain parts of the Education Act to which we will give our first attention. Progress cannot be rapid until administration is simplified and decentralised . . .

There are far too few technical schools and colleges for a nation which relies for its very life on the goods it can produce and export. Our survival depends on our skill. A Conservative Government will give first priority to increasing the number and status of technical schools and colleges, which must be fully equipped and staffed. Secondly, we would reduce the size of classes as soon as possible and particularly in the primary schools . . . It will be part of our policy to see that canteens and equipment are provided as soon as possible so that we can make available to all the free school meals which we promised when we passed the Family Allowances Act.

. . . We regard with suspicion the tendency to create enormous and unwieldy multilateral schools. Under certain circumstances, variations of the multilateral idea may well be adopted. But we shall not allow them to become so big that individual attention and a sense of community cannot be given to the children.

It is of vital importance to the nation that the standards of the grammar schools, and particularly of their sixth forms, should be kept at the highest level . . .

The Universities are, rightly in modern times, the recipients of large grants from the Government. Conservatives will continue these grants and guarantee the present freedom of the Universities from Government interference. We shall help them to equip themselves in staff and buildings to deal with the greatly enlarged student population. The Working Party on University Awards has recommended a much larger number of county scholarships. We favour these proposals in general, but we do not believe that every place in a University should of necessity be free.

Women

The proposals put forward in this statement of policy are designed for the benefit of the whole nation irrespective of class or sex. Conservatives recognise that there are, in addition, some questions, particularly in matters of law, which are of special concern to women. In some cases the law has, through lapse of time, ceased to correspond to the status of women in a modern society. We will revise the law relating to domicile and institute an enquiry into out-of-date legislation affecting women.

The Health Scheme

The nation has been warned by the Socialist Chancellor of the Exchequer that unless there is economy in the use of the Health Services some special charge or tax may have to be imposed. Conservatives share this anxiety about the maladministration and lack of foresight displayed by the Minister of Health and any Government may find itself forced to establish priorities based on need and urgency. We shall, therefore, see that the large sums of money spent on these Services yield their full value.

The Health Services depend in the end upon the efficiency and goodwill of the family doctor. A Conservative Government would strengthen his position by restoring his freedom to practise anywhere and by offering a weighted capitation fee would give further security to doctors, particularly those in rural areas, with small lists. We shall allow an appeal against dismissal to go to the High Court instead of to the Minister.

The scheme is intended to be comprehensive and any part of it should be available to any member of the public. We shall, therefore, allow private patients to obtain free of charge drugs prescribed by their doctor on a parity with people in the State scheme.

From *The Right Road for Britain* (Conservative and Unionist Central Office, 1949)

B13   One Nation, 1950

Social Effects of the Redistribution of Wealth

Some redistribution of wealth is an inevitable consequence of all progressive taxation. The consequence is the more marked the more the proceeds of taxation, instead of being applied to collective purposes (like defence), are distributed to individuals in the form of benefits or payments.

For many years, however, it has been regarded not merely as a consequence but as an *object* of taxation and of the social services to bring about redistribution of wealth.

A sharp division between the economic and social consequences of redistribution is, of course, not possible. The basic well-being of individuals clearly depends both upon the national income per head and upon the manner in which it is distributed between individuals. Redistribution may be so limited that many individuals remain below the minimum level of well-being with which the nation could afford to provide them. Conversely, redistribution may be pushed to a point where it produces economic evils which directly or indirectly affect everybody, such as the tendency to consume the country's capital assets instead of to increase them, or the repression of energy and enterprise by reduction of incentives.

Now, there must exist, even though it may not be possible to ascertain it in practice with mathematical accuracy, a certain degree and method of redistribution which would *in the long run* produce the optimum result in a purely economic sense. Whether that economic optimum has already been reached or passed in the Britain of 1950 is a matter for dispute. We believe that in fact it has been passed, and that the future well-being of even the poorest is already being endangered by the economic effects of redistribution.

Our contention here, however, is a different one. We wish to speak of the social consequences of redistribution, by which we mean the effect upon the relationships between men, and between classes of men, and upon the well-being of individuals in all but the most narrowly economic sense. We contend that the optimum has quite certainly been passed on social grounds, and that the social well-being of the nation has already been endangered by the redistribution of wealth. We base this contention on the view that in our society the possession and transmission of property can and should produce desirable results which are not to be procured by any other means. It is, of course, immaterial to our argument whether the man who sets out to accumulate private property and to transmit it to his heirs is, by origin, a Duke or a dustman.

Rights and Duties   The first consideration which we advance is a moral one. The existence of a nation depends on the steady and indeed instinctive acceptance by those who compose it of a scheme of *duties*. It may also imply a scheme of *rights*; but the health and life of the nation are endangered as soon as the rights come to be regarded as more important than the duties, or even as their prior condition. Whatever may be true in the legal sphere, in the political or moral sphere there is no more dangerous fallacy than the idea that rights and duties are equal and opposite, and that every duty implies a corresponding right. For example, the commandment 'Thou shalt love thy neighbour as thyself' never meant, 'Thou hast the right to be loved by thy neighbour as he loves himself.' When the State redistributes income and property to give everyone the largest amount possible, the citizen who has paid his taxes has discharged in full his obligations to the huge benefit pool to which he belongs. The State is now the keeper of his conscience and duty; he gives and receives exactly what the State thinks right. Perhaps this is the millennium of 'fair shares for all'. It is certainly the death of a human society.

As capital, in money and land, is progressively fragmented by redistribution, the State must come to fill for an increasing proportion of people the positions of employer and landlord. However unavoidable this may be for a small percentage of employment and land, we regard it as of most evil consequence when extended to the majority. That the State, when it fills these roles itself, must cease to be the arbiter and moderator of relations between individuals and become instead the judge in its own cause, is a familiar though important consideration. There are others as important: the humanity and adaptability of these relationships is lessened. The private employer (even a large firm) and the private landlord have more discretion in administration, in dealing with special cases, than the bureaucrat, administering on behalf of the State, either can or should possess. In the long run no employer has to be so heartless and no landlord so grasping as the State. It is perfectly true that a bad employer or landlord may fall, in the short run, below the average standards of the State, and we fully support State intervention to force upon them acceptable standards of behaviour. But we refuse to judge, as Socialists do, whole classes of men by their renegades, and to abolish the opportunity for great good in an attempt to prevent occasional abuses.

Similar evils result from the assumption by the community of the exclusive role of Grand Almoner, which must also follow from the elimination of private fortunes. The expenditure of public money necessarily involves parity of treatment and tends to eliminate discretion. In large things and small, this necessity impoverishes the social services. Special needs, which lie outside the scope of the services demanded by contemporary public opinion, or standards higher than those at which the public purse can aim, are the proper objects of private gifts and foundations. In education, in the treatment of the sick and in the care of the young and the aged, it will be found that historically the course of the social services has been piloted by private initiative — whether it be Dr Barnado's or Manchester Grammar School, Guy's Hospital or the village almshouses. That leadership, which by its nature the State cannot exercise, depends on the existence of aggregations of wealth at the disposal of individuals.

One last consideration, too often overlooked. Private property is an equipoise to political power. If it ceases to exist, rank in the bureaucracy, or perhaps in the Party, will be the sole means by which men can fulfil their natural ambition. When this happens, personal liberty is gone. The more men and women there are whose property gives them a security, a status and an influence independent of officialdom, the greater is the guarantee for the freedom of their fellow subjects.

If the views which we have just set out contain even an element of truth, the obligation is inescapable to see that our policy takes account of them. This means that those features of taxation and other policy which are promoting the fragmentation of property and hindering its accumulation and transmission must be checked and to some extent reversed.

Paying for the Social Services

We have accepted as the objective of our social policy the establishment and maintenance of a basic minimum standard of life and labour below which none shall be allowed to fall. In this book we have discussed our idea of what goes to make up this minimum standard. Our attempts to formulate a practical policy by which it can be provided have been governed throughout by two considerations. First, our total requirements for the social services must be kept within the bounds of what the country can afford. Secondly, our policy must be one which can be introduced by stages as the country's economic resources permit.

To speak of 'what the country can afford' will infuriate those Socialists who believe that the only criterion of social expenditure is the so-called 'need' of the recipients. They will argue that the State must provide by way of social services whatever a man is unable to afford for himself, owing to prior claims on his income. They forget that there are prior claims on the national income before the social services; and that a point can be reached, and Conservatives believe has been reached, when the State does more harm in taking a further share of the national income than it does good by using it for the social services.

On the other hand, our theories will be derided by those who hold that full employment — and Socialism — can be maintained only by controlled inflation, and that heavy Government expenditure through the social services is the easiest way of ensuring it. The effect on an economy which is not isolated from the rest of the world, which indeed depends for its very existence on its competitive power, is ignored. That way lies a rising cost of living, hardships for the recipients of fixed social service and other payments, pressure for increases in these payments, further inflation, repeated devaluation and, finally, chaos. We do not deny that in the past Governments have, on the plea of inability to afford more, spent far too little on social services. But today the dangers involved in spending too much are only too plain.

What principles should decide what the country can afford in expenditure on the social services? First, their place in the priorities for Government expenditure. Just as we have accepted a system of priorities for expenditure inside each social service, and for each service in relation to the others, so we must accept priorities between the different branches of Government expenditure.

It is convenient to classify this expenditure under four heads. There is first the service of the National Debt; that is to say, the cost of making interest payments to all those who hold Savings Certificates, War Loan and other Government bonds. Secondly, there is the cost of government, the expenditure on the general administration of the country. Thirdly, there is the cost of Defence; and fourthly, there is the cost of the social services.

It is clear that expenditure on the social services must in general come after payments for the National Debt and the cost of government, both of which would have to be made even if there were no social services at all. Until there is national security there can never be social security, so that until this country is adequately defended it is not possible to make further extensions in the social services. Expenditure on Defence must always be kept to the minimum commensurate with the safety of the country, but today the war against Communism makes the burden of Defence a heavy one. A Budget estimate for 1950–51 of £780 million has already been increased to at least £850 million, and the cost is to become greater. Total expenditure on Defence over the three years 1950–53 is now estimated at £3,600 million.

The second general principle governing the size of the social services budget is that the good it does must outweigh the burden which it places on the individual and on industry. We believe that the individual's or the company's income is best spent by them. But, after the State has collected taxes for the general cost of government, it must also tax the strong in order to help the weak. It must not tax to help everybody. Nor, in helping the weak, must it weaken the strong to the extent that all suffer. It must not so tax industry that it cannot replace its own capital, with the result that its prices become uncompetitive in world markets. It must not burden the individual so that he loses his initiative and enterprise, or is driven to emigrate.

In the light of these general principles, let us look at the present financial position. The national income for 1950 is estimated at £11,630 million. The receipts from all forms of national and local taxation are estimated at £4,470 million. Of this, the Chancellor of the Exchequer takes £3,896 million. Thus, some 40 per cent of the national resources are taken in taxation. This necessitates a high tax on companies' undistributed profits, high death duties, an immense burden of income tax, and heavy indirect taxation on all individuals.

We believe that this level of taxation is harmful in its effect on industry and the individual, that it is more than the public can go on bearing in normal times, and that it must be reduced. It is unlikely that the interest charges of the National Debt can be brought down. The present cost of government could certainly be lowered by enforcing those economies for which the Conservative Party has so long been pressing. But the financial saving would not be large enough to allow any considerable change in taxation. The costs of Defence are increasing, and will continue to increase if the country is to be prepared. There remain the social services, including Food Subsidies.

The main increases in expenditure on the social services since the war have been on the Health Services, the Insurance Schemes, and on Education. The estimates for these for 1950–51 are as follows: for the Health Service, £393 million; for Insurance, £381 million; and for Education, £242 million. Nor will this expenditure remain static. If present policies are followed it will increase automatically. This is especially the case with the cost of retirement pensions, which in 1948 was £238 million, but which will increase to £421 million by 1968. The other large item of expenditure in the social services is the Food Subsidies, costing £465 millions annually.

The Present Choice

Looking to the future, we see other demands for Government expenditure looming large. Continued rises in the cost of living make it unjust to resist claims for increased salaries for civil servants, doctors and teachers, and there are other claims to be met.

The position can be summarized as follows:

(1) The level of Government expenditure is already too high for normal times.
(2) We are now entering abnormal times, involving a rearmament programme, but there is little taxable capacity in reserve.
(3) Our resources of men and materials are almost fully employed. We shall require more of them for Defence purposes.
(4) The social services — involving at present a high and automatically increasing level of expenditure — are therefore in danger.

After nearly half a century of almost uninterrupted expansion of the social services, we are faced with three choices. We can continue with the present policy of apparently uncontrollable expenditure, which will imperil not only our defence but our whole way of life. For us that is unthinkable. Secondly, we can build up our defences at the cost of our social services. That is undesirable, and must be done only in the last resort. Thirdly, we can make a supreme effort to meet the needs of Defence, and at the same time to maintain the social services. Our task is plain. Our emphasis now must be on finding ways of maintaining the social services.

This can be done only if there is a speedy increase in national production which will supply the growing needs of the Armed Forces as well as the existing demands of the social services. It is doubtful whether this increase in production can be achieved by the normal improvements in technical efficiency. They result in an annual increase of about $3\frac{1}{2}$ per cent. More is required, and more quickly. We cannot generalize, except to say that it will mean more efficient work from all. Each industry must be treated separately. For some the solution may lie in improved organization by management, for others it may be the introduction of a shift system for the workers or — if necessary — it may mean longer hours.

Whether this increase in production can be obtained or not will therefore depend to a large extent on all those engaged in industry. We must call on them for a great effort to save the social services.

There must be no further increases in the total cost of the social services, other than those which are automatic and inevitable. These could of course be met by increases in the insurance contributions paid by employers and employees. These would bear hardest on the lower-paid workers and would tend to increase the pressure for higher wages. This is not a course we would like, though we have suggested . . . that some increase may ultimately be necessary.

We accept the declaration of the Chancellor of the Exchequer that no more money can be spent on the National Health Service. It follows that either the Service must remain exactly as it is, or, if new priorities are to be established, and parts of the Service expanded, this can only be at the expense of other parts of the Service. We take the latter view . . . we have made proposals for charges for hospital board, for appliances and for prescriptions. These should produce a net saving of some £35 millions a year. This sum, if not needed to cover rising costs, will be available to finance the more urgent of the priorities we have indicated. It is recognized that it cannot cover all improvements that are desirable, and the less urgent must be met as and when the financial commitments of the country allow.

We hold the view that in education the money available should be used in a way which will ensure that what is done is done thoroughly, and that the highest standards are maintained. The danger is that with rises in costs all aspects of education will suffer and that standards as a whole will deteriorate. We believe it is better that items of expenditure which we have rated as a low priority should be omitted altogether, and the standard of the remainder maintained.

From *One Nation: A Tory Approach to Social Problems* (Conservative Political Centre, 1950)

B14   The Welfare State, 1952

Labour . . . looks upon social security and social services as the birthright of every citizen, normally speaking without test of means. There will, of course, always be special circumstances when an assessment of need is inevitable, but this must be the exception and not the rule. Labour, then, reasserts its belief in the development of social services democratically organised to meet the essential needs of the whole community and in which the whole community participates as a matter of course. It does so because it accepts the moral obligation of making provision for the needs of the old and the weak. It does so because it believes in the economic gain to the whole community as well as to the individual concerned of public spending on the social services. And it does so because it believes that as we develop our social services we can encourage a growing understanding of our common needs and reduce the pressure of the narrow personal acquisitive instincts of a capitalist society.

We recognise, however, that this aim can only be achieved over a period of time and with the positive encouragement of a much closer association of the social services with effective local democracy. It should be made much easier for all who want to do so to help in the work. Much more has to be done to explain the work of the services and how they affect each one of us as individuals. A responsible attitude towards the services can be developed only if we can feel a much closer contact with and pride in them, not merely as users but as providers, too.

Future Developments

We are proud of the great structure of social welfare legislation which has been implemented by the Labour Government, but at the same time we must guard against complacency, as there is still much to be done. The five giants have been subdued. But the battle for freedom from want is not yet over. There is still much avoidable distress, for which social action and social effort are needed. Our social services will need extending in the years ahead if we are to succeed in building a fairer and juster society, and that means that they will cost more.

However, social services are not the only claim on the British economy at the moment. There are others no less important and no less urgent. We have to carry out our commitments within the

United Nations Organisation and contribute our share towards the efforts of the Atlantic Treaty countries. We must play our part in the struggle 'towards world plenty' by building up the standard of life in the under-developed countries. We must export more of our resources in the fight to attain economic independence. We can only achieve all these ends by greater production through the sustained effort of the whole community. If we do not secure this greater output we shall not be able to extend our social services, unless it is at the expense of commitments no less vital and no less urgent. The balance of payments battle is not something remote that only concerns financial experts. It is of day to day concern to all of us.

Meanwhile we have to think not only of expanding our social services where it is necessary, but we must also review our existing services so as to eliminate avoidable waste, and get the greatest value for money. When appropriate the services must be simplified, and overlapping between various departments must be cut out. At the same time, we must not allow our welfare services to become cold, impersonal or hidebound. These are the evils that standardisation and centralisation can bring with them. Provision must always be made, in some way or another, for the exceptional case, while opportunities for local action and voluntary initiative must be extended.

We must also consider priorities within the main groups of the social services. For instance, given the limited resources available, would it be better to raise the school-leaving age to sixteen or to make provision for children to start in nursery classes at the age of three? This, and many other problems of a similar character, have to be decided, and it is the purpose of this pamphlet to consider some of the issues of policy that must be faced in the future.

Conclusion

Many critics do not openly attack the great work of Social Welfare legislation of the Labour Government. Instead they concentrate their criticism on two points. First they argue that the Social Services cost too much and are an important influence on our balance of payments difficulties. Second they suggest that comprehensive Social Services cannot be provided without high taxation. Such taxation is undesirable, they say, it reduces incentives and it removes from the citizen the responsibility of spending his own money, which instead the State spends for him. In fact both these criticisms are grossly exaggerated.

. . . The figures for Social Service expenditure of £1,896.6 million for 1949/50 and £1,921.2 million for 1950/51 are not completely up to date. Social Service expenditure accounted for about 16 per cent of the national income in those years and a fair estimate for the present day would be about 17–18 per cent. A recent survey of Social Service expenditure carried out by the International Labour Office covering over twenty nations indicates that some other countries are spending a larger percentage than this on Social Services. These estimates effectively dispose of the argument that social services are swallowing up an unduly large part of the national income, and that Britain is the heaviest Social Service spender. In particular it should be noted that Social Service outlay, both by central and local government, on the widest possible definition, . . . accounts for less than half the budget of national and local authorities. Moreover the amounts shown as transfer incomes are, of course, incomes which were spent by the public in the way they thought fit and not by the Government at all. As transfer incomes amounted to as much as 54 per cent of the national income in 1950–51 only 11 per cent of the national income was in fact spent by the Government directly on the other Social Services including food subsidies. Some may still consider that this proportion is too high. We do not think so. Humane and extensive Social Services are a safeguard for the democratic way of life. They further the principle of human equality and they relieve distress and suffering. As such they bring with them a positive economic gain to the community. Social Service expenditure is an investment in human capital, the most valuable capital that a people have.

What of the future? We want to safeguard our existing services and extend them when need is great. It is here that our difficulties arise and we must face up to them. In the long run the call of the Social Services on the national income will increase despite the ceilings that have been imposed on the health and education services, and despite the cuts in food subsidies. These measures will for the time being more than compensate for the increased allowances that are being paid, but it is unlikely that they will cover the amounts needed as the proportion of old people in the population begins to rise appreciably. Also it is extremely doubtful if these ceilings can be held if existing services are to be adequately maintained.

Many people regard the Social Services as a first charge on the community. But they are not the only charge and consequently the money which can be spent on them is limited. We must also face our commitments in the field of defence; the colonies and the undeveloped countries need our aid badly; our own industry needs plant and machinery; houses, power stations and factories must be built besides schools, clinics and hospitals; our export trade must be expanded.

Future problems of Social Service policy are all concerned with priorities. We have to start with an acceptance of the need for planning the use of our resources, and as we have seen, Social Service expenditure cannot be satisfactorily planned in isolation from all the other relevant facts in the economy. If priorities are to be properly considered, Social Service expenditure must be related to national income as a whole. There is therefore a strong case for ear-marking a proportion of the national income for Social Service purposes. This proportion would of course be subject to review from time to time in the light of economic circumstances, social developments, size of the national income and the demands of competing resources. It would be a great advantage if Social Service expenditure could be looked at from this point of view . . .

However hard we try we can only get a pint out of a pint pot. Therefore a large expansion of expenditure on Social Services is only possible if we increase our national income. But we must never forget that increased effort can only go hand in hand with social justice. That was the secret behind the effort of the British people in wartime and under a Labour Government. Our Social Services must be based on principles of fairness that are plain for all to see. Where the Tories abandon the principle of fairness we must be prepared to put things right. But we need to be ready to do more than that. We have to look at our own handiwork in a critical spirit and strive when necessary to improve it. By our Social Services we can secure freedom from want and at the same time enshrine the principle of equality on which a democratic Socialist Society must be based.

From *The Welfare State* (The Labour Party, 1952)

B15   Equality and Opportunities, 1956

Another objection to our schools system is the very different and unequal quality of education which the three types of school provide. Entry to universities, the professions, the State service and to managerial and technical posts in industry, increasingly depends on the attainment of academic qualifications or upon success in competitive examinations. It follows that if a school's curriculum is not geared to these requirements, its pupils' choice of careers will be automatically restricted. In practice, the curricula of the grammar and public schools are geared to these requirements, but the curriculum of the modern school is not. Moreover, with few exceptions, a child who goes to a modern school leaves at 15 — whereas education continues beyond that age for many grammar and most public school pupils. Thus, while in the grammar and public schools the doors of opportunity are wide open, in the modern schools they are, at best, only ajar.

It is obvious too, that the quality of education provided by the different schools will largely determine success in competitive examinations. That the grammar schools have better facilities and smaller classes than the modern schools is common knowledge. The public schools, with their larger financial resources, can often provide still better teaching and still smaller classes than the grammar schools.

It is not surprising therefore to find that pupils from public schools win State scholarships to universities, and success in the highly competitive examinations for entrance to the Foreign Service and to the Administrative Class of the Home Civil Service, out of all proportion to their numbers. Since entry to the public schools is determined more by the wealth of the parent than the ability of the child, it cannot be assumed that these successes are due solely to the innate intelligence of their pupils. To a considerable extent they must be attributed to the character of the education they receive.

The point we wish to emphasise is not that competitive examinations are unfair, but the different types of schools are bound to give very unequal chances of success. Even if all the nation's children had equal educational facilities, the competitive advantage would lie strongly with those whose family background was materially and culturally enriched. As it is, the child from a poor family with a grammar school education enters the competitive race against the public schools with severe handicaps. The child from the modern school is, as far as the professions and the senior grades of the State service are concerned, virtually a non-starter.

Of course, only a small minority of the more interesting and highly paid positions are open to competitive examinations. In industry, nepotism still plays a major role in determining many executive and directorial appointments. While this is becoming less true of some at least of the big companies, it is still the rule in medium, small and family businesses. In the professions, too, family connections play a considerable role. But the critical factor here is what might be called 'financial staying power' rather than direct personal connections. Many of the professions — law and medicine are outstanding examples — require such a long period of unpaid or low-paid training before the necessary qualifications can be obtained, that only those with considerable financial aid or with quite exceptional determination can hope to finish the course. State grants and scholarships have, it is true, helped to open the professions; but in many cases grants have not been generous enough to enable the student from a poor family to continue his studies.

Clearly, we have a long way to go before equality of opportunity becomes a reality. In spite of the postwar changes in our schools and universities, the greater equality of incomes and the greater use of competitive selection, opportunities are still far from equal.

From *Towards Equality* (The Labour Party, 1956)

B16   The Future of the Welfare State, 1958

It has lately become a cliché of Right-wing rhetoric to proclaim the need for an Opportunity State to match and sustain the Welfare State. Neither of these terms is defined with any precision. But we may take it that, if the Welfare State is a mechanism for distributing golden eggs, an Opportunity State denotes the conditions under which the goose will most readily lay them. These conditions do not exist in Britain today. They can scarcely exist, I think, so long as we offer to people of responsibility and skill incentives that are laughable by American or Russian standards, and fiscally punish our top productive talents with the heaviest weight of direct taxation imposed anywhere in the world.

It is a thundering great fallacy to imagine that an economic advance such as is postulated in talk of doubling our standard of living in twenty-five years is to be obtained, in this of all countries, through the sheer momentum of technological change. The significant growth of our national income is going to depend, as it always has done, largely on the activities and decisions of exceptional men and women. To induce them to do the exceptional things of which they alone are capable is part of the very mechanism of creating the necessities (and the luxuries) of life for the nation as a whole. In penalising them, exploiting them, and ultimately driving them abroad, the nation puts a brake on its own progress. By rewarding them, by reducing disincentives to work and save, it can enrich itself.

No one who genuinely cares about contemporary social conditions would, on a long-term view, shrink from such (among other) means to guarantee their improvement. There is so little now that can be achieved in any positive sense by spreading existing wealth more thinly; so much that could be done, and desperately needs doing, out of the resources of a dynamic and healthily expanding economy. I only wish my Socialist (and some of my Conservative) friends would apprehend that what disfigures our modern society is not class but squalor.

The Welfare State as it exists today is the delayed reaction to Victorian poverty and inter-war unemployment. As standards of living continue to rise, many of the assumptions upon which it is based are seen to have been falsified; not least Lord Beveridge's assumption in framing his 'Social Security Budget' that the post-war rate of general unemployment would average about $8\frac{1}{2}$ per cent. More and more people of working age are becoming capable of standing on their own feet; more and more can afford to make provision out of their earnings, either directly or through insurance, for the necessities and against the hazards of ordinary life. Public policy has in the last few years begun to take account of this. Why, now, do we not push public policy further and faster in this direction? Why, looking further ahead, do we not turn to good account the popular prejudice in favour of genuine insurance benefits 'earned by contributions and paid as of right', by remodelling the social security system on principles that do not treat its ultimate beneficiaries as needful of charity or posterity as a pack-horse to be loaded with our deficits? Why, above all, do we not give maximum and consistent encouragement to people to be self-providing, to become owners as well as earners, to pay for their own homes, to make their own superannuation arrangements, to insure themselves privately against ill-health — even, if most can and are so minded, to educate their children outside the public system?

If in an expanding economy, with full employment and heavy (I would hope heavier) fiscal discrimination in favour of the family, we can in this coming generation lift the standard of living to a level where people may, in some at least of these respects, freely exercise social responsibility for themselves, why should we regard this otherwise than as a consummation devoutly to be wished? I confess I am not greatly impressed by the classic argument about the fate of the shiftless or luckless 5 per cent who might always require (and for whom there should always be) a safety net; I am much more concerned that the other 95 per cent should not be seduced into decadence, into thinking that no matter how much they are earning, it is someone else's responsibility to look after them, and not their own.

I hope not to be misunderstood, and therefore not to be misrepresented. It is no part of my argument to say that we should spend less on social provision. My argument, on the contrary, is that we should aspire to spend more, much more, and establish conditions in which our resources will expand to match these aspirations. It does, however, seem to me that there is both a need and an opportunity now and in the years ahead for a major shift in the nature, direction and emphasis of social spending — away from the crude services which working people ought increasingly to be able to provide for themselves, and towards modern services crying out for community effort or finance: namely, the vigorous creation and maintenance by public authority of the finest environmental conditions for our people, and the generous application of public money to the subtler problems of personality, social adjustment and education in its widest sense.

From Peter Goldman's preface to *The Future of the Welfare State* (Conservative Political Centre, 1958)

B17 Enoch Powell: The Welfare State, 1961

The Plowden Report on *Control of Public Expenditure* contained, amongst other nuggets of wisdom, the following sentence which I should like to take as my starting point: 'The social changes of the last fifteen years have altered the incidence of hardship, so that there now may well be excessive social services for some purposes and inadequate ones for others.'

I should have thought that, in the abstract, no one was likely to quarrel with that statement. Indeed, the reference to 'the social changes of the last *fifteen* years' makes it an understatement: for there is not a single social service today which was not framed more than fifteen years ago. The conception of all of them, in more or less their present form, dates from the social revolution of 1942 to 1944. Yes, you heard me correctly: I said 1942 to 1944. The General Election of 1945 was in some ways only a consequential recognition of the revolution which took place under, and inside, the Coalition Government at the height of World War II, and was announced to the outside world by a cloud of White Papers — on planning, social insurance, employment, a national health service — much as the election of a new Pope is first evinced by the smoke from the burning ballot papers.

But not only does the framing of the existing social services date back twenty years already. The conditions in the light of which those services were then framed were the conditions of the inter-war years — the only available peace-time background for the war-time revolutionaries to use. If the Plowden Committee had referred therefore to 'the social changes of the last *thirty* years' instead of fifteen, they would have been guilty of no inaccuracy. Those thirty years span some of the sharpest changes of trend in modern history, from persistent deflation, for instance, to persistent inflation, or from unemployment averaging 10 per cent to unemployment averaging 2 per cent, as well as a rise of at least one-third in national income per head.

Inertia and Institutionalisation

Acceptance of a proposition in principle and rejection of it in practice is a perfectly normal human attitude, as common outside politics as inside. It is, I suppose, one manifestation of man's indomitable urge to 'have it both ways at once'. None the less an examination of the special reasons why the Plowden proposition is accepted as a truism in general but treated as an abominable heresy in particular may be worth while.

The most obvious of these reasons are political ones, in the pure, Party, vote-catching sense of that term. In politics it is more blessed not to take than to give. The termination of a benefit or a payment or a service is a sharp, specific assault upon identifiable individuals: it gives political opponents something solid to talk about: they can actually produce the bodies and point to the wounds. By contrast, the failure to introduce new benefits, payments or services is a much blunter grievance: political opponents have only something hypothetical to discuss; individual electors do not easily identify themselves with the deprived. Moreover while the *minus* is always identifiable and indisputable the *plus* is often not identifiable separately or not identifiable as a consequence of the *minus*. Similarly the citizen as a taxpayer does not identify himself — and indeed is only partially identical in fact — with the citizen as a recipient of tax-financed benefits.

Finally, there is the fact of human nature summed up in the saying, 'There's no gratitude in politics.' Even if there were equal numbers of equally identifiable gainers and losers, the political resentment of the losers would outweigh the political gratitude of the gainers. When an addition is made to the system of State-provided services, it is only made because there is a general opinion that the time is ripe for it and that such provision is 'only right'. The beneficiaries thus regard themselves as having received no more than their due, to which they were entitled anyhow, while those whose benefits are discontinued regard themselves as cheated of what they had a right to and had been encouraged to expect.

Politically, therefore, the inducements to continue what the Plowden Committee call 'excessive social services' are much stronger than the inducements to discontinue them or to supplement any which may happen to be 'inadequate'. But it would be a cynical mistake to limit the forces of inertia to these narrowly political ones.

It is the characteristic of social services that they become rapidly and strongly institutionalised. True, all acts of government policy create a presumption that they will remain in force and are an invitation to the citizen to adapt his private behaviour accordingly; but the tendency of decisions in the social service field to create vested interests is of a quite peculiar order . . . We see a range of existing social services, entrenched to varying degrees in institutional form, reflecting to varying degrees needs and economic conditions which have passed or are passing away. We see new needs, born of newer economic and social conditions, which call to be met. We recognise that logically this demands a transfer of resources and effort from the former to the latter, that in the words I have so often quoted, some social services are 'excessive' and others 'inadequate' — that it was bound to be so and that it is so.

The question for us, for the Conservative Party, is whether, having seen this, we put the file into the 'Too Difficult' tray and 'pass by on the other side'. I can see the expediency of that course; I can see the expediency of Ministers not making addresses which explore this kind of territory and arrive at this kind of conclusion . . .

However, I confess that I do not believe a Party, any more than the society which it serves, can fail to suffer if it knowingly allows institutions to fall more and more out of correspondence with contemporary needs. In Britain of the 1960s this challenge of the Welfare State is not isolated: it is but one aspect of the challenge which confronts us throughout the whole political field . . .

The question falls to be posed in different terms in the different fields of policy. Here in the social services, which, in volume of resources involved, represent between one-third and one-half of the activities of the State, the question, it seems to me, cannot be posed by disconnected, spasmodic *pluses* and *minuses* but by presenting a broad and large conception of the manner in which resources ought to be redeployed to meet modern realities, and this will not be done without soberly assessing but boldy facing the in-built obstacles to that redeployment.

From Enoch Powell, *The Welfare State* (Conservative Political Centre, 1961)

B18 Agreement on More Spending, 1973

Two political factors emerge strongly from this 20 years' experience [1950–70]. First is the force of the momentum that drives public expenditure forward. One can identify some slowing-down and acceleration (in addition to the rising cost from pay increases, etc.), but it is difficult in retrospect to link these with specific Government actions, such as 'stop-and-go'. Secondly, one cannot deduce from the figures the existence of a 'high-spending' party and a 'low-spending' party: one cannot even identify party differences on questions of priorities between, e.g. defence and social services, or between one service and another.

The first turning-point in this story was the decision by Sir Winston Churchill's Government to abandon 'Korea' rearmament and drastically curtail defence spending: by 1959 this had gone so far that it had to be reversed. The second turning-point was in the late 1950s, when Mr Macmillan's Government decided implicitly that the expansion of social and environmental programmes then being launched was more important than the desirability of reducing taxation: 'implicitly', for without PESC [The Public Expenditure Survey Committee], government cannot consider such strategic issues with any knowledge of the numbers at stake and thus of the practical implications. The third came in the middle period of Mr Wilson's Government, when the fact had to be faced that this great complex of programmes was hypothecated upon an assumed rate of economic growth that would not happen. This illustrates the darker face of PESC, which is self-destructive if actual spending plans are related to 'targets' or 'objectives' for the rate of growth of resources. In this case, the original growth rate of 4 per cent a year used as the basis for 'Neddy' studies in May 1962, and endorsed as an 'objective' by the 'Neddy' Council in February 1963 was politically inevitably endorsed by Mr Maudling as the basis for the Government's medium-term planning (and of course tacitly by the Labour Opposition also). None of these three turning-points were related to political party issues.

Over the whole 20 years there has been deeply fundamental agreement between the parties that the social and environmental services should be pressed forward hard, with not very much regard for the implications for the national economy (and other widely held political objectives) of the rate of their development. This is not a British phenomenon alone: it has been common to all the advanced democratic countries in the period since Europe's recovery from the war, and it has been one of the powerful pressures making for inflation everywhere. It is nevertheless remarkable that something so huge both in economic terms (now over £16,000 million a year) and in terms of social policy should have advanced over so many years with so little political controversy except on details which over quite short periods show themselves to be unimportant.

From Sir Richard Clarke 'Parliament and Public Expenditure', *The Political Quarterly*, vol. 44, no. 2 (April-June 1973), pp. 137–53. The above extract has been taken from pp. 141–2

B19   Politics and Public Spending, 1978

The Scale and Growth of Public Spending

As Table 1 shows, public expenditure has been rising at a faster rate than Gross Domestic Product (GDP) and has thus increased its share of the latter. This share has risen from approximately 39 per cent. in 1950 to 52 per cent. in 1976 . . . .

Following the rise in the share during the early 1950s, largely

Table 1: Total Public Expenditure and Gross Domestic Product, both at current market prices, 1950–1976 (£'000m)

Year	Total public expenditure (1)	Gross domestic product (2)	Column (1)/Column (2) %
1950	4.87	12.47	39.1
1951	5.54	13.73	40.3
1952	6.21	14.82	41.9
1953	6.51	15.90	40.9
1954	6.67	16.92	39.4
1955	7.06	18.11	39.0
1956	7.53	20.89	36.0
1957	7.94	22.09	35.9
1958	8.31	23.08	36.0
1959	8.77	24.25	36.2
1960	9.40	25.72	36.5
1961	10.31	27.47	37.5
1962	11.01	28.87	38.1
1963	11.67	30.35	38.4
1964	12.76	33.18	38.5
1965	14.14	35.61	39.7
1966	15.32	37.96	40.4
1967	17.52	40.11	43.7
1968	19.10	43.37	44.0
1969	19.78	46.42	42.6
1970	21.86	51.02	42.9
1971	24.33	56.94	42.7
1972	27.38	63.09	43.4
1973	32.32	72.09	44.8
1974	41.93	81.59	51.4
1975	54.47	103.29	52.7
1976	63.34	122.28	51.8

Source: National Income and Expenditure Blue Books (various).

associated with the Korean War, there is then a decline through the 1950s, a rise throughout the 1960s until 1968, a decline in the late 1960s and early 1970s and a very sharp rise in 1974. A further rise in 1975 is followed by a fall in 1976.

Party Influences on Total Public Spending

For those years of our study when the Conservative Party was in office (17 years, i.e. including election years) the average rate of growth of public spending measured in *current market prices* was 9.28 per cent. For Labour (nine years in office) it was 12.98 per cent. Labour Governments, therefore, increased public spending, on average, at a significantly higher rate than Conservative Governments. However, to put the tendency to spend into the context of

GDP increases and also to allow partially for differential rates of inflation experienced by the two parties, we have divided the average rate of growth in total public expenditure by the corresponding rate of growth of GDP (Conservative 8.30 per cent and Labour 11.07 per cent) to produce a spending ratio.

For the Conservative Party's total period in office this spending ratio was 1.12 compared with a ratio of 1.17 for Labour periods of office. When set in the context of GDP growth and measured over the long term, Labour governments emerge with a tendency to increase public spending only marginally faster than Conservative governments. This is a somewhat surprising finding, given what might have been expected on the basis of differing published ideologies of the two parties on the desirable degree of State intervention, public ownership, etc.

In Table 2 the ratios of rate of growth of public spending to rate of growth of GDP are shown separately for each period of office.

Table 2: Rate of Growth in Public Spending as a Ratio of Rate of Growth in GDP for Each Period of Government, 1950–1976

Date	1950–1951	1951–1955	1955–1959	1959–1964	1964–1966	1966–1970	1970–1974	1974–1976
Party	Lab.	Cons.	Cons.	Cons.	Lab.	Lab.	Cons.	Lab.
Spending ratios	1.42	0.78	0.80	1.23	1.41	1.23	1.44	1.00

Although over the whole period under study the two parties emerge with little difference between them in terms of overall spending ratio, the trends for each particular party are quite different. Successive Labour Governments have steadily reduced their tendency to spend at a faster rate than GDP growth, the ratio falling from 1.42 in 1950–51, through 1.41, 1.23, to 1.00. Conservative Governments, on the other hand, have steadily increased their spending ratio, from 0.78 in relation to GDP growth in 1951–55, through 0.80, 1.23 to 1.44 during their last period in office. The two parties have thus moved in opposite directions to that expected, each becoming more like the other once was.

This convergence of spending ratios prompts a number of questions. Are we to assume that such a convergence is a reflection of the postulated broader tendency for political parties to move towards the centre (and thus towards each other)? Do these spending trends reflect a deliberate change of fundamental policy about which the parties have been publicly less than frank? Do they reflect overwhelming external circumstances which have pushed the parties in a direction other than that intended? (To the latter we might suggest that this sort of explanation seems more plausible in the case of external pressures forcing reductions in spending, e.g. 1966–70 post-devaluation and 1974–76 IMF pressures) but the same reasoning can hardly be applied when the movement is towards increasing public spending, e.g. 1970–74, the latter part of which, as we have already shown, witnessed the biggest single jump in public spending in all 26 years of the study.

Table 2 also indicates that in relation to GDP growth, public spending has not simply steadily increased, with each government forced into the spending mould of the previous government, but that governments have been able to alter the inherited pattern. There are sharp contrasts between different electoral periods when government changed party, e.g. after 1951, after 1970 and after 1974 and even when the same party remained in office, e.g. 1959–64 compared with 1955–59.

Comparison of Growth Rates of Individual Programmes during Total Period of Office for Each Party, 1950–1976

In this section we examine the progress of the individual programmes under different governments to see if the different parties, over their total period in office have exhibited different spending patterns. Programme spending priorities for each party are shown in descending order in Table 3. A comparison of programme priorities between the two parties is shown in Table 4.

At the aggregate level we have seen . . . that adjusted public spending increased only marginally faster during Labour periods of office overall than Conservative. A study of the individual programmes on the same basis, however (Tables 3 and 4), reveals some major differences.

The Conservative Party in office can be seen in retrospect to have pursued the following programmes (in descending order) considerably more forcefully, in spending terms, than Labour Governments: Housing, Agriculture, Research, Environmental Services, External Relations and to a lesser degree, Roads and Public Lighting, Other Industry and Trade and Education. We might note in particular Housing (which grew on an adjusted basis by 1.57 per

Table 3: Spending Priorities for Each Party as Indicated by Individual Programme Growth Rates adjusted by Growth Rates of GDP, during all Labour and during all Conservative Years of Office, 1950–1976

Labour		Conservative	
Employment Services	2.67	Research	1.67
Personal Social Services	1.76	Personal Social Services	1.62
Transport & Communication	1.57	Housing	1.57
Law & Order	1.38	Environmental Services	1.56
Social Security Benefits	1.28	Transport & Communication	1.39
Education, etc.	1.26	Other Industry & Trade	1.36
Other Industry & Trade	1.25	Education, etc.	1.33
Defence	1.19	Law & Order	1.33
Roads & Public Lighting	1.16	Roads & Public Lighting	1.31
National Health Service	1.15	External Relations	1.26
Research	1.10	Social Security Benefits	1.24
Finance & Tax Collection	1.07	National Health Service	1.13
Environmental Services	1.04	Employment Services	1.00
External Relations	.84	Finance & Tax Collection	.87
Housing	.80	Defence	.70
Agriculture, etc.	.44	Agriculture, etc.	.69

cent annually under Conservative governments against 0.80 per cent under Labour governments). The other item which might cause some surprise is the slightly faster growth rate of Education spending under Conservative governments than Labour (1.33 per cent, against 1.26 per cent).

On the other hand, the Labour Party in office can be seen in retrospect to have pursued the following programmes (in descending order) considerably more forcefully in spending terms than Conservative governments: Employment Services, Defence, Finance and Tax Collection and, to a lesser extent, Transport and Communications, Personal Social Services, Law and Order, Social Security and N.H.S.

It is surely surprising that there was so little difference between the two parties in those programmes which are considered to be so fundamental to the Welfare State idea — Personal Social Services, Social Security and Health, to all of which Labour in its public pronouncements would claim a greater commitment than Conservatives.

It is also perhaps surprising to find Defence spending increasing substantially more rapidly under Labour governments than Conservatives, given the greater public commitment of the latter to Defence, although part of the relatively higher rate can be attributed to the high level of Korean War spending which particularly affected Labour in the year 1950–51. It is in fact now the policy of both parties to increase Defence spending by 3 per cent in real terms per annum. It would not seem unreasonable to assume, where there are substantial differences in the long-term spending ratios between the two parties, that this implies a clear difference of priorities.

Table 4: Comparison of Individual Programme Spending Growth Rates, adjusted by Growth Rate of GDP, during all Labour and during all Conservative Years of Office, 1950–1976, ranked by Relative Party Priorities

	Labour	Conservative	Ratio (higher to lower)
Total Public Expenditure	1.17	1.12	1.04
Programmes increasing faster under Conservative Governments			
Housing	.80	1.57	1.96
Agriculture, etc.	.44	.69	1.57
Research[a]	1.10	1.67	1.52
Environmental Services	1.04	1.56	1.50
External Relations[a]	.84	1.26	1.50
Roads & Public Lighting	1.16	1.31	1.13
Other Industry & Trade	1.25	1.36	1.09
Education, etc.	1.26	1.33	1.06
Programmes increasing faster under Labour Governments			
Employment Services	2.67	1.00	2.67
Defence	1.19	.70	1.70
Finance & Tax Collection	1.07	.87	1.23
Transport & Communications	1.57	1.39	1.13
Personal Social Services	1.76	1.62	1.09
Law & Order	1.38	1.33	1.04
Social Security	1.28	1.24	1.03
National Health Service	1.15	1.13	1.02

[a] 1955–76 figures, as comparable figures not available for earlier governments.

From F. Gould and B. Roweth, 'Politics and Public Spending', *The Political Quarterly*, vol. 49, no. 2 (April-June 1978), pp. 222–27. Certain omissions have been made from the original article.

PRINCIPLES AND TECHNIQUES OF RESOURCE ALLOCATION

B20   Crosland: Universality and Social Equality, 1956

It appears that while social equality of course requires universal *availability* of the public service (though not necessarily completely universal use), it does not always require universal *free* availability. And there is all the difference, from the point of view of avoiding social differentiation, between a test of means which determines the right to use a service, and one which determines only the question of payment. Thus if beds in state hospitals were to be provided only for national assistance beneficiaries, or if old-age pensions were to be paid only subject to a means test, the sick or the elderly would be denied the right of unconditional *access* to the service; they would first have to apply to the State, and produce evidence of destitution. This would lay a clear mark of social inferiority on those who applied, who would openly confess themselves as incapable of self-support. The test of means is here both a denial of access unless certain conditions are satisfied, and a means of isolating the poorest section of the community.

But granted the right of access, an income-test to determine the question of completely free access — one, that is, which requires the state to apply to the citizen for a recovery of charges, and not the citizen to apply to the state for the right to use the service — need neither offend against social equality, nor cause humiliation, provided that two conditions are fulfilled. First, the benefit or service must not be so essential, and so large in relation to the recipient's means, that he may reasonably consider he has a social right to it, so that both his real income and self-esteem would be severely affected by a test of means. This rules out an income-test both for the basic cash benefits, which often constitute almost the whole of the recipient's income, and for the central, essential health and education services. Secondly, the income-line should be set as high as possible. If only paupers are excluded from the need to pay, there is more danger of inferior feelings arising than if only surtax-payers are compelled to pay. The income-test applied to University awards, for example, which exacts no payment below a certain level, then a graduated payment, with full payment only above £2,000, cannot be said to cause social inequalities — especially as tutors and fellow-students have no means of detecting who is grant-aided and who is not.

Thus the link between free universality and social equality is rather tenuous. On the one hand, social equality is not necessarily threatened by an ascertainment of means, subject to certain conditions. And on the other, the provision of free and universally available services will not enhance social equality if they are much inferior to the corresponding private services. They will then simply not be used by better-off people; and class differentiation will be in no way diminished.

Social equality mainly requires the creation of standards of public health, education, and housing so high that no marked qualitative gap remains between public and private provision. It will then matter little whether or not occasional charges are imposed, subject to the above conditions. While as for universal use, this will either follow automatically (or perhaps be enforced by a growing equality of incomes); and even if it does not, and some diehard snobs continue to prefer their private doctors, this will really be of little moment. But the important point is that 'universality' must follow *from* social equality, and cannot itself create it.

From C.A.R. Crosland. *The Future of Socialism* (Jonathan Cape, 1967 ed.)

B21 Titmuss: The Real Challenge in Welfare, 1968

Today, with this heritage, we face the positive challenge of providing selective, high quality services for poor people over a large and complex range of welfare; of positively discriminating on a territorial, group or 'right' basis in favour of the poor, the handicapped, the deprived, the coloured, the homeless, and the social casualties of our society. Universalism is not, by itself alone, enough: in medical care, in wage-related social security, and in education. This much we have learnt in the past two decades from the facts about inequalities in the distribution of incomes and wealth, and in our failure to close many gaps in differential access to and effective utilization of particular branches of our social services.

If I am right, I think that Britain is beginning to identify the dimensions of this challenge of positive, selective discrimination — in income maintenance, in education, in housing, in medical care and mental health, in child welfare, and in the tolerant integration of immigrants and citizens from overseas; of preventing especially the second generation from becoming (and of seeing themselves as) second-class citizens. We are seeking ways and means, values, methods and techniques, of positive discrimination without the infliction, actual or imagined, of a sense of personal failure and individual fault.

At this point, considering the nature of the search in all its ramifying complexities, I must now state my general conclusion. It is this. The challenge that faces us is not the choice between universalist and selective social services. The real challenge resides in the question: what particular infrastructure of universalist services is needed in order to provide a framework of values and opportunity bases within and around which can be developed socially acceptable selective services aiming to discriminate positively, with the minimum risk of stigma, in favour of those whose needs are greatest.

This, to me, is the fundamental challenge. In different ways and in particular areas it confronts the Supplementary Benefits Commission, the Seebohm Committee, the National Health Service, the Ministry of Housing and Local Government, the National Committee for Commonwealth Immigrants, the policy-making readers of the Newsom Report and the Plowden Report on educational priority areas, the Scottish Report, *Social Work and the Community*, and thousands of social workers and administrators all over the country wrestling with the problems of needs and priorities. In all the main spheres of need, some structure of universalism is an essential pre-requisite to selective positive discrimination; it provides a general system of values and a sense of community; socially approved agencies for clients, patients and consumers, and also for the recruitment, training and deployment of staff at all levels; it sees welfare, not as a burden, but as complementary and as an instrument of change and, finally, it allows positive discriminatory services to be provided as rights for categories of people and for classes of need in terms of priority social areas and other impersonal classifications.

Without this infrastructure of welfare resources and framework of values we should not, I conclude, be able to identify and discuss the next steps in progress towards a 'Welfare Society'.

From R.M. Titmuss, *Commitment to Welfare* (Allen & Unwin, 2nd edn, 1976)

B22   Seldon: Universal *and* Selective Benefits? 1968

It would seem clear that social services and benefits can be supplied either to everyone or only to people identified by a financial measure of income, means, or need. State education is either available universally or only to children of parents with income below a stated figure; medical care is available to all social insurance contributors or for payment of a charge that is reimbursed to people below a given income; housing is available at below-market rents either to everyone on a waiting list or at market rents partly reimbursed to people with income below a given level; pensions are paid to everyone aged 60 or 65 or only to those with an income below a stated amount; and so on.

British social services and benefits are predominantly universal. There are many means tests for individual services and benefits, which are therefore selective. But the distinction in principle is unambiguous; and the overwhelming area of expenditure is on universal benefits. Of £1,350 million spent on education in the latest year only £175 million was paid on a means test, almost none of the £1,250 million spent on the National Health Service, an unknown proportion of the £750 million on housing subsidies and only £300 million of the £2,450 million on social security benefits. All the rest went on services or on transfer payments available for all who otherwise qualified for them by age, residence or other condition that had little or nothing to do with income, means or needs.

Until recently the academic and political debate was clearly between the *principles* of universality and selectivity. The arguments for universality ranged from high moral invocation of the badge of citizenship through the avoidance of the stigma of financial segregation to the mundane administrative convenience and simplicity of general distribution: they either accepted abortive benefits as a price of simple administration or tried to mop up some of the waste by taxation. Recently two of the leading academic advocates of universality seem to have changed their minds. Professor Abel-Smith now accepts that 'the most obvious remedy is to concentrate help where it is needed and to stop giving it where it is not' but believes it may take a decade to develop the required means tests; and he also accepts the possibility of a negative income tax administered by the Inland Revenue. Professor Titmuss's change of mind has taken a more interesting turn. In his Official War History, *Problems of Social Policy*, he argued eloquently for universalism; he now agrees, in circumlocutory sociological language, that the choice between universality and selectivity is false:

> The challenge that faces us is not the choice between universalism and selective social services. The real challenge resides in the question: what particular infrastructure of universalist services is needed in order to provide a framework of values and opportunity bases within and around which can be developed socially acceptable selective services aiming to discriminate positively, with the minimum risk of stigma, in favour of those whose needs are greatest.

In simple English, it is now proper for some services to be universal and for others to be selective. Or is it acceptable for some to be universal (or selective) at some periods in life, or in given circumstances, permanently or temporarily? Whatever the meaning, it is apparently no longer essential to make all services universal in order to respect human dignity. Discrimination, singling out, social divisiveness, segregation by a financial measure, is acceptable in some circumstances, or for some people. Social benefits need no longer be wholly universal, equal without regard to (varying) individual circumstances. The welfare state may now properly comprise universal and selective services; social benefits may now be both equal and unequal.

The academic advocates of unqualified universalism on principle are in an intellectual dilemma from which they cannot escape except by concession of error. If selectivity is morally repugnant there can be no room for selective benefits, even as a superstructure for a substructure of universal benefits. If selectivity is, at last, morally acceptable, there can be no moral reason for insistence on a substructure of wasteful universal benefits. Economic circumstance, intellectual argument and the belated recognition that generalised benefits are inhumane have destroyed the case for universalism. Nor should refuge be taken in attempts to pay lip service to both principles, formerly regarded as moral opposites, now joined in an administrative *mariage de convenance*.

The universalist/selectivists have been reduced to their parlous straits by the mounting evidence of inadequacy in tax revenue and misdirection in universal benefits that show no signs of removing the persistent pockets of need among old people, large families, incapacitated and others and of the evident desire of many with rising incomes to provide for themselves education, medical care and housing and pensions better than the state can provide in a centralised, standardised, stagnant service. These are the underlying two socio-economic trends that are making the Beveridge doctrine of universal benefits out of date barely 20 years after they were introduced. They are also provoking a disturbing revolution in thinking among social administrators who can distinguish between human needs and social philosophy. They are causing a rift between the academic universalists and the politicians who have had to change their minds in two years of office. And they will produce social policies in the coming two decades far different from those envisaged by the two main political parties three years ago.

From A. Seldon, *Taxation and Welfare* (Institute of Economic Affairs, London, Research Monograph 14, 1968)

B23   Universality and Selectivity — Ideological Irrelevancies, 1971

It is arguable that if a discipline is to play any effective part in the short-term amelioration of social problems, its practitioners must be prepared to compromise on issues of principle. At the same time, the moral commitment must and will survive so long as the practitioners themselves differ over the means and ends of social-welfare provision. The most generalized and clearly articulated forms of these ideological differences over ends are expressed in the 'institutional' and 'residual' models of social welfare. As means of achieving these ends, universalism and selectivity are more interchangeable procedures than is often supposed.

The key conceptual distinction may therefore lie between 'institutional' and 'residual' models of social welfare rather than 'universalism' and 'selectivity' as methods of allocation. In these ideal forms, the 'institutional' model of social welfare is one in which there is a powerful value commitment to universalist forms of welfare provision, supplemented where necessary by selectivist services. Allocation takes the form of positive discrimination programmes rather than means tests. In practice, however, means tests tend to proliferate on an *ad hoc* basis because positive discrimination programmes are unable to differentiate between individuals and groups with sufficient finesse.

Residualist models of social welfare display a strong value

commitment to selectivist form of welfare provision, supplemented where necessary by universalist services. Allocation takes the form of means tests, which in practice often affect receivers as negative acts of discrimination. Again, in practical terms, some minimum framework of universalist services tends to emerge and become institutionalized, usually for reasons of administrative convenience.

So long as conditions of scarcity prevail and demand potentially exceeds the supply of social services, forms of rationing prevail. The institutionist begins with generosity and is driven reluctantly towards stringency in allocation. The residualist starts with stringency and is driven reluctantly towards generosity. The overall effect on the recipient is a more uniform one than ideologists of either the left or the right will care to admit. Only if one group ceases to press its case will the balance shift markedly.

We can therefore identify the 'institutional' and 'residual' models of social welfare as the two major value-orientations amongst specialists in social administration. In the actual context of policy-making and administration, compromises of one kind or another are the rule. The persistence of scarcity, the existence of many different kinds of claim upon national resources and the desire to do the best for those in greatest need combine to weaken the appeal of uncompromising universalism or selectivism to policy-makers. None the less, radical minorities still attempt to influence policy and to negate the real or imagined influence of their rivals. The radical right favours selectivity in order to prevent waste, encourage thrift and give effective aid to the social groups in greatest need. In order to achieve these ends, forms of statutory intervention such as a 'reverse income tax' are proposed. (Such schemes would have been interpreted by Dicey as examples of rampant collectivism.) Similarly, the radical left is prepared to countenance superannuation schemes of graduated contribution and benefit which represent drastic modifications of traditional forms of universalism. This seems to be as far as radicalism goes in the context of social policy and administration, where relatively frequent contact with the realities and complexities of human need quickly sobers the enthusiasm of ideologists and utopians.

In the context of democratic politics, the related concepts of relativism and proportionate justice act as a kind of catalyst, inexorably transforming universalists into reluctant selectivists and selectivists into reluctant universalists. Universalism and selectivism may therefore be seen to be alive in principle but dead in practice, just as the nineteenth-century struggle between collectivist and individualist doctrines was largely the invention of an intellectual minority. The conflict that breaks out from time to time is largely a battle between ideological ghosts, but the echoes of their gunfire serve as necessary reminders to policy-makers that issues of principle are involved. In different metaphorical terms, the ideological skeletons may hang in separate cupboards, but the same political wind rattles both sets of bones.

From R. Pinker, *Social Theory and Social Policy* (Heinemann Educational, 1971)

SOCIAL POLICY AND POVERTY

B24 Titmuss: The Need for a New Approach, 1962

To study the rich and the sources of power in society is not the kind of activity which comes easily to social workers attempting to understand the human condition. Traditionally, they have been concerned with the poor and the consequences of poverty and physical handicap. They have thus tended to take — perhaps were compelled to take — a limited view of what constituted poverty. It was a view circumscribed by the immediate, the obvious and the material; a conception of need shaped by the urgencies of life daily confronting those they were seeking to help. In so far as they looked at relativities and inequalities in society — which they seldom did — they restricted their studies to the day-to-day differences in levels of expenditure on the more obvious or more blatant necessities of life. Daily subsistence was both the yardstick and the objective.

Far-reaching changes affecting the structure and functions of social institutions; general improvements in material standards of living; and the growth of knowledge about the causes and consequences of social ills in the modern community, are now forcing on us the task of re-defining poverty. Subsistence is no longer thought to be a scientifically meaningful or politically constructive notion. We are thus having to place the concept of poverty in the context of social change and interpret it in relation to the growth of more complex and specialized institutions of power, authority and privilege. We cannot, in other words, delineate the new frontiers of poverty unless we take account of the changing agents and characteristics of inequality. How then is poverty to be measured today and on what criteria, secular, social and psychological?

Each generation has to undertake anew this task of re-interpretation if it wishes to uphold its claim to share in the constant renewal of civilized values. Yet the present generation, it must be conceded, has been somewhat tardy in accepting this obligation. It has been too content to use the tools which were forged in the past for measuring poverty and inequality.

These tools are now too blunt, insensitive and inadequate. They do not go deep enough. These also are the lessons thrown up by this particular study of one of the primary sources of knowledge about the distribution of incomes. They yield a surface view of society which is increasingly at variance with other facts and with the evidence of one's eyes.

What, it may be asked, has prevented us from sharpening these tools of inquiry and applying them with more precision to contemporary Britain? Three by no means inclusive reasons may be provocatively advanced.

First it may be said that modern societies with a strongly rooted and relatively rigid class structure do not take kindly to self-examination. The major stimulus to social inquest in Britain during the present century has come from the experience of war. On each occasion this experience was sufficiently mortifying to weaken temporarily the forces of inertia and resistance to change. In the absence of such stimuli in the future, we may have quite consciously to invent and nourish new ways and means of national self-examination. This task may be harder to discharge in the face of rising standards of living and the growing influence of the mass media of complacency. Perhaps the most powerful challenge of all will come from the notion that economic growth will solve all our social problems involving choice, distribution and priorities.

Secondly, it becomes clearer as we learn to distinguish between the promise of social legislation and its performance that the present generation has been mesmerised by the language of 'The Welfare State'. It was assumed too readily after 1948 that all the answers had been found to the problems of health, education, social welfare and housing, and that what was little more than an administrative tidying-up of social security provisions represented a social revolution. The origins and strength of this climate of opinion — some illustrations of which are given later — will no doubt continue to absorb historians for a long time to come.

Thirdly, and concomitantly, the 1950s saw the spread of the idea that some natural built-in 'law' was steadily leading to a greater equality of incomes and standards of living. It followed implicitly from this theory that further economic growth would hasten the operation of the natural law of equalization. This was not a new thesis; Marshall had stated it hopefully over seventy years ago: 'the social and economic forces already at work are changing the distribution of (income) for the better; . . . they are persistent and increasing in strength; and . . . their influence is for the greater part cumulative.'

From R.M. Titmuss, *Income Distribution and Social Change* (Allen & Unwin, 1962)

B25   Abel-Smith and Townsend: The Rediscovery of Poverty, 1965

The limited object of the work upon which this report is based was to find out from data collected in government income and expenditure surveys in two post-war years as much as possible about the levels of living and the social characteristics of the poorest section of the population in the United Kingdom. In the process we have defined and used a national assistance standard of living, have re-applied a subsistence standard adopted in an earlier study of poverty (by Rowntree and Lavers in 1950), and have given some account of the extent to which households range in income and expenditure from the average for their type. In this chapter we will first of all discuss whether the evidence for 1953–54 and 1960 allows us to draw conclusions about changes in living conditions between the two years. We will then discuss briefly some of the implications of this report for future research, for government information services and for government action.

This is not the place for a searching discussion of reforms in social security. All that we wish to point out is that there is a two-fold implication for social policy of the evidence in this report — not only that a substantial minority of the population in addition to those receiving national assistance live at or below national assistance standards, but also that a substantial minority are not receiving national assistance and yet appear to qualify for it. The legitimacy of the system of national assistance is therefore called into question.

Possibly the most novel finding is the extent of poverty among children. For over a decade it has been generally assumed that such poverty as exists is found overwhelmingly among the aged. Unfortunately it has not been possible to estimate from the data used in this study exactly how many persons over minimum pensionable age were to be found among the $7\frac{1}{2}$ million persons with low income in 1960. However, such data as we have suggest that the number may be around 3 million. There were thus more people who were not aged than were aged among the poor households of 1960. We have estimated earlier that there were about $2\frac{1}{4}$ million children in low income households in 1960. Thus quantitatively the problem of poverty among children is more than two-thirds of the size of poverty among the aged. This fact has not been given due emphasis in the policies of the political parties. It is also worth observing that there were substantially more children in poverty than adults of working age.

There is a simple if relatively expensive remedy for the problem of poverty among children — to substantially increase family allowances, particularly for the larger family. Alternatively, part of the problem could be dealt with at relatively low cost by allowing national assistance to be drawn despite the fact that the breadwinner is receiving full-time earnings. Such a proposal would mean overriding more than a century of conventional wisdom about incentives. However assistance is paid to families receiving full-time earnings in several States in the United States and this policy enjoys the tacit support of the American trade unions. The acceptance of this principle would make it possible to deal with the problem of poverty among 'wage stopped' families already receiving assistance and among large families with a breadwinner in full-time work. In the case of the latter group, however, there would remain the problem of families who were not prepared to apply to the Board for help.

. . . Between 1953 and 1960 the Ministry of Labour surveys suggest that the number of persons living at low levels increased from 7.8 per cent to 14.2 per cent. Of the difference of 6.4 per cent we would estimate that about $1\frac{1}{2}$ per cent was due to a better representation in the sample of aged persons in 1960 than in 1953 and another 0.5 or 1 per cent to a fuller representation in the sample of national assistance recipients other than the aged. Very little of the difference seems to be due to a change, relative to wages, in the definition of 'low levels of living', but part of it (about 2 per cent) seems to be due to the fact that the definition was based on income in 1960 and expenditure in 1953–54. None the less, some part of the apparent increase from 7.8 to 14.2 per cent seems attributable to (*a*) the relative increase in the number of old people in the population, (*b*) a slight relative increase in the number of men in late middle age who are chronically sick, and (*c*) the relative increase in the number of families with four or more children, at a time when family allowances have increased much less than average industrial earnings and when the wages of some low-paid workers may not have increased as much as average industrial earnings. On the whole the data we have presented contradicts the commonly held view that a trend towards greater equality has accompanied the trend towards greater affluence.

In general, we regard our figures for 1960 to be the more accurate even though we believe that they understate the numbers of the population with low levels of living because of the under-representation of the aged and the sick. We may summarise our findings for that year by saying that about 5–6 per cent of the population were in low income households because wages, even when supplemented by family allowances, were insufficient to raise them above the minimum level. A further 3–4 per cent were in households receiving social insurance benefits (principally pensions) but the latter were insufficient. Many such households would probably be entitled to national assistance but for various reasons had not applied for it. A further 4–5 per cent of the population were in low income households because, under various regulations, they were not entitled to the full scale of national assistance grant or because the minimum we have taken is considerably above the *basic* national assistance scale.

Even if we take a substantially lower base line — the basic assistance scale plus rent — we find that about 2 million people (3.8 per cent of the population) were living in households with exceptionally low incomes. For about a quarter of them the problem was inadequate earnings and family allowances; for nearly half of them the problem was inadequate social insurance benefits coupled with unwillingness to apply for national assistance, and for the remainder the amount of national assistance being received was apparently inadequate.

In terms of national information we conclude from the evidence that steps should be taken by the government to ensure that regular surveys are made of the living conditions of the poorest households in our society and that reports should be published showing their sources of income and how their social characteristics compare with those of other households.

Finally, we conclude that the evidence of substantial numbers of the population living below national assistance level, and also of substantial numbers seeming to be eligible for national assistance but not receiving it, calls for a radical review of the whole social security scheme. Moreover, the fact that nearly a third of the poor were children suggests the need for a readjustment of priorities in plans for extensions and developments.

From B. Abel-Smith and P. Townsend, *The Poor and the Poorest* (George Bell & Son, 1965)

B26   The Cycle of Disadvantage, 1976

To What Extent Are Problems of Disadvantage Still With Us?

The concept of a cycle of deprivation (or disadvantage, as we have preferred to call it) began with the question: 'why is it that . . . deprivation and problems of maladjustment so conspicuously persist?' It is appropriate to begin, therefore, with a consideration of how far the assumptions behind the question are correct. As we have seen, it is indeed true that disadvantage is still very much with us. Although there have been marked improvements in the overall standards of living in this country, poverty remains. Moreover, inequalities in income and wealth are almost as great as they were at the turn of the century, and regional variations in patterns of disadvantage with respect to employment have continued with little change since the First World War. The quality of housing in Britain has steadily improved during this century but even so, one in four children is reared in a home which is overcrowded or lacking in basic amenities.

On the whole, educational attainments (as assessed by reading age) have shown a substantial improvement since the Second World War and the average level of intelligence may also have shown a marginal rise. Nevertheless, the level of illiteracy remains high and there are marked differences between geographical areas in reading standards. Low attainments are especially marked in inner city areas. Furthermore, the rise in reading standards after the war seems to have halted . . .

The net amount of social mobility has probably changed little during this century but there has been a reduction in the proportion of unskilled and semiskilled workers, with a corresponding overall upward mobility. However, the gap between the social classes with respect to infantile mortality, educational progress, economic resources, working conditions, and ill-health remains almost as wide as it has ever been.

Crime rates have markedly risen during the last 50 years and it seems that this reflects an increase in both the amount of crime and the number of criminals, and not simply changes in the law or police practices. No adequate data exist regarding changes over time in the rates of psychiatric disorder, but it seems unlikely that the rates have fallen appreciably. Again, there are large differences in the prevalence of crime and psychiatric disorder according to area, with inner city areas showing the highest level of troubles.

The patterns of parenting and of family life have altered considerably in recent years, with marked trends towards earlier marriage and earlier child-bearing, a higher proportion of illegitimate children, more frequent divorce and smaller families. The concept of 'problem-families' is too vague to allow any accurate estimate of changes in frequency, but what evidence there is indicates that there continues to be a substantial number of families with multiple problems, some of which involve prolonged dependency on social services.

A second question is how far the continuing presence of disadvantage is due to some form of intergenerational continuity and how far it arises afresh in each succeeding generation. Undoubtedly there are continuities over time. However, only some of these involve familial continuity. Regional continuities in disadvantage, for example, are very striking. Thus, for many years Scotland and the northern parts of England have had particularly high rates of unemployment and of poorly paid workers. Since the First World War, geographical differences in suicide rates have remained remarkably stable. During a similar time period, the same parts of London have maintained the highest rates of delinquency. Over a decade at least, variations between schools in delinquency rates have been shown to be remarkably persistent. Both psychiatric disorder and reading difficulties are very much more prevalent in inner city areas. Continuities may also be evident within socio-cultural groups. During the two generations or so that black people have been in this country, they have continued to be disadvantaged in educational attainment, employment and housing. All of these patterns constitute a form of cycle of disadvantage but in no case is the continuity familial.

Nevertheless, familial continuities do occur. With respect to intelligence, educational attainment, occupational status, crime, psychiatric disorder and 'problem-family' status there are moderate continuities over two generations. Continuities for many aspects of family life are generally fairly slight although they are substantial in the case of severe abnormalities in parenting such as child-battering. Almost no information is available on their strength with regard to normal patterns of parenting, poverty or poor housing.

However, several qualifications have to be made concerning intergenerational continuities. In the first place, even with forms of disadvantage where they are strong, discontinuities are striking. At least half of the children born into a disadvantaged home do not repeat the pattern of disadvantage in the next generation. Over half of all forms of disadvantage arise anew each generation. On the one hand, even where continuity is strongest many individuals break out of the cycle and on the other many people become disadvantaged without having been reared by disadvantaged parents. In short, familial cycles are a most important element in the perpetuation of disadvantage but they account for only a part of the overall picture.

A second qualification is that continuities are much weaker over three generations than they are over two. Reed and Reed found that a third of mentally retarded individuals had mentally retarded parents but only one in six of their children and one in twenty-five of their grandchildren was retarded. Even in cases with the strongest family histories of retardation only 16 per cent of the grandchildren were retarded. The same marked reduction in continuities over several generations has been found for all other forms of disadvantage which have been systematically studied.

Thirdly, not only does the extent of continuity vary according to *type* of disadvantage but also it varies considerably according to *level* of disadvantage. Thus, social mobility is much less marked in professional groups than it is amongst skilled manual workers. Similarly, severe mental retardation (IQ below 50) shows almost no intergenerational continuity whereas continuity is moderately strong for mild degrees of retardation or for intelligence within the normal range.

From M. Rutter and N. Madge, *Cycles of Disadvantage, A Review of Research* (Heinemann Educational, 1976)

B27   Townsend: Stratification and Resources, 1979

Living standards depend on the total contribution of not one but several systems distributing resources to individuals, families, workgroups and communities. To concentrate on cash incomes is to ignore the subtle ways developed in both modern and traditional societies for conferring and redistributing benefits. Moreover, to concentrate on income as the sole criterion of poverty also implies that relatively simple adjustments, as might be made in a single scheme for negative income tax, will relieve it.

A plural approach is unavoidable. Thus, the list given below shows the types of resource arising from the principal systems of resource distribution. Even a fleeting reference to the different systems in society which distribute and redistribute resources, such as the wage system, insurance and banking, social security and services like the National Health Service, may suggest that poverty is the creation of their complex interrelationship, or perhaps, more fundamentally, of the values and norms upon which they rest or which they continuously reinforce. The practical implication is that the abolition of poverty may require comprehensive structural change in not one but several institutional systems. The problem is to establish, first, the part that the different types of resource play in determining the overall standards of living of different strata in the population, and secondly, which of the systems underlying the distribution of that resource can be manipulated most efficiently to reduce poverty. The list is as follows:

1. Cash income:
   (a) Earned.
   (b) Unearned.
   (c) Social security.

2. Capital assets:
   (a) House/flat occupied by family, and living facilities.
   (b) Assets (other than occupied house) and savings.

3. Value of employment benefits in kind:
   (a) Employers' fringe benefits; subsidies and value of occupational insurance.
   (b) Occupational facilities.

4. Value of public social services in kind:
   Including government subsidies and services, e.g. health, education and housing but excluding social security.

5. Private income in kind:
   (a) Home production (e.g. of smallholding or garden).
   (b) Gifts.
   (c) Value of personal supporting services.

To obtain full information about all these types of resource for a representative cross-section of households is an ambitious but necessary task. Each of the types of resource can be defined in detail and converted (sometimes though arbitrarily and with difficulty) into equivalent cash-income values. The distribution of each in the population can be examined. Individual income units and households can be ranked according to each dimension and a measure of total rank achieved. The way can be opened for the measurement of the contribution made by different resource systems to both inequality and poverty . . .

One of the purposes of combining the ranking of resources in different dimensions would be to allow *total* and *partial* poverty to be distinguished. If resources are distributed by different institutional systems, then it follows that while some people may lack a minimal share of any of these resources, there will be others who lack a minimal share of one or two of these types of resource but have a substantial share of others. Alternatively, the level of total resources may be sufficient to avoid deprivation in one or more but not all major spheres of life. Thus in Britain there are, for example, fatherless families with identically low cash incomes, but whose other resources differ sharply. There are those who live in the slum areas of cities in very bad, overcrowded housing, with schools and hospitals of poor quality near by. And there are those who live in new council housing estates on the fringe of cities or in new towns, in good housing with spacious, modern schools and hospitals near by with modern facilities and equipment. The standards of living of these two sets of families are not at all equivalent. Whether instances such as these are common is unknown.

Another advantage is to trace more clearly the differences between *temporary* and *long-term* poverty. The distribution of resources changes over time. People are promoted within the wage system; they change jobs, and become unemployed or sick; they obtain new dependants. Clearly there may be major changes in the possession of resources both in the long term, over the entire life-cycle, but also in the short term, from month to month and even week to week. The life-cycle of poverty, first described by Seebohm Rowntree, requires contemporary documentation. A proportion of the population may always have been poor, but a much larger proportion have had occasional or periodic but not continuous experience of poverty.

Just as I have argued that a wider concept of 'resources' should replace 'income' in the study of inequality and poverty, so I would argue that 'style of living' should replace 'consumption' (or more narrowly still, 'nutritional intakes') in determining what levels in the ranking of resources should be regarded as constituting deprivation.

There are subtle gradations of styles of living ramifying through society as well as different mixes of national and local styles for different communities and ethnic groups. Different classes may engage in similar types of activity, such as going on a holiday or holding a birthday party for children, but do them differently. In developing an operational definition of style of living it is therefore necessary to distinguish (a) types of custom and social activity practised or approved, and home, environmental and work conditions enjoyed or expected by a majority of the national population; (b) the types of custom and social activity practised or approved by a majority of people in a locality, community, class, racial group, religious sect or work group; and (c) the specific content and manner of individual and group expression of both national and local customs or practices. It is hypothesized that, with a diminishing level of resources, people will engage less fully in the national 'style of living'. At relatively low levels of resources people find they are unable to enjoy a wide representation of consumer goods, customs and activities and are able to enjoy only cheaper versions of some goods, customs and activities. The range is reduced proportionately to falling levels of resources. The reduction is more gradual than the diminishing resources would suggest, because of the need to maintain social cohesion or integration. Through state, industry, community, church and family, means are found, for example, through mass production and the mass media, to satisfy and integrate the relatively hard up. But at still lower levels of individual and family resources, economical forms of social participation become impossible to provide. People's participation in the national style of living diminishes disproportionately.

From P. Townsend, *Poverty in the United Kingdom* (Allen Lane, 1979)

B28   The Causes of Poverty, 1979

Among those with earnings, does poverty mainly stem from low pay? It appears not. Of workers in the bottom 10 per cent of income relative to SB only one fifth were in the bottom 10 per cent of hourly earnings. The reason is that the poorest workers are men with large families, many of whom earn a reasonably high wage, while most of those on the lowest pay are married women, whose earnings ensure that the family is not among the poorest.

In fact, whether a wife works is a crucial determinant of whether a family is financially speaking poor. Even when the husband has very low earnings, only 18 per cent of families have incomes below 140 per cent of SB if the wife works, compared with 76 per cent if she does not. (This comparison of course ignores the greater cost of child-care that may accrue to the family if the wife works and the loss of the time she would otherwise spend on housework or on leisure.) Not surprisingly the lower the husband's wage, the more likely the wife is to work. If the husband is sick or unemployed, the family is much more likely to be poor, especially if the wife does not work.

Unemployment

The unemployment rate for unskilled men is about four times as high as the average unemployment rate, and for professional men about half the average rate. Thus, among men with low earnings when in work, the proportion who are unemployed is much higher than among men with higher levels of earnings. The unemployment benefit of a low-earner is also a higher fraction of his earnings than is the case for a high-earner. In consequence, the unemployment rate is in general higher the higher the replacement ratio (i.e. the higher net income out of work relative to net income in work). But why are the unskilled so much more likely to be unemployed?

We try to separate out the demand-side reasons (no jobs) from the supply-side reasons (lack of incentive to take the first job that comes along). We find that if, holding constant the availability of jobs, the replacement ratio rises by 10 per cent, the unemployment rate is likely to rise by about 5 per cent. However this effect comes entirely from the effect on people who have been unemployed for less than six months. The replacement ratio has no effect on the probability that a person who has been out for over six months will become employed. So there is no incentive argument in favour of reducing the level of unemployment benefit after six months, as is now done. Moreover in terms of equity, it is relevant that the average household income relative to SB of men that have been unemployed for over twelve months is 104, compared with 171 for men unemployed for one to six months and 200 for society as a whole. It is obviously much easier to raise benefits for the long-term unemployed than the short-term unemployed since their replacement ratios are now so much lower. But if there are difficulties arising from high replacement ratios, the answer may not be to leave the unemployed where they are, but to raise the incomes of the working poor by some form of income support programme.

While the effect of unemployment on the current weekly income of an unemployed family is on average a decline of around a quarter, the effect on the *annual* incomes of those who are unemployed at some point in the year is obviously less, unless they are unemployed throughout the year.

Any realistic approach to unemployment policy must bear in mind that unemployment means loss of psychic income as well as money income. Presumably the psychic hardships as well as the financial hardships of unemployment grow with duration. The average uncompleted duration of unemployed men in 1975 was around 28 weeks. Duration is longer for the unskilled than for the average unemployed worker, and shorter for the young worker. Young workers are more prone to be unemployed than the average because of the high rate at which they flow into unemployment, and not because of any excessive duration. For all types of workers the chances of getting back to work fall progressively after the first few weeks of unemployment. This poses a real challenge to the Employment Services and raises the issue of whether the long-term unemployed can be adequately helped without specific measures to encourage employers to take them on.

Children in Two-parent Families

Of all children 8 per cent live at or below SB level, of whom nearly two-thirds are in two-parent families. Poverty is closely related to family size, and 20 per cent of children in families with 5 or more children are below the SB level. However, because there are so few large families, the bulk of family poverty is in families with 3 children or less — these include over half the children in two-parent families living at or below the SB level.

Another crucial factor determining poverty is whether the mother works. Very few families in which the mother works are poor. But the main factor influencing absolute family income is the husband's earnings. So, among families of a given size, this is the main determinant of poverty or otherwise. As between families of different sizes, fathers of large families have a much higher probability than average of being out of work and they also have lower average hourly earnings. But these differences are small, compared with the effect of having more mouths to feed. The main reason why so many large families are poor is that they are large.

One-parent Families

Though only 8 per cent of all children live in one-parent families, they include over a third of all children living at or below SB level. This is because most single-parents are mothers (rather than fathers). As such, they have relatively low earning capacity and the needs of the children plus the workings of the social security system discourage them from working enough to lift themselves above the SB level. This is not true of families headed by men or widows, which are substantially better off than families headed by single, separated or divorced women.

Of the last two groups rather over half get regular allowances from the father of their children, but the average receipt in 1975 was about £9 a week. Thus the receipt of allowances seems to make less difference between poverty and sufficiency than does the fact of working or not working. About the same fraction of single-parent mothers go out to work as of all mothers, but since there are no male earnings coming in, even the families of single-parent mothers who work tend to be below the average level of economic welfare.

Disability and Ill-health

Health is an important factor affecting income. Among workers, 'long-standing illness' lowers a person's hourly wage by a few per cent, and in 1975 it raised a man's probability of being unemployed by 2.5 percentage points. It also raised his uncompleted duration of unemployment by 14 weeks. Except in the younger age-groups, male manual workers are a good deal more prone to long-standing illness than non-manual workers. The same is true to an even greater degree of short-term sickness, causing absence from work and loss of earnings.

Permanent disability is of course more serious than long- or short-term sickness affecting those normally able to work. It not only involves severe psychological hardship but also generally causes low income, except when it affects a married woman, with an able-bodied husband to look after her. Thus, the proportions of the permanently disabled living with family incomes at or below SB level were:

Disabled man	32 per cent
Disabled single woman	68 per cent
Disabled married woman	12 per cent

Altogether 1.7 per cent of men below 65 and 0.9 per cent of women below 60 were disabled. In each group a half were within 5 years of pension age. So the disabled are a small but important group of the poor.

The Elderly

Over half of the poorest people are elderly. The reason is that about half of the elderly have little income other than from social security. Since the basic pension is below SB level, they end up with incomes close to the SB level.

However, old people who work or have occupational pensions or who own their own homes typically do better than this. Thus, whereas 36 per cent of all elderly families have family incomes at or below SB level, the comparable proportions are as follows:

Families where the head works	7 per cent
Families where the head has an occupational pension	13 per cent
Families owning their homes	19 per cent

Not many old people work, due in part to the earnings rule for pensions and the working of the Supplementary Benefit system. Among men aged 65–69, just over 20 per cent work, mainly part-time. Among women of the same age the proportion is about 12 per cent. Those whose life was spent in non-manual occupations are slightly more prone to continue work, but the difference is not sharp.

Occupational pensions are received by 51 per cent of elderly men, 32 per cent of spinsters and 19 per cent of widows. A man's previous wage has a profound effect on his occupational pension. A 10 per cent increase in the wage raises the probability of his having an occupational pension by 10 per cent of itself. And, if he has an occupational pension, it raises its amount by something like 40 per cent.

The situation is similar for home-ownership, where a 10 per cent increase in a man's former wage increases his probability of home-ownership by 14 per cent. On average, 46 per cent of men live in owner-occupied homes, compared with 39 per cent of lone women. Given the sex differences we have mentioned, it is not surprising that the proportion of the elderly living at or below SB level is lowest for men and highest for widows, where it is no less than 48 per cent.

Conclusion

Thus there is no one cause of poverty. But two basic facts emerge. Most of the poorest families have little or no earnings. In some cases they lack earnings because they cannot work, as for example with many old people and with the sick and the disabled. In other cases it is difficult for them to work because of the need to look after children — this is most likely to lead to poverty when there is only one parent. And finally there is the case of the unemployed, who cannot find work. Since the social security system provides a basic level of support that is lower than normal earnings in work, it is the presence or absence of earnings rather than the level of pay in work that mainly determines which families are the poorest.

Our second fact is a consequence of the first. It is social security which determines the *level* at which the poorest members of our community live. It may be reasonable that benefits for those without earnings should be set below incomes in work. But this does not of itself mean that real benefits for those without earnings could not be raised. For there is already a parallel social security system for the working poor (Child Benefit, FIS, rent and rate rebate, free school meals). Particularly if this could be made automatic, so that the curse of claiming was abolished, the living standards of the working poor, and also of the non-working poor, could within limits be set at whatever level society chose.

How much income equality is desirable depends on ethical judgements about the relative importance of equity and efficiency and on the relevant facts. Two of the main factual issues concern incentives and the existing pattern of incomes, on both of which we have tried to throw light. Beyond this, judgements are needed on many questions: How far do existing income inequalities reflect the need to compensate people for unpleasant work or prolonged study? How far do income differences divide society and make it less efficient? How much will a rich man lose and a poor man gain in happiness, when the rich man's pound is transferred to the poor man? and How much ethical value should be attached to a change in happiness accruing to the poor, and to the rich?

These are age-old questions, but inescapable. One of the difficulties in resolving them is that those who concern themselves with the allocation of resources often know little about the poor, and those who know the poor often know little of resource-allocation. But one must try to understand both, if one really wants to grapple with the problem of poverty.

From R. Layard, D. Piachaud and M. Stewart, *Royal Commission on the Distribution of Income and Wealth: Background Paper No. 5, The Causes of Poverty* (HMSO, 1979)

B29   Townsend and the Concept of Poverty: A Critique, 1983

Townsend argues that 'A new approach to both the definition and measurement of poverty is called for'. . . In support of his conclusion, Townsend attacks Rowntree's definition of 'poverty' in terms of the attainment of a level of physical efficiency and suggests that '. . . an alternative, and more objective conception might be founded on "relative deprivation" — by which [he means] the absence or inadequacy of those diets, amenities, standards, services and activities which are common or customary in society'. I shall argue that what Townsend considers to be Rowntree's definition of the term 'poverty' is defensible against Townsend's attack and that Townsend has yet to demonstrate the superiority of his own definition of the term 'poverty' over other definitions . . .

To define a term 'X' is simply to say what the term means; it is to present the concept of an 'X'. There is a distinction between defining the term 'X' and identifying actual X's as X's. For instance, an 'alcoholic' might be defined as someone who has an acute psychological and/or physiological dependence upon alcohol. However, one might recognise particular people as alcoholics on the basis of possession of other non-defining features of alcoholics such as, say, cirrhosis of the liver. Arguments over the definition of terms are either about what conventionally is or was meant by particular terms or else they pertain to proposals as to how — for whatever reasons — particular terms should be re-defined. Notice that re-definitions, like any definitions, are tautologies; unlike factual claims, they are neither true nor false; they are, rather, useful or useless, advantageous or disadvantageous, desirable or undesirable. Such usefulness or uselessness will be relative to particular purposes.

According to Townsend, Rowntree:

. . . defined families whose 'total earnings are insufficient to obtain the minimum necessaries for the maintenance of merely physical efficiency as being in primary poverty' . . . He estimated the average nutritional needs of adults and children, translated

these needs into quantities of different foods and hence into cash
equivalents of these foods. To these costs for food he added
minimum sums for clothing, fuel and household sundries
according to size of family. The poverty line for a family of man
and wife and three children was 17s. 8d. per week, made up of
12s. 9d. for food, 2s. 3d. for clothing, 1s. 10d. for fuel and 10d. for
household sundries. Rent was treated as an unavoidable addition
to this sum, and was counted in full. A family was therefore
regarded as being in poverty if its income minus rent fell short of
the poverty line. (Townsend, 1979, p. 33.)

Notice that there are two procedures involved here, although they
are not explicitly distinguished by Townsend. There is that of
defining the term 'poverty' and that of indicating how, in terms of
this definition, those in poverty might be identified. In other words,
there is a difference between defining the term 'poverty' and
measuring poverty.

In *Poverty* (1979), Townsend presents the following case against
Rowntree's and other similar studies of 'poverty':

. . . the standards which were adopted proved difficult to defend.
Rowntree's estimates of the costs of necessaries other than food
were based either on his own or other's opinions or, as in the case
of clothing, on the actual expenditure of those among a small
selection of poor families who spent the least. Does the actual
expenditure of the poorest families represent what they *need* to
spend on certain items? Neither in his studies nor in similar
studies were criteria of need, independent of personal judgements or of the minimum amounts actually spent on certain
goods, put forward. (Townsend, 1979, p. 34.)

Townsend proceeds to elaborate on these points but the
elaboration does not strengthen his argument. It is difficult to see
why Townsend thinks that these claims in any way invalidate the use
of Rowntree's definition of 'poverty'. According to Townsend,
Rowntree says that (by definition) families are in (primary) poverty
if their ' . . . total earnings are insufficient to obtain the minimum
necessaries for the maintenance of merely physical efficiency . . . '
(Townsend, 1979, p. 33). Nothing that Townsend says here tells
against this as a definition of the term 'poverty'. Townsend points
out that R wntree might well have mis-identified those who were, in

terms of Rowntree's definition, in 'poverty' but that is not in itself a criticism of Rowntree's definition — indeed, it seems a tacit acceptance of its viability. There is a difference between disagreeing over what is meant by the term 'X' and disagreeing over what is correctly classified as an X. And disagreement of the latter sort presupposes an agreement — albeit temporary — over the meaning of the term 'X'. Rowntree might well have miscalculated the precise monetary amount required to purchase the 'minimum necessaries' in question. But, so what? This is a criticism of his *method* rather than of his definition of the term 'poverty'. As Townsend points out, the monetary figure will change over time and differ from one family to another. Again, this is no criticism of Rowntree's definition.

Townsend draws two conclusions from his quoted criticism of Rowntree:

> The first is that definitions which are based on some conception of 'absolute' deprivation disintegrate upon close and sustained examination and deserve to be abandoned. Poverty has often been defined, in the words of an O.E.C.D. review, 'in terms of some absolute level of minimum needs, below which people are regarded as being poor, for purposes of social and governmental concern, and which does not change through time'. In fact people's needs, even for food are conditioned by the society in which they live and to which they belong, and just as needs differ in different societies so they differ in different periods of the evolution of single societies. Any conception of poverty as 'absolute' is therefore inappropriate and misleading. (Townsend, 1970, p. 38.)

Townsend is confusing various issues here. He is confusing the issue of 'poverty' with that of governmental intervention to secure minimum levels of economic welfare. The concept of 'needs' is a problematic one; it is not adequately analysed by Townsend. This leads him to fail to identify among 'needs' those whose non-fulfilment constitutes 'poverty' and/or should provoke governmental intervention. After all, it would be curious to say that anyone with an unmet 'need' is in 'poverty' or that the government should intervene to meet all the needs of the governed. Townsend is also confusing the question of providing an 'absolute' definition of the term 'poverty' and that of providing an absolute measure of poverty. He is also assuming, wrongly, that, in order to be an 'absolute' measure of 'poverty', the measure must be the same for all people. One could give, in Townsend's terminology, an 'absolute' definition of 'poverty' and say that people are in 'poverty' if they have insufficient resources to attain a specified level of physical efficiency. It is quite beside the point, and no criticism of the definition, to do what Townsend does and try to show that different people require different amounts of resources to attain that particular level. Furthermore, it does not seem in principle impossible to establish that, above a particular absolute level of possession of resources, no one is in 'poverty' and that below some other particular absolute level of possession of resources, every one is in poverty. Townsend does not establish that 'Any conception as "absolute" is . . . inappropriate and misleading' (Townsend, 1979, p. 38).

Townsend continues:

> The second conclusion which might be drawn is that, though the principal definitions put forward historically have invoked some 'absolute' level of minimum needs, they have in practice represented rather narrow conceptions of relative deprivation and deserve to be clarified as such. Thus Seebohm Rowntree's definition amounted in effect to a conception of nutritional deprivation relative to the level believed to be required for members of the manual working class at the turn of the century to function efficiently. (Townsend, 1979, pp. 38–39.)

But this is merely a reiteration of Rowntree's definition; it does not amount to a criticism. The adjectives 'poor' and 'tall', like their nouns 'tallness' and 'poverty' are *necessarily* relative terms. Rowntree can hardly be criticised for making explicit his particular reference. Why should Rowntree not have chosen this particular reference? Any state of poverty, like any state of tallness, will constitute poverty relative to some other states and the same state will not be one of poverty if some other points of reference are chosen.

According to Townsend:

> The main fault in the standards used has been their lack of relation to the budgets and customs of life of working people. Many who are considered to be above the poverty line because their income exceeds the total cost of meeting basic needs do, in fact, spend less on the individual items included in the standard—

— food, clothing, fuel and light and household sundries — simply because they spend their money on other things . . . How those on the borderline of poverty ought to spend their money is a very different thing from how they do spend their money. It would be unrealistic to expect them, as in effect many social investigators have expected them to be skilled dieticians with marked tendencies towards puritanism . . . (Townsend, 1954, pp. 132–3.)

It is difficult to see to what extent this constitutes a valid criticism of Rowntree's definition of the term 'poverty'. Townsend's point here is obscure. I would imagine that what he is trying to say here is that people might not be in 'poverty' in terms of Rowntree's definition or in accordance with Rowntree's proposed measure of 'poverty' and yet still suffer hardship and that Rowntree's derived 'poverty line' provides an insufficiently generous measure for the provision of social security payments. This would seem to be unobjectionable, but, in defence of Rowntree, it could be pointed out that no definition or study of 'poverty' is likely to identify all forms of inequality and hardship. (See, for instance, Townsend's own account of 'poverty'.) Furthermore, we need not expect any definition or measure of a 'poverty-line' to generate acceptable political prescriptions. It is an unfortunate but not an inevitable fact that some people have concluded that the 'poverty-line' should be the level of social security payments: that the state should intervene solely to secure the maintenance of 'merely physical efficiency'.

From H.V. Maclachlan, 'Townsend and the Concept of Poverty' in *Social Policy and Administration*, vol. 17, no. 2 (Summer 1983), published by Basil Blackwell, Oxford, and edited by R.A.B. Leaper

POLITICAL ECONOMY AND SOCIAL WELFARE

B30 Sir Keith Joseph on Social Security: The New Priorities, 1966

So the Tory approach is both more selective and less dependent on the State. We desperately want to end hardship but because our resources are limited we shall end it the sooner if we concentrate our efforts and the taxpayers' money on those in need and if we try wherever possible to help people to help themselves. To us self-help and voluntary action are more desirable and more likely where practicable to be effective than State intervention.

We can state our objectives: to strengthen the family, thrift and self-reliance; to strengthen voluntary service; to remove crutches from those who can walk; to strengthen the social network; to help those in need better than ever before, setting to work forces that will of themselves reduce need and poverty, particularly in old age; to reduce delinquency, boredom and purposelessness; to reinforce the growing volume of voluntary effort so as to give far more people the grace of helping others.

These are not simple things to achieve, and there are no simple solutions. Men and women, even boys and girls, who are not ready for the responsibilities of bringing up children cannot be prevented from producing them. Bad parents are not transformed easily, and certainly not by dependence on the State. Of course we cannot end all misery and unhappiness and grief, but some of it *is* avoidable and some of what is avoidable gets handed on to the next generation. We can reduce its impact and we can reduce its transmission.

We know some of the breeding-grounds of warped lives; we know the close interaction of poverty, bad housing, over-sized classes, inadequate parents.

In face of these multiple evils of today, breeding often the evils of tomorrow, action is needed on many fronts. For some, money; for others, money and more supporting services — voluntary or public — in their homes; for very many, better housing; for children, more teachers, perhaps even special tuition; for all children, a chance to succeed in some worth-while activity, however small. The urban young need the challenges and satisfactions of sport and of activities like music, climbing and sailing. We must try in all we do to foster family strength. We must encourage and help the voluntary services, who do so much already. But we can only effectively do these things if we have a strategy and if we establish priorities: with money and people necessarily limited, we *must* establish priorities.

These problems and these objectives reach into so many aspects of life that they are beyond the powers of any one department. They call not only for a series of programmes — in the social services, in pensions, in housing, in education, in recreation, in law and order, in finance and in voluntary work. They call for something new in our complex, specialist age. They call for a social policy, with a social strategy: social priorities and a social programme on all these and on other fronts. And all this requires a number of changes, in Whitehall, in local authorities, in social and voluntary services.

First, in Whitehall itself: there is no department which covers enough of these varied fields to have the overall vision required . . . What we need is a new department close enough to the fieldwork to be well-informed, and large enough to carry and put to full use a new brand of civil servant and of research — the social administrator, served by research in the department, commissioned by the department or studied by the department.

Of course, we could not put in one Ministry all the social responsibilities. But we could form a department which was primarily responsible for evolving, with the other departments concerned, a social strategy.

That is why in our last General Election Manifesto we announced our intention to amalgamate the Ministries of Health and Pensions and National Insurance into a new Department of Health and Social Security and merge with this new Ministry a new and more positive welfare executive, to carry out the work done by the National Assistance Board.

In no single department is there now a social policy research organisation or indeed a group of civil servants concerned with social policy as a whole. The new Department would fill this gap. The policy would need regular and constant review as factors change and as new knowledge comes in, but at the heart of any effective policy must be a view on priorities. It would provide a more unified and central machinery for deciding social policy, but the implementation of the policy would still be very much in the hands of local authorities and voluntary services.

But as we assume new community responsibilities we must try to relieve ourselves of others. We must always be redeploying public resources to where they are most needed. We must shift the taxpayer's money from purposes which can now be left to people privately to purposes where only the public can help.

If we do not do this we shall cripple the community's power to do what only the community can do, and shall stunt the willingness of more and more people to provide in some directions, helped by insurance, more and more for themselves. Indeed we must start no new service without trying to organise it on a self-liquidating basis wherever practicable.

We must use our resources sensibly — they cannot be unlimited. We must concentrate our effort where the most good can be done. Above all, we must try to prevent predictable trouble.

We envisage, therefore, more strategic initiatives from the centre, from government, because it is here that we can collate new knowledge and experience and redeploy or, if need be, increase our effort as needs change. But we would still depend on local offices of central departments, local authorities and health authorities, and voluntary bodies to do the work on the ground. We must look to them and the academic world for information and recommendations on which we can work at the centre.

From Sir Keith Joseph, *Social Security: The New Priorities* (Conservative Political Centre, 1966)

B31 Negative Sum Welfare/Efficiency Interactions, 1979

It may tentatively be concluded that the growth of the relative size of the nonmarket sector is a necessary but not a sufficient condition for the adverse market-sector/nonmarket-sector interactions sketched above. Institutional capabilities and social values, attitudes and norms of behavior also play essential roles in these interactions. A country — e.g., Germany — whose institutions and behavioral norms remain conducive to innovation, managerial dynamism and conscientious work effort may be able to sustain a bigger income share for its nonmarket sector relative to that of its market sector without adverse consequences than another country — e.g., the United Kingdom — in which sociocultural conditions are significantly less favorable to these prerequisites for productivity increases and efficiency. But, at some point in the relative growth of the nonmarket sector's income share, the former nation, too, would begin to experience negative-sum welfare/efficiency interactions.

More empirical research than funds and time permitted for this study will be needed to determine with reasonable certainty for any country the approximate percentage of GDP at which the growth of the nonmarket sector generates significant adverse effects.

Specific indicators at the macro level that negative-sum welfare/efficiency interactions may be occurring include changes in:

▶ the size and components of the nonmarket sector's income;

▶ the percentage of marketed goods and services acquired by the nonmarket sector;

▶ the number of people employed in the nonmarket sector and of nonworking welfare recipients relative to the number of people working in the market sector;

▶ the size of the disposable income for purchasing marketed goods and services of the people employed in the nonmarket sector and of the nonworking welfare recipients relative to the total output of the market sector;

▶ the rate of growth of productivity in the market sector;

▶ the relative returns to labor and capital in the market sector;

▶ the preference for leisure as manifested in participation rates, absenteeism rates, the length of the work week and of vacation time, retirement age, etc., relative to changes in productivity and wage incomes;

▶ the basic and marginal rates of income tax, the rates of payroll taxes and social security contributions, the rate of indirect taxes affecting consumption (such as value-added tax and excise taxes), and the proportions of the total tax revenue that are paid by those employed in the nonmarket sector and by the various kinds of wage and other income earners in the market sector;

▶ the subsidies provided to local governments, public enterprises and market-sector enterprises;

▶ the amounts of research and development undertaken by the market sector and available to it from the nonmarket sector;

▶ the rate of productive investment in the market sector;

▶ the level of employment and the rate of new job creation in the market sector;

▶ the rate of inflation;

▶ the shares of domestic and export markets obtained by a country's industrial producers;

▶ the deficit on goods and services in the balance of payments.

It is readily apparent that many of these variables can serve as indicators of changes not only in welfare/efficiency relationships but also in other important relationships in the economy — such as cyclical trends, demographic developments and international shifts in technological capabilities.

From T. Geiger, *Welfare and Efficiency* (Macmillan, 1979)

B32   Joseph and Sumption: Poverty is not Unfreedom, 1979

If it it were a mere accident that the pursuit of equality has in practice led to inequality and tyranny these examples would be of little relevance. But it is not mere accident. It is the direct result of contradictions which are inherent in the very concept of equality. Egalitarians rely for the achievement of their objects on the coercive power of the State, as they are bound to do by the nature of the human material with which they deal. A society in which the choices fundamental to human existence are determined by coercion is not a free society. It follows irresistibly that egalitarians must choose between liberty and equality.

This proposition, although we regard it as irresistible, is very frequently denied. The choice between equality and liberty is an uncomfortable one. Whence come the commonplace attempts to avoid it by an argument which goes something like this. Liberty has no meaning except in relation to an individual's opportunity to make use of it. Men are not in any meaningful sense equally free if their freedom can only be of use to them when joined with some other advantage (such as money) which some of them do not have. To put it crudely there is no point in telling us that we are all free to run newspapers or lunch at the Ritz if only a millionaire can afford to do either. A proponent of this view would say that the only meaning which can usefully be attached to the concept of equality of opportunity is equality to buy things. It is not enough in his view to be free *from* something; if freedom is to have any meaning one must also be free *to do* what one wants or needs to do . . . Poverty is one kind of personal incapacity. But it is not coercion. The possession of the money one would like is not the same thing as liberty, simply because both of them are desirable. How much money we have is one of the factors which determines the choices open to us. Liberty means that we, not others, choose between these alternatives. A person who cannot afford to buy food may well have a justifiable grievance which ought to be rectified politically, but it would be misleading to describe his grievance as lack of freedom . . . Freedom consists in the absence of external coercion and no man is unfree unless other people intentionally use coercion to prevent him from doing something which he is able and willing to do and which could be done without encroaching on the freedoms of others.

Is inequality a denial of freedom? Not long ago Mr James Callaghan gave it as his opinion that liberty had been denied when he was a young man by the fact that he could not afford to go to university; then since he would presumably not have made that observation if everyone else had been in a like predicament we must assume that what he meant was that his liberty had been diminished because others had an advantage which he did not have. If Mr Callaghan had thought sufficiently deeply about it he might have put this in two ways. He might have said that his poverty as a young man was due to the excessive appetites of other men who had taken more than their due proportion of the national cake, and this thus extended their own freedom by encroaching upon his. In other words he might have said that those greedy persons had exceeded the limits beyond which, as even the classical liberal theorists agreed, one man's freedom was another man's slavery. Alternatively he might have said (as Marx would have said) that his poverty really did amount to external coercion by other men, because it was the result of certain economic arrangements which other men had intentionally contrived whereby he was prevented from having enough for his needs while others were not.

To prove that inequality is the result of an economic system contrived by some men for their own advantage one must do more than show that another economic system could be contrived which would do away with it. One must show that differences of income which would not naturally exist are artificially brought into being. But the very methods on which egalitarians rely refute this view. Those who advocate the use of the coercive power of the State to create equality presumably recognise that without active intervention inequality would survive. And they are right. Inequality is a state of affairs which results when the natural aptitudes of men are allowed to manifest themselves in natural differences. It may be suggested that another and better state of affairs is conceivable, but it does not follow from that that inequality is a contrivance of men. Yet if it is not a contrivance of men it is not coercion and it is not a denial of liberty.

Those who confuse liberty and equality would no doubt hope to harness their cause to a word which commands instinctive emotional support even when emptied of all meaning. By doing so they conceal a real dilemma behind a screen of verbiage. But it is more than a rhetorical device. It is an attempt to deny that we must choose between liberty and equality by pretending that we can have both. It would be quite fair (although irrelevant in modern Britain) to say that liberty is not in all circumstances the highest good and that in some conditions of extreme starvation and squalor one might reasonably prefer to be fed and housed than to be free. In other words if one believed that in an unfree society one would have a better chance of being fed one could make a case for having less liberty and more equality. But one cannot without dishonesty pretend that the liberty which has been lost in the process has been replaced by some other kind of liberty, 'economic liberty', 'social liberty' or the like. Liberty is liberty, not something else. And the slave is a slave; you do not set him free by feeding him.

From Sir Keith Joseph and J. Sumption, *Equality* (John Murray, 1979)

B33 Breaking the Spell of the Welfare State, 1981

There are four reasons for looking critically at the welfare state and, where appropriate, vigorously pruning its many departments. First, there is the urgent need to reduce public expenditure. Second, some important areas of the welfare state have been subjected to quite specific and powerful criticism — for example, ILEA secondary schools and social workers taking children into 'Care'. Third, there is a need to keep under constant critical review experimental arrangements like those of the welfare state, especially as they are not directly accountable to their customers through the market and are, often, a near monopoly. Fourth, there is no excuse for complacency where people's welfare is concerned. That welfare demands a ceaseless search for better standards, initiatives and alternatives.

. . . How should analysts and critics approach the welfare state? What questions should they ask? What criteria should they use? What is to count as evidence in the absence of market choice? What should they do to see that the debate does not turn into an unproductive 'roundabout' debate of the 'Yes, it is — No, it isn't' variety?

Should they ensure that criticism is more than a vague, loud noise and actually specifies changes which reduce public expenditure? Can analysis be extended to show how such changes could be implemented? How can critics make positive and imaginative suggestions for the improvement of health, education and social welfare and avoid a stance which, taking the agenda as set by current provision, merely argues for former means of provision, the 'opposite means' of provision or the reverse of current provision? . . . For today's critic of the welfare state is not debating in ideal circumstances. He is dealing with a complex of ideas, official reports, half-hidden practices, undisclosed assumptions, alliances of vested interests, value and sentiment-laden appeals and ideology.

I think it more appropriate to call this complex thing a 'spell' than a proposition and I argue that to analyse the welfare state involves breaking that spell.

Four Inadequate Criticisms

1. Tokenism   The welfare state has been criticised from a variety of angles. Marxists have found its performance 'dismal' in achieving any appreciable change in the condition of the working classes. Free marketeers argue that it has changed from 'the expression of compassion to an instrument of political repression' stifling innovation in education and health care, denying choice, and voraciously and insatiably consuming people's money. The media have brought particular departments and practices of the welfare state under scrutiny. Welfarists themselves have suggested changes in functions and organisation. The last fifteen years have seen the creation of comprehensive schools, mixed-ability teaching, a raised school leaving age, a re-organised national health service, a Manpower Services Commission, an expanded social work 'profession', new laws on Race Relations, Equal Opportunities, Health and Safety at Work, housing and consumer 'protection', and an explosion in higher education.

The first sort of inadequate criticism is one that scarcely deserves the name of criticism at all. I have called it 'Tokenism' because one of the forms it takes is to accept critical attention provided there are no consequences. Reports are made, investigations carried out and everything carries on as before. A second form even welcomes investigation as a means of expanding the bureaucracy by introducing monitoring, inspection, evaluation, working parties, research, commissions and the rest. And a third sees investigation as a way of permanently expanding the 'service' under investigation. It is dangerous to make calls for the critical evaluation of a bureaucracy, for bureaucrats are skilled in using such criticism to initiate change in one direction only — expansion. Last, there are criticisms which pull a service apart and put it together again in a different form — 're-organisation'.

Even investigations which do reveal faults in the welfare state can be neutralised or turned to advantage. Such faults occur, say welfare employees, because of lack of money, or staff shortages, poor pupil-teacher ratios, heavy case-loads, inexperienced staff, which all result from insufficient salaries. They occur because of inadequate training, because the scope of the department is not wide enough, because of poor communication, and so on. More posts, more money, higher salaries, newer buildings, more research and more training are what is needed. Faults are not usually attributed to individuals. Very rarely are incompetent teachers or social workers sacked; how many ILEA teachers will be sacked as a result of the HMI 1980 report on London schools? Very rarely are those responsible for failed projects sacked. If criticism is made, it is *neutered*, i.e. attributed to rates, statistics, levels, and other abstractions rather than to human beings.

Even the acceptance of these criticisms is contained. Blame is not allowed to reach and reduce a whole department. Scandals in social work do not lead to less or smaller social service departments. Schools which can be persuaded to admit to being unsuccessful neither sack teachers nor close down. They blame external sources; the home background of pupils, 'wicked government cuts', the social structure or simply organisational problems. This understanding of criticism that welcomes talk, investigation and report, as long as they have no effect, or lead to the expansion of the welfare state is token criticism.

Moreover the system has an inbuilt credibility gap. Very, very few students fail their social work (C.Q.S.W.) or teaching (Cert. Ed., P.G.C.E. or B.Ed.) qualifications and very few are sacked. At no point from initial college interview to retirement is there a tough evaluation. What those who are content with token criticism are asking others to believe is that a vast bureaucracy of people with good intentions but with all the usual human failings can, without significant exception, continue to achieve high standards in the absence of selection, customer choice and tough accountability.

There is a similarly unbending refusal to consider the aims of the various welfare state 'services' in anything other than a token way. The constant re-affirmation of the original 'aims' of the nationalised health service or state education and the incantation of slogans drawn from founding fathers and the holy texts of the 1940s have all the features of a cult. The failure of the cult to 'bring rain' is but the excuse for extending the magic — if state education fails to raise the social mobility of the lower classes, we do not challenge it but add to it a comprehensive system, new and easier examinations, the minist-rations of education welfare officers and more careers advisers, culminating in attempts to destroy private schooling and externally assessed examinations. The cult cannot be wrong. If it does not seem to work, it is factors outside it that are to blame.

The cult of the welfare state is not sustained by evidence or proof. The ideas behind its various departments and practices were, in their day, hunches. They were not scientific conclusions nor were the 'institutions' which resulted from them proven institutions. No one could foresee how these institutions would work. Social policy is not a predictive science in any true sense. This is not to say that the ideas were wrong but to admit the possibility that, when advanced, they could have been. Certainly they need re-consideration in a world that is very different from that in which they were introduced. It is the opposite of a token criticism which is needed — a criticism which is prepared to look with an open mind at all the levels and practices of the welfare state and, where appropriate, to discard out-dated and inefficient personnel, practices and departments.

2. Utopian Criticism   If Tokenism confines and emasculates criti-cism, what I shall call Utopianism inflates it. The Utopian sees problems in the welfare state as 'aspects' of far wider problems. Utopians live in the subjunctive and the conditional. They are not much interested in problems as they are constituted in present society. They have little interest in education, health or welfare but see these as convenient excuses to fight hypothetical battles about 'the State' or a 'free-market economy'. Utopians are a good deal more interested in 'positions' than in analysis and they like 'general positions' most of all. From these 'general positions' they start. Each individual problem of health, education and welfare is converted into the cardboard cast and standard plot of the general position. Utopianism afflicts many Marxists and is a potential hazard for some free marketeers especially those given to macro-theorizing and aggregation . . . The issue Utopians wish to avoid is — what is to be done with the nationalised health, education and welfare services—the services we have, not the ones we 'ought to have', over the next five years.

3. Abuse A third form of criticism is that of Abuse. There is no shortage of abusive criticism, or what appears to be abusive criticism, of 'trendy' teachers, 'interfering' social workers, 'self-serving' bureaucrats and 'ludicrous' polytechnic courses. The welfare establishment points out that such Abuse is based on personal or political prejudice, on ignorance, dislike, over-generalisation and misunderstanding rather than on research.

4. Book-keeping Butchery The last inadequate criticism I call Book-keeping butchery. By that I mean an approach which is only or largely interested in cost, especially immediate and obvious cost. It is an approach to welfare that cares little about the substance or contents of welfare, about what goes on in classrooms and social work teams, examining welfare institutions only to find opportunities for saving money. It is currently to be seen in the behaviour of those who are being pressed to reduce public expenditure.

Failure to make these reductions imperils the Government's economic strategy. It fuels the rates bill. It makes the private sector bear disproportionately the burden of economic sacrifice. Where, if anywhere in the welfare state have there been redundancies on the scale of those in the private sector? Where in the welfare state are the departmental closures that correspond to the bankruptcies of the private sector? This disproportionate burden may well contribute to recession, unemployment and all that is antithetical to *welfare*.

But if this pressure is justified and to be heeded, if the welfare state is to be reduced, then the pressure should be heeded thoughtfully and quickly. Utopian talk is of little use for the problem is an immediate one. But there is no sense either in the thoughtless butchery of the welfare state. Those who manage private industry have no responsibility to manage the allocation of welfare cuts. It is the job of government and its bureaucrats.

The temptation is to respond to pressure from economic interest groups with purely economic measures, such as cutting the Rate Support Grant or freezing education and social services posts. None the less, the external pressure for reduced welfare state spending will serve a more useful function if it leads to a hard, detailed and critical look at the content of the welfare state. The problems generated by high spending welfare will continue regardless of a few *ad hoc* cuts. In the end they will have to be addressed by changing structures in a critical and creative manner. So often in the last decade demands for economies have been made under both Labour and Conservative administrations. So often it has seemed that, at last, a re-assessment of the welfare state was about to be made. Each time the government of the day turned back from the brink after balancing its books by a few *ad hoc* cuts. The welfare state, fudged, botched and re-organised, its parts re-titled and its members mildly inconvenienced by inconclusive investigations and superficial debate, continued.

It looks a little tattier now after several unco-ordinated botchings. Its elderly functionaries retire prematurely. Its unfavoured but inexpensive part-time staff are reduced. Its offices close earlier. Its customers are inconvenienced. Its queues grow and its stationery changes with yet another minor re-structuring. Its pupils buy the odd books for themselves. Some mothers have to feed their own children and the bureaucrats only use the telephone in the afternoon. Productive and efficient departments are hit as hard, or as soft, as inefficient ones. Useful staff suffer as much or as little as useless staff. No one makes significant policy decisions about which departments, units or individuals should go, which should continue and which should be rewarded with more resources. A general, indiscriminate stagnation prevails. The efficient and the inefficient, the main grade teachers and social workers and the expensive upper ranks, the Assistant Directors of Social Services Departments and Polytechnics, the advisers and inspectors, the heads of this and that, remain in static and demoralised profusion.

It was thought by some in 1979 that this time it would be different. This time there would be a severe and sustained examination of public expenditure and the welfare state. This time the 'open secrets', the abuses within the system that every teacher, lecturer, bureaucrat and social worker knows about, the 'insider' knowledge would be publicly revealed and some sort of purge would follow. This time there would be a comparison of departmental efficiencies, a rewarding of merit, and expansion of successful work and a sacking of the inefficient and the tired. This time there would be an end to failed experiments. This time decisions would be taken to close some ailing departments. This time alternative ideas and new ways of delivering education and health would be considered. This time experiments of a different sort, experiments on charging, mutual aid, vouchers, tax credits, subscription, tender and voluntarism would be encouraged. But those who expected these changes would seem to have been wrong. The welfare establishment has won again.

It should be clear by now that while an economic analysis is indispensable in the assessment of the welfare state, book-keeping butchery has no part to play. Lopping off bits and pieces of the system to attain this year's solvency is not evaluation nor is it adequate criticism. Sacking the weakest staff has nothing to do with promoting value for money. Freezing posts regardless of function has nothing to do with efficiency.

And if we can do without Book-keeping butchery, we can do without Tokenists and Utopians as well. Re-organising the health service again and having another 'education debate', let alone turning England into Albania, are inadequate substitutes for criticism. The welfare state requires evaluation because it affects a lot of people through its 'services' and costs a lot through taxes. Evaluation cannot avoid the details of practice, of what the welfare state does to, as well as, for its customers. Expenditure levels are important but attention to them should not act as an escape from criticising practice. Perhaps one way to express this is to say that a *social* analysis of the welfare state is an indispensable part of an adequate criticism, and a *social policy* is an indispensable part of action to cut welfare state expenditure.

From D. Anderson, J. Lait and D. Marsland, *Breaking the Spell of the Welfare State* (The Social Affairs Unit, 1981)

B34   Thatcherism and the Welfare State, 1983

Thatcherism is a political formation that combines the principles of the 'social market economy' with a new 'authoritarian populism'. The social market economy represents a return to some of the precepts of nineteenth-century liberalism; a limited role for government, an emphasis on the responsibilities of the individual and so forth . . . Populism represents an appeal to national interests which are supposedly above class interests, drawing on the ideology of a neutral market place working in the interests of all. In its attack on immigrants, welfare recipients and unions, for example, it stresses the need for a strong state to represent national over sectional interests, though Thatcherism clearly differs from a truly authoritarian movement. Crudely speaking then Thatcherism = monetarism + authoritarian populism though the two threads of this ideology clearly complement each other.

What is striking for our purposes is the position of the welfare state at the heart of these two strands. The welfare state is the central target for the radical right on both counts. First, because it allegedly generates even higher tax levels, budget deficits, disincentives to work and save, and a bloated class of unproductive workers. Second, because it encourages 'soft' attitudes towards crime, immigrants, the idle, the feckless, strikers, the sexually aberrant and so forth. Economic prescriptions and populist incantations are harnessed together, and their prime target is the expanded sphere of state responsibility, state regulation and state-provided benefits which constitute the modern welfare state . . .

The process of restructuring the welfare state can now be situated within the political formation of the radical right. First, the *quantitative* role of cuts follows from the precepts of monetarism: strict control of the money supply, a substantial reduction in the level of government expenditure and taxation and a shift towards indirect taxation. A reduction in the public sector borrowing requirement is a key object of policy because of its impact on the money supply (or on interest rates if government securities are to be sold to the non-banking sector). Given the commitment to lower tax levels in order to encourage incentives to work and invest, this must involve even faster cuts in public spending. Given the commitment to higher defence spending, this must involve still greater cuts in social and economic expenditures. This has as another aim the weakening of the power of organised labour via higher rates of unemployment (and the threat of still higher levels if wage claims are 'excessive'). The goal is to use market forces (together with new legal restrictions) to reduce real wages and augment profits. A cut in the 'social wage', for example reducing housing subsidies or personal social services, augments this pressure to reduce labour's share in the national income. It thus provides an indirect route to encourage profitability and re-investment in British industry . . .

Second, the *qualitative* shifts in social policy are designed to reassert individualism, self-reliance and family responsibility, and to reverse the collective social provision of the post-war era. Present attempts to impose a national curriculum and 'raise standards' in public education provide a striking example of the social programme of the new conservatism. In many ways, though not all, these qualitative shifts complement the absolute cuts in expenditure: cutting social benefits to working age adults saves money and panders to the anti-scrounger mentality of the new populism. Together these two sets of forces have generated the most sustained attack on the welfare state since the war. The restructuring of the welfare state has begun in earnest ... In part the post-war Keynesian-welfare state generated its own momentum for further state intervention, to secure economic growth and capital accumulation within a new balance of class forces that it had itself helped to shape. It follows from this that the development of Keynesian economic policy and modern social policy were interlinked and formed the two central planks of the post-war political consensus between the parties. It therefore comes as no surprise to find that both planks are simultaneously under attack from the new radical right.

But what, if any, is the link between an expanded welfare state and a declining economy? Is the British economic crisis the result of an overgrown public sector, as the present Government would have it, or are the two unconnected? My own view is that there is a link, but that it is not so straightforward or unambiguous as the new conservatism suggests. After all, a recent EEC report showed that government spending as a share of GDP is lower in the UK than any other country in the EEC. On the other hand socialist reformers and others who deny any link and who reiterate Keynesian nostrums about the need for more public spending in order to pull us out of recession do a disservice to the socialist movement. The Keynesian welfare state *has* generated new contradictions working as it is within the framework of a private capitalist economy. It is not possible for state spending to rise inexorably as a share of GNP without adverse consequences for its domestic capital. What then are these limits?

I believe there are two main limits. First, a growing level of state expenditure exacerbates the post-war conflict between capital and labour over the *distribution* of national output. Given the centralisation of capital within an expanding international economy, and given a stronger, more organised labour movement, then inflation becomes inbuilt within advanced capitalist countries, as capital and labour can in turn offset higher wage costs or higher prices. When the state then lays claim to a higher share of resources this two-way conflict becomes a three-way conflict adding to the inflationary pressure. For however the state seeks to finance this expenditure —

via higher taxes on the working class, or on corporations (very unusual), or via higher indirect taxes, or via higher state borrowing — the result is to exacerbate the spiral of wage costs and prices . . .

Second, the growing level of state expenditure and intervention interferes with the *production* of surplus value and profit. The growth of the 'social wage' and 'collective consumption' means that the operation of the labour market and the reserve army of labour is impaired, and the bargaining strength of the working class increased. Unemployment benefits, family benefits, public assistance, state health and social services, housing subsidies, etc., all remove part of the real living standards of the working class from the wage system, and allocate this part according to some criteria of social need and citizenship. Citizenship rights are counterposed to property rights, and the ability of capital to transform labour power into labour performed is impaired.

In the light of this what has been the impact of the welfare state on British capitalism? Two peculiar facts about Britain must be borne in mind in answering this question. First, the position of Britain within the world economy is a declining one, and the deep-seated weaknesses of our economic structure are now super-imposed on a worldwide recession which has marked the end of the post-war boom. Second, the defensive economic strength of the British trade union movement has prevented the strategy of industrial restructuring attempted by Labour and Conservative administrations since the early 1960s from being successfully implemented. This defensively strong, decentralised labour movement with extensive shop-floor organisation has also hindered the restructuring of the welfare state.

It is perhaps not surprising, then, that monetarist and populist attacks on the welfare state have established themselves here. Given the failure of Keynesianism, and the progressive degeneration of the Labour Governments' corporatist experiments after the 1974 Social Contract, a vacuum opened up which first Powell, then Thatcher, Joseph *et al.* were quick to exploit. The defeat of the left in the EEC referendum of 1975 under a Labour government helped prepare the ground for this move to the right. The indigenous populist ideology, analysed by Hall and Gamble; the reluctance of British capital to opt for Continental-style interventionism; and the failure of the Labour leadership to develop an alternative strategy to replace the wilting nostrums of Keynesianism, all left the way open for a tax-welfare backlash culminating in the victory of the new conservatism in the last election.

The result is that Britain is experiencing the most far-reaching experiment in 'new right' politics in the Western world . . . Its underlying aim is to attack the labour movement on the economic and ideological fronts. The policy shifts outlined earlier on can all be seen to contribute to this aim: legal sanctions against unions, mass unemployment by means of tight monetary controls, the cutting of social benefits for the families of strikers, a reduction in the social wage on several fronts, and a shift to more authoritarian practices in the welfare field. It represents one coherent strategy for managing the British crisis, a strategy aimed at the heart of the post-war Keynesian-welfare state settlement.

From I. Gough, 'Thatcherism and the Welfare State' in S. Hall and M. Jacques (eds), *The Politics of Thatcherism* (Lawrence & Wishart, 1983)

B35   Socialist and Communist Social Policy, 1983

Under socialism more of the available resources will be allocated to the meeting of welfare needs. Under communism, once the material needs for clothing and housing, etc. have been readily satisfied, the percentage of society's resources devoted to the meeting of welfare needs may diminish again because of the priority now given to the satisfaction of non-material welfare needs such as creative work or the developing of rewarding relationships. There may also be other reasons, connected with detailed considerations of particular social services, for suggesting that under communism the proportion of a society's resources devoted to these services will be reduced. Medical care, for example, might require less spent on it if a system based on giving priority to the consumption of commodities such as drugs has given way to a system that gives priority to the eradication of the causes of much ill-health.

Under communism, self-management would apply as much to the welfare sector as to any other. Some form of democratic workers' control of, for example, hospitals within a framework that ensures that the self-management body is answerable to a democratic form of local community government is to be envisaged . . . The self-managed welfare institutions would also permit the full participation of the users of these institutions in decision-making, but the exact form that the power-sharing between workers in and users of the institutions would take is an open question. The changed division of labour would ensure that the contributions of those carrying out technically different tasks such as, say, doctoring or portering in a hospital, would be equally valid in the decision-making forums, though, of course, the advice of those with some particular technical competence in a specialist area of medicine (to continue with the same example) would continue to be more important. Under communism it is also to be expected that each of the local community bodies would have considerable freedom to determine the extent and form of welfare provisions in its locality, but that this freedom would operate within some centrally-but-democratically laid down guidelines to ensure a degree of territorial justice and ease of geographic mobility.

Under socialism, while progress towards these communist goals would be expected, there are at least two factors inhibiting their immediate realisation. First, the necessity of greater central control over policy to iron out the inherited inequalities of capitalist provision, and second, the need for a strong central state to protect these developments against possible counter-revolutionary sabotage at a local level by the old dispossessed ruling class. Furthermore, there would be great reliance on the old 'capitalist' expert, who would of course be answerable to the bodies of the workers' state until such time as the projected changes in the division of labour could be brought about. There would also be a necessary part to be played under socialism by activists and members (cadres) of the governing socialist party in the formulation and implementation of policy at all levels of administration, until such time as the unified collective experience of everybody makes this dependence on a party political form of administration involving cadres unnecessary. How quickly reliance on 'capitalist experts' and party policies and party cadres could be brought to an end is a matter of controversy.

Agency of Service Provision

The case of communism is largely straightforward. If human need dictates the production and distribution of goods and services; if resources for them are plentiful; if the centralised state has withered; if the division of labour has been transformed and if privatised forms of nuclear family life have given way to more communal forms of living, then the local community will predominate in the providing of services for itself. The state, as a separate central institution, will not exist, the market will probably

have outlived its role as an allocater of goods, work will have
receded in its importance in the life of people, and the family as we
know it will not be so important in people's lives. The local
community will assume prime importance. The question as to
whether there will be a limited role for the market in helping to
shape the priorities of production of welfare 'goods' is the only one
to which different answers could be given from the literature
reviewed.

Socialism, however, presents a far more complex picture. It will
still be necessary to some extent for the central state to provide on
behalf of people. The market's role in socialist provision depends on
the interpretation of Marxist theory adopted. Following
Bettelheim, commodity exchange would still, of necessity, be
expected to operate even, presumably, in social welfare areas such
as housing provision. Other interpretations would suggest that
commodity production and exchange would not determine social
welfare provision and that total planning would prevail. Whatever
view is taken, however, money will still exist under socialism and
will still be the reward for work done; and people's welfare needs
will still be expressed in terms of their willingness to pay some
smaller or larger part of their wages for services such as housing.
This use of money to express a preference which could then register
in the state's plan of provision is to be distinguished from the
provision of alternative types of similar goods by competing
providers in a commodity market. The first is an essential
component of socialism. Whether the second is, too, is a matter of
dispute. The workplace is likely to feature significantly as an agency
providing welfare because of the importance of work in the
allocation of rewards in a socialist society. The family would not
have changed immediately and old forms of care would continue
into the new society. A complete mix of providers is therefore likely
to exist under socialism, but the tendency would be towards decentralised, community-controlled forms of provision.

Relationship between Welfare User and Provider

Under communism the relationship would be between equals who
may happen to have differences in their current abilities in particular
technical skills. Doctor and patient would be two equal people
agreeing upon a diagnosis and treatment. Teacher and student
would learn almost as much from each other. The social worker, if
such were to exist, would be merely a catalyst for the further

development of the self-analytical skills of the client. All traces of professionalism and its converse, the experience of helpless and ingratiated dependence of the client, would have been eradicated. In other words, deprofessionalisation would go hand-in-hand with the already projected democratisation.

Of socialism, all that can be concluded is that there would be substantial progress in this direction but that the inequalities between people inherited from capitalist days, and the legacy of past attitudes to professional providers, would continue to influence policy.

Rationing Procedures

Under communism, the work-income connection would have been broken by the abolition of the wage system. There would be no further reason why, for example, the rules governing the allocation of social security should reflect the need to motivate people for work. A social dividend available to all could be envisaged and work be a quite separate matter, done because of transformed motivations and attitudes and transformed working relationships. The vision might be pursued further and all traces of even a social dividend removed from the picture. All may indeed take freely, from the stock of available goods, those which they require to meet their material needs. These material needs would rank much lower in people's perception of their requirements. The appropriate availability of goods and services could be ensured by a computerised projection of likely needs based on past usage or random surveys, operated in the context of a political system that allows for the resolution of political disagreements as to which of these needs should be satisfied, always bearing ecological questions in mind.

Under socialism, however, the work-income connection would not yet be broken. The allocation of benefits in cash and kind would therefore continue to be affected by the necessity of motivating people to work. The care of those who are not willing to work is likely to be less desirable than the care of those who are. The social benefits of hard work are likely to be high.

A socialist society will . . . attempt to gear the distribution of services towards those who most need them, notwithstanding the overriding considerations of the work principle. In a choice between rationing techniques for the allocation of housing and health services, for example, those techniques most likely to ensure that the services are delivered to those who most need them would be preferred. Thus rationing devices based on deterrence, on keeping people ignorant of their rights, on professional discretion, on delay, would be avoided and replaced by explicit, publicly discussed and approved, *a priori* rationing devices that clearly embody within them the ways in which those with competing needs would be found and chosen.

Family Policy/Sexual Division of Labour

1. The equalisation of male and female employment generally, but also in the social services; in particular the ending of the situation in which women do all the caring jobs and manage none of them;
2. the abolition of the family wage and the consequent provision of a separate child's income to those who have the care of children;
3. the breaking down of the distinction between home and work to permit men to share in child care;
4. the progressive communalisation of forms of living and housework; and
5. the shift of caring functions for the young, disabled and elderly from the privatised nuclear family and from its converse, the remote bureaucratic institution, to a system of democratic, decentralised, community-run provisions.

From B. Deacon, *Social Policy and Socialism* (Pluto Press, 1983)

B36   Equality, Markets and the State: Democratic Equality, 1984

Equality of Opportunity

Equality of opportunity seems on the face of it to be a very persuasive conception of equality, and perhaps the most consensual form which it could take in British society. It is concerned with fair recruitment procedures to jobs, and can be portrayed as an important factor in increasing efficiency because it matches recruitment to ability, not to birth, race or sex. However, the principle has to be subjected to a good deal of interpretation, and when this is done it becomes clearer that it is at bottom very vague and ambiguous and its widespread acceptance in society may well depend upon its remaining ambiguous. On a minimalist interpretation of the principle we might say that it is concerned with the progressive removal of legal impediments to recruitment and giving all children a fair start in schools. It is a procedural notion concerned with making sure that the race for positions is a fair one. It is this procedural aspect of equality of opportunity which makes it attractive to liberals. Liberals argue that more substantive forms of equality such as equality of outcome will involve intolerable interferences with personal freedom, whereas a procedural form of opportunity will involve few if any interferences with freedom.

However, this easy compromise is illusory. A fair equality of opportunity cannot be attained on a purely procedural basis . . . If we are concerned with an equal or fair opportunity for the development of talent and ability, then more substantial policies than the removal of legal and procedural limitations on recruitment will have to be involved. Granted that background inequalities between individuals and families are going to affect the development of talent, if we are to equalise opportunities we shall have to act on these background inequalities.

However if we do this two problems arise for the liberal commitment to the principle. In the first place, if we try to compensate for background inequalities which bear upon the developments of talents in children then it might seem that this is going to threaten the personal freedom of families to live their own lives in their own way; and thus the claim that equality of opportunity and personal freedom may not be so compatible as is usually supposed. Secondly, if a policy of seeking to compensate for background inequalities which make a difference to the development of talent is adopted seriously, the redistributive consequences of such compensation would make the principle of equality of opportunity merge into that of greater equality of outcome which liberals reject. Equality of opportunity is the equal opportunity to become unequal but, as I have argued, unless we are to stick to a disingenuous procedural conception of equality of opportunity, the idea of equalising starting places in the competition will take on very substantive aspects in the sphere of compensating for unmerited inherited disadvantage and in restricting rights of bequest for the better off. Only strategies of this sort are likely to be able to equalise opportunities, but such strategies pose exactly the same problems for liberty as do socialist conceptions of equality.

The basic socialist objection to equality of opportunity is concerned with the fact that there is no critical approach to the differential positions to which equal access is being proposed. It takes the existing structure of inequality for granted and is concerned about recruitment to it. However, this is not satisfactory for socialists: they will want to probe the legitimacy of the differential reward structure, otherwise greater equality of access may give a greater legitimacy to a structure of rewards which the socialist may regard as unjust . . .

Equality of Outcome

The obvious alternative to equality of opportunity, given the difficulties which it involves, would be to endorse greater equalities of outcome in terms of income, wealth and welfare. The reasons for this can be developed out of an internal critique of equality of opportunity . . . If we seek to compensate those who do not have a fair chance to develop their talents because of circumstances beyond their control — their genetic endowment, their famiiy background, their sex, their colour — there will in fact be very definite limits to which this can be done consistently with the maintenance of the family and individual freedom. There is a point at which the attempt to secure a fair background for the development of talent cannot go without being intolerably intrusive.

So what do we do at this point? There are two alternatives. One is to endorse the existing differential reward structure, admit that there are limits to which equality of opportunity can go, and argue that it is an unfortunate fact that some individuals will be penalised in realising their life chances because of factors which are outside of their control but cannot be altered in a way compatible with individual freedom. The other alternative is to argue for a greater compression of the reward structure and in favour of greater equality of outcome. If the family is to be maintained and personal liberty secured so that equality of opportunity must be limited, then it is wrong to reward as prodigiously as we do a narrow range of talent for which the individual does not bear entire responsibility and to make the costs of failure so heavy for those whose opportunities have been more modest and who similarly do not bear full responsibility for their condition.

This is the general ground for equality of outcome, and it follows fairly naturally from a recognition of the defects of equality of opportunity. The obvious difficulty with it is that in endorsing a wholesale critique of an income and status hierarchy it may well embody very weak demands in terms of efficiency, while at the same time failing to recognise the positionality of certain goods which cannot be distributed in a substantively equal manner. The obvious solution to this difficulty is to seek to develop a theory of legitimate

238 *Political Economy and Social Welfare*

inequality. This I believe is the central socialist task in this field, and one which will have to involve a social consensus if it is ever to be supported electorally. In what follows I can only give the broad parameters within which such a theory could be developed . . . As purposive creatures, liberty to pursue our own good in our own way is central to us; but this means that we cannot be indifferent to the worth of liberty to individuals, and to the resources they have to pursue their conception of the good. Consequently a socialist theory of equality will be concerned with the distribution of those resources which are necessary basic goods for experiencing a life of purpose and agency and making full use of the rights of citizenship. In our society these will include health services (unless people have the greatest degree of physical integrity of which they are capable they will not be able to act effectively), education and welfare goods generally. These resources are also going to include income because, as Le Grand has shown, differences in income lead to marked differences in the use of other sorts of basic welfare goods. A fair distribution of the worth of liberty is therefore going to involve far greater equality of income and wealth as well as the provision of services. It also follows from what I argued earlier that these basic resources which are necessary to live a life of active citizenship should so far as possible be distributed in cash rather than in kind, in order to enhance the ability to live life in one's own way and avoid bureaucracy and paternalism. This linking of equality and a more equal worth of liberty should demonstrate to critics that we are serious about freedom and value equality as a means to liberty.

However, we have to take into account the points about incentives and positional goods which I emphasised earlier. It follows from these points that while I have talked interchangeably so far about a fair worth and an equal worth of liberty, these may diverge and this marks the difference between the view which I am advocating and a stricter equality of result. Moves away from equality in the worth of liberty would be justified on this view if such moves would lead to a greater value of liberty, i.e. resources, both financial and welfare, for all. If incentives need paying for reasons of economic efficiency, to produce more goods without which the worst off members of society would actually be worse off than they would be under a differential system of rewards, then a theory of legitimate inequality would justify incentives on the grounds that they still secure a fair, but not an equal worth of liberty to all members of the society including the worst off. Similarly, positional goods such as limited educational opportunities which *ex hypothesi* cannot be distributed more equally would also be consumed legitimately if their consumption by particular individuals benefited society as a whole.

It might of course be argued that this argument goes too far away from a genuine socialist outlook because it does not *constrain* the extent to which inequalities could exist if they were for the general good. There are I believe two answers to this point. In the first place, if we are concerned with individual liberty then it would be irrational to prefer a more equal distribution of goods in which the worth of liberty to many citizens would be less than it would be under some degree of inequality. The second point is to emphasise the values of community and fraternity operating here as an independent value. There is a point, which cannot easily be specified in advance, at which the inequalities linked to efficiency to pursue a greater value to freedom will threaten a sense of community and fraternity because of the social distance which would be created between those occupying differential positions and the rest of the society. However, this social distance would be lessened to some degree, because the argument . . . presupposes common and not private services in the spheres of health, education and welfare, and despite the earning of differential rewards it is likely that this sort of provision will limit any social distance which might occur. However, it is still true that there may come a point at which we would want to say that we would prefer community to efficiency if the structure of incentives required for the former threatened to override the latter.

There is no point in pretending that thinking about values can provide us with a detailed blueprint for the future. Political values and principles are always going to be ambiguous and susceptible to many interpretations. Nor are all our values capable of being reconciled in one coherent schedule. There are trade-offs and choices to be made. Nevertheless, while this is true, a moral theory is still central to socialism. Unless it is explicitly grounded in a clear moral standpoint, the claim for greater equality can be misrepresented by our opponents as just the product of class resentment or the politics of envy. In the view developed in this pamphlet, however, by securing a fairer value for liberty, and thus a share in the common rights of citizenship, the greater equality can be seen as an essential means both to liberty and fraternity: it is thus central to any restatement of the socialist position.

A good many of the bureaucratic and regulatory features of the welfare state are a consequence of attempting to tackle the symptoms rather than the causes of inequality. Intervention, subsidy, compensation and the network of rules which go along with these could to some extent be offset by a straightforward and more egalitarian approach to the taxation of wealth, income and inheritance. This would require less bureaucracy and less paternalistic interference in the lives of individuals.

From R. Plant, *Equality, Markets and the State* (Fabian Society No. 494, 1984)

B37   The Reform of Social Security: A New Approach, 1985

1.4 This Green Paper aims to define a system which is founded on public understanding of the purposes and the workings of social security; which is more relevant to the needs of today; and which is capable of meeting the demands into the next century. It sets out a new approach to social security — but it recognises and seeks to build on what has been achieved over the past forty years.

1.5 Fundamental to this approach is a belief that the system of social security provision should be based on a clear understanding of the relative roles and responsibilities of the individual and the state. In building for the future we should follow the basic principle that social security is not a function of the state alone. It is a partnership between the individual and the state — a system built on twin pillars.

1.6 Most people not only can but wish to make sensible provision for themselves. The organisation of social security should encourage that. It should respect the ability of the individual to make his own choices and to take responsibility for his own life. But at the same time it must recognise the responsibility of government to establish an underlying basis of provision on which we as individuals can build and on which we can rely at times of need.

1.7 Such an approach does not lead, as some have suggested, to a system based on a single concept: whether it be universality or means-testing. For such concepts almost invariably concern only the state dimension of social provision. They regard state provision as good or bad: they postulate that it should do as much or as little as possible. Either analysis misses the central point. State provision has an important role in supporting and sustaining the individual; but it should not discourage self-reliance or stand in the way of individual provision and responsibility. 1.8 This was a central theme in the 1942 report of Sir William Beveridge:

> The state in organising security should not stifle incentive, opportunity, responsibility; in establishing a national minimum, it should leave room and encouragement for voluntary action by each individual to provide more than that minimum for himself and his family.

Much has changed in the forty years since then. The ability of most people to make more of their own provision has substantially improved. For instance, the spread of home ownership among those previously relying on public provision of housing underlines the wish of most people for greater independence.

1.9 Yet the scope and scale of the state social security system has extended greatly. The decision at the outset of national insurance to pay pensions at once rather than after a build-up of entitlement substantially changed Beveridge's concept. The later development of earnings-related benefits and contributions was a further step away from the 1942 report.

1.10 We should not be deceived about the nature of national insurance today. It is *not* the same as private insurance and owes little to normal insurance principles. It is a pay-as-you-go scheme. Today's contributions meet the cost of today's benefits. As for tomorrow, the most we can do is to create a liability to be met by our children. Even with the elaborate State Earnings-Related Pension Scheme the contributor is doing no more than helping to pay for the present cost of pensions. His own entitlement is a claim to a pension which he hopes future generations of contributors will finance.

1.11 Forty years on from Beveridge there is little point in seeking to replicate private insurance arrangements inside the state organisation. We should certainly recognise the debt we are building up for the future. But the better course is to distinguish between what can and should be organised by individuals and their employers and what can and should be organised by government. This is what the twin pillar approach seeks to do. It recognises the importance of the state provision but it seeks to define its limits.

1.12 In developing this approach the Government believe that three main objectives should underlie the reform of social security.

First, the social security system must be capable of meeting genuine need. This is a basic responsibility of any government. No individual should be left in a position where through no fault of his own he is unable to sustain himself or his family. Supplementary benefit is based on that principle and — while it has many faults — it is more effective than many equivalent schemes overseas. At the same time the overall system must be flexible enough to recognise that what constitutes need changes and that those groups most in need also change. In the 1930s working-age families were seen as the main group in poverty: the main causes being unemployment and low earnings among men with large families. By the 1950s and 1960s pensioners were the major cause for concern. Now the position has changed again and in 1985 it is families with children who face the most difficult problems.

Second, the social security system must be consistent with the Government's overall objectives for the economy. Social security is already by far the largest government programme — more than twice defence spending and larger than health, social services, education and housing put together. It is responsible for a major share of the current heavy tax burden on individuals and companies. As many other countries recognise, continued growth of this burden could severely damage the prospects for economic growth. Yet in the longer term, the scope for sustaining and improving social security provision depends on the performance of the economy. But there are other issues. While it is one of the functions of the social security system to help those who are unemployed, it is self-defeating if it creates barriers to the creation of jobs, to job mobility or to people rejoining the labour force. Clearly such obstacles exist if people believe themselves better off out of work than in work; or if employers regard the burden of national insurance as a substantial discouragement to providing new jobs. Equally restrictions in areas like pensions can discourage people from changing jobs. If we wish to encourage individuals to provide for themselves then the social security system — public and private — must not stand in the way.

Third, the social security system must be simpler to understand and easier to administer. Forty years of tinkering have resulted in complexity and confusion. Nobody can be happy with the system as it stands today. The supplementary benefit system alone requires some 38,000 staff to administer it. The rules of entitlement are so complex that the manual of guidance to staff runs to two volumes and 16,000 paragraphs. Nor is it only the rules which cause confusion. All the main income-related benefits — supplementary benefit, housing benefit and family income supplement — use different measures of income and capital. Not surprisingly, therefore, some benefits are shrouded in an obscurity which at times is virtually total. As for administration, much of the social security system is run from local offices which largely lack the kind of aids which modern computer science can provide. The result is that the service for the public too often fails as the staff hunt for files in a Dickensian paper-chase.

1.13 These three objectives are not independent of each other. At times choices have to be made. Thus it is quite possible to construct a scheme under which all benefits — including pensions — would be means-tested on the basis that this was concentrating public resources on those who needed them most. Yet the objective of relieving need does not lead simply to the conclusion that the state should provide *only* where all else fails. It is an entirely proper function for the government to provide a basis on which individual provision can rest. In particular, such support can come at times when expenses are high (as when raising children) or when income is limited (as in retirement). Here government is underpinning individual effort: encouraging it not replacing it.

1.14 The Government's proposals are not based on a grand design for a new state system but on a view of social security which allows important roles for both state and individual provision. In that respect it takes a radically different direction from some of the developments over the last forty years. We want to give greater responsibility and greater independence to the individual. But the proposals have also been framed in the clear belief that our tradition of state support of those in need is one which should be maintained and developed.

From *Reform of Society Security*, vol. 1, Cmnd 9517 (HMSO, 1985)

SECTION C: STATISTICS

C1 Age Distribution of the Population of the United Kingdom: 1871–1981

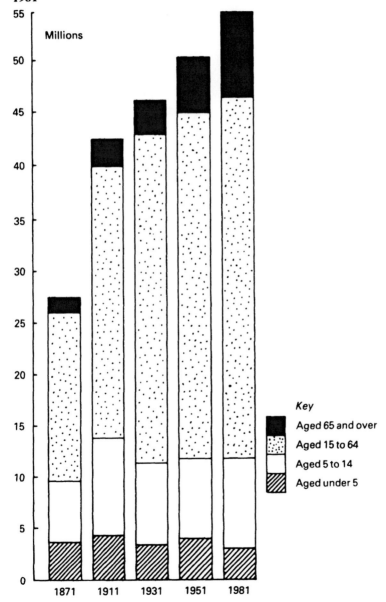

Sources: Based on figures in the *Annual Abstract of Statistics,* 1938–50 & 1984 (HMSO)

C2 Crude Birth and Death Rates, 1885–1982

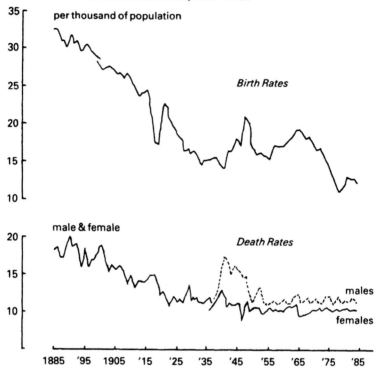

Sources: Based on figures from B.R. Mitchell and P. Deane, *Abstract of British Historical Statistics* (Cambridge U.P. 1962); *Statistical Abstract of the United Kingdom*, 1899–1913, 1929, 1938 and *Annual Abstract of Statistics*, 1938–50, 1960, 1970, 1985 (all HMSO)

Notes.
Figures for the period 1885–99 relate to England and Wales. Those for 1899–1982 relate to the United Kingdom except that the death rates for 1916–20 are based on civil deaths and the population of England and Wales.

C3 Causes of Death in the United Kingdom: 1913, 1938, 1981

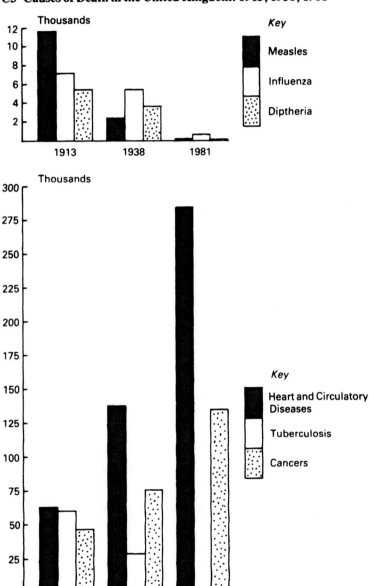

Sources: Based on figures from the *Statistical Abstract of the United Kingdom,* 1929 and the *Annual Abstract of Statistics,* 1938–50, 1984 (all HMSO)

C4 Local Authority Expenditure on Poor Relief: England and Wales, 1885–1949

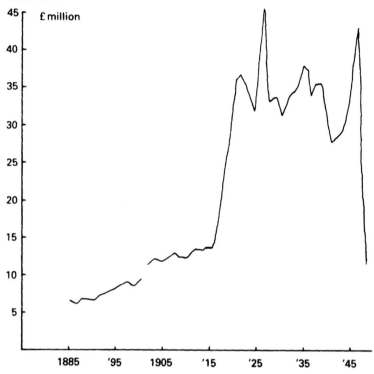

Sources: Based on figures in B. R. Mitchell and P. Deane, *Abstract of British Historical Statistics* (Cambridge University Press, 1962) and B. R. Mitchell and H. G. Jones, *Second Abstract of British Historical Statistics* (Cambridge University Press, 1971)

Note.
Figures relate to the financial year ending (for most authorities) in March of the year given. Expenditure on paupers in asylums is not included. Loan charges are included from 1903.

C5 Numbers Receiving Old Age Pensions: 1914, 1932, 1952, 1982

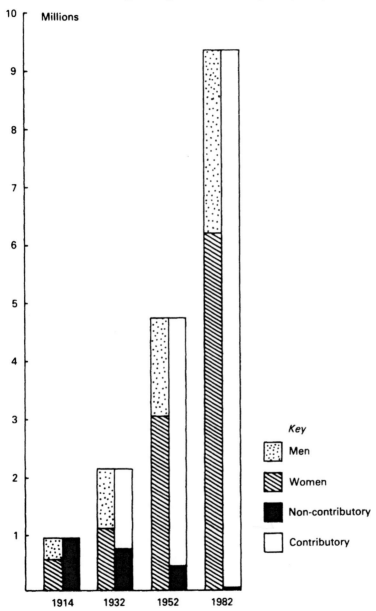

Key
Men
Women
Non-contributory
Contributory

Sources: Based on figures in the *Statistical Abstract for the United Kingdom,*
1929, 1938; *Annual Abstract of Statistics*, 1960, 1984 (all HMSO)

C6 Insured Unemployed, 1885–1982

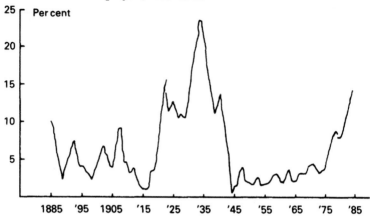

Sources: Based on figures in B. R. Mitchell and P. Deane, *Abstract of British Historical Statistics* (Cambridge University Press, 1962); London and Cambridge Economic Service, *British Economy: Key Statistics, 1900–1970* (Times Newspapers, 1975); *Annual Abstract of Statistics,* 1980, 1985 (Both HMSO)

Note.
Statistics for the period 1885–1922 relate to returns from certain insured trades; those for 1922–82 to those insured under Unemployment or National Insurance schemes.

C7 Housing Stock and Forms of Occupancy: 1911, 1951, 1981

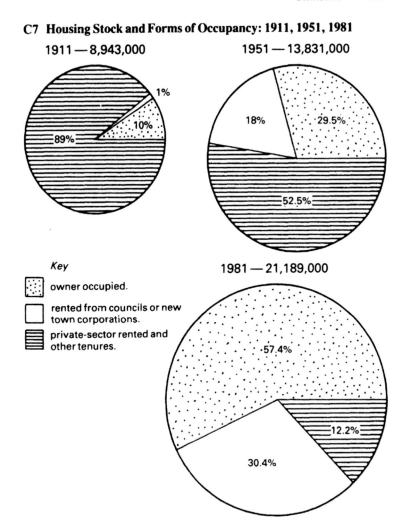

1911 — 8,943,000

89%
10%
1%

1951 — 13,831,000

18%
29.5%
52.5%

Key

owner occupied.

rented from councils or new town corporations.

private-sector rented and other tenures.

1981 — 21,189,000

57.4%
12.2%
30.4%

Sources: based on figures from the *Annual Abstract of Statistics*, 1960, 1984; *Statistical Abstract of the United Kingdom*, 1929 and *Social Trends*, 1971 (all HMSO). For the breakdown of occupancies in 1911, we have accepted the estimate for 1914 in S. Glynn and J. Oxborrow, *Inter-war Britain: a Social and Economic History*(Allen & Unwin, 1976)

C8 Public Expenditure on Welfare Services: 1949/50 and 1958/9

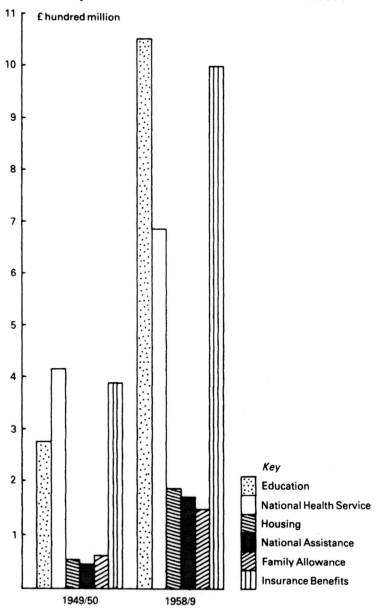

Sources: Based on figures from the *Annual Abstract of Statistics*, 1938–50, 1960 (both HMSO)

C9 Public Expenditure on Welfare Services: 1972/3 and 1981/2

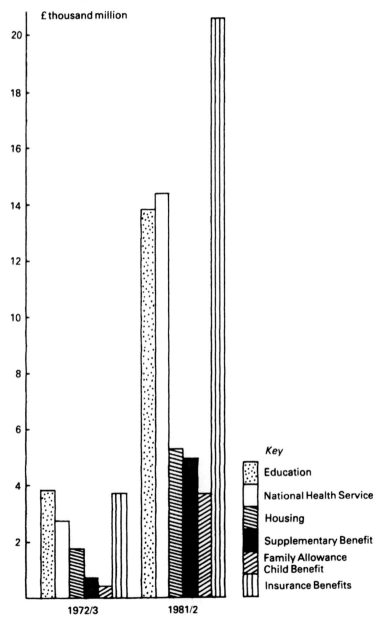

£ thousand million

Key
Education
National Health Service
Housing
Supplementary Benefit
Family Allowance
Child Benefit
Insurance Benefits

1972/3   1981/2

Source: Based on figures from the *Annual Abstract of Statistics*, 1984 (HMSO)

C10 Expenditure on the National Health Service and on Education, 1980/1 (in £ million)

National Health Service

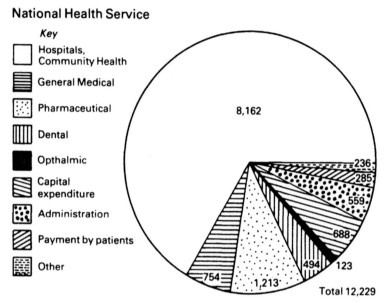

Key

☐ Hospitals, Community Health

▤ General Medical

▦ Pharmaceutical

▥ Dental

■ Opthalmic

▧ Capital expenditure

▦ Administration

▨ Payment by patients

▦ Other

8,162

236
285
559
688
494
123
754
1,213

Total 12,229

Education

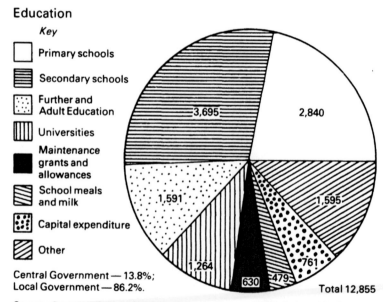

Key

☐ Primary schools

▤ Secondary schools

▦ Further and Adult Education

▥ Universities

■ Maintenance grants and allowances

▧ School meals and milk

▦ Capital expenditure

▨ Other

3,695
2,840
1,591
1,595
1,264
630
479
761

Central Government — 13.8%;
Local Government — 86.2%.

Total 12,855

Source: Based on figures from the *Annual Abstract of Statistics*, 1984 (HMSO)

SOME FURTHER READING

Books Relevant to Sections A and B

D.H. Aldcroft, *Full Employment: the Elusive Goal* (1984)

P. Barker (ed.), *Founders of the Welfare State* (1984)

T. Barker and M. Drake (eds.), *Population and Society in Britain, 1850–1980* (1982)

A. Briggs, *Social Thought and Social Action: A Study of the Work of Seebohm Rowntree* (1961)

A.H. Halsey (ed.), *Trends in British Society since 1900* (1972)

J. Harris, *William Beveridge: A Biography* (1977)

J.R. Hay (ed.), *The Development of the British Welfare State, 1880–1975* (1978)

J.S. Maclure (ed.), *Educational Documents: England and Wales, 1816–Present Day* (1979)

T.H. Marshall, *Social Policy* (1975)

W.J. Mommsen (ed.), *The Emergence of the Welfare State in Britain and Germany* (1981)

R. Pinker, *Social Theory and Social Policy* (1970)

R.M. Titmuss, *Essays on 'The Welfare State'* (1963)

B. Watkin (ed.), *Documents on Health and Social Services: 1834 to the Present Day* (1975)

Books Relevant to Section A

R. Barker, *Education and Politics, 1900–1951: A Study of the Labour Party* (1972)

M. Bruce, *The Coming of the Welfare State* (1968)

J. Burnett, *A Social History of Housing, 1815–1970* (1978)

F.F. Cartwright, *A Social History of Medicine* (1977)

S. Constantine, *Unemployment in Britain Between the Wars* (1980)

M. Daunton, *House and Home in the Victorian City: Working-class Housing, 1850–1914* (1983)

A. Deacon, *In Search of the Scrounger* (1976)

E. Evans (ed.) *Social Policy, 1830–1914* (1978)

D. Fraser, *The Evolution of the British Welfare State* (1973)

B.B. Gilbert, *British Social Policy, 1914–1939* (1970)

—— , *The Evolution of National Insurance in Great Britain* (1966)

J. Harris, *Unemployment and Politics: A Study in English Social Policy, 1886–1914* (1972)

J.R. Hay, *The Origins of the Liberal Welfare Reforms, 1906–14* (1975)

J. Hurt, *Elementary Schooling and the Working Classes, 1860–1918* (1979)

P. Keating (ed.), *Into Unknown England, 1886–1913* (1976)

A. Lynes, *The Unemployment Assistance Board: the Origins of Supplementary Benefit* (1985)

J. Macnicol, *The Movement for Family Allowances, 1918–45* (1980)

M.E. Rose, *The Relief of Poverty, 1834–1914* (1972)

B. Simon, *Education and the Labour Movement, 1870–1920* (1965)

—— , *The Politics of Educational Reform, 1920–1940* (1974)

G. Stedman Jones, *Outcast London* (1971)

J. Stevenson, *British Society, 1914–45* (1984)

—— (ed.), *Social Conditions in Britain Between the Wars* (1977)

M. Swenarton, *Homes Fit for Heroes* (1981)

P. Thane, *The Foundations of the Welfare State* (1982)

—— (ed.), *The Origins of British Social Policy* (1978)

Books Relevant to Section B

P. Addison, *The Road to 1945: British Politics and the Second World War* (1975)

W. Beckerman and S. Clark, *Poverty and Social Security in Britain since 1961* (1982)

R. Berthoud, J.C. Brown and S. Cooper, *Poverty and the Development of Anti-Poverty Policy in the United Kingdom* (1981)

D. Blake and P. Ormerod (eds.), *The Economics of Prosperity. Social Priorities in the Eighties* (1980)

Lord Blake and J. Patten (eds.), *The Conservative Opportunity* (1976)

M. Brown, *Introduction to Social Administration in Britain* (1982)

N. Bosanquet, *After the New Right* (1983)

—— and P. Townsend (eds.), *Labour and Inequality* (1972)

—— and P. Townsend (eds.), *Labour and Equality. A Fabian Study of Labour in Power* (1980)

K. Fenwick and P. McBride, *The Government of Education* (1981)

V. George and P. Wilding, *Ideology and Social Welfare* (1976)

I. Gough, *The Political Economy of the Welfare State* (1979)

K. Jones, W. Brown and K. Bradshaw, *Issues in Social Policy* (1983)

S. Lansley, *Housing and Public Policy* (1979)

R. Levitt, *The Reorganised National Health Service* (1977)

S. Macgregor, *The Politics of Poverty* (1981)

N. Madge and M. Brown, *Despite the Welfare State* (1982)

A. Murie, P. Niner and C. Watson, *Housing Policy and the Housing System* (1976)

N. Parry, M. Rustin and C. Satyamurti (eds.), *Social Work, Welfare and the State* (1979)

D.A. Reisman, *Richard Titmuss. Welfare and Society* (1977)

E. Sainsbury, *The Personal Social Services* (1977)

B. Showler and A. Sinfield (eds.), *The Workless State* (1981)

R.M. Titmuss, *Social Policy. An Introduction* (1974)

B. Watkin, *The National Health Service. The First Phase 1948–74 and After* (1978)

INDEX

Lightning Source UK Ltd.
Milton Keynes UK
UKOW02f0413050815

256415UK00001B/6/P